The Mid-Antrim Narrow Gauge

Second edition of

The Ballymena lines

With two additional chapters by Norman Johnston

Dr EM Patterson

Colourpoint

Dr EM Patterson, BSc, MSc, DSc, MPhil, MRIA, FRSE was born at Bangor, Co Down, in 1920 and educated at Bangor Grammar School and The Queen's University, Belfast. He was trained as a geologist but in 1941 he moved to Scotland to take up employment as a research chemist at ICI (Explosives) at Ardeer, Ayrshire. His interest in geology continued to flourish and in 1947 he moved to St Andrews University where he lectured in the Department of Geology and Mineralogy. In 1953 he married Violet Kirk (neé Adams), a Queen's graduate, and returned to ICI at Ardeer the following year, working there until his retirement in 1981. In Ireland his focus of interest was the railways in the north of the island. He wrote nine books, covering seven of the narrow gauge lines (two in this book, formerly published as *The Ballymena Lines*), as well as *The Great Northern Railway of Ireland* and *The Belfast and County Down Railway* (two books). An updated edition of *The Clogher Valley Railway*, with additional text, was published by Colourpoint Books in 2004 and a similarly updated version of *The Ballycastle Railway* in 2006. His last book was *The Castlederg and Victoria Bridge Tramway* (Colourpoint 1998), published just after his death. The posthumous award of MPhil in 1997 by The Queen's University was for his work on the industrial archaeology of gunpowder manufacture.

Dr EM Patterson, at Tiriach, Pitlochry, Scotland in October 1995.

First impression

© Dr EM Patterson 1965 and Anna Singer 2007
Additional text © Norman Johnston 2007

Designed by Colourpoint Books, Newtownards
Printed by ColourBooks Ltd

ISBN 978 1 904242 70 3

Colourpoint Books
Colourpoint House
Jubilee Business Park
21 Jubilee Road
NEWTOWNARDS
County Down
Northern Ireland
BT23 4YH
Tel: 028 9182 0505
Fax: 028 9182 1900
E-mail: info@colourpoint.co.uk
Web site: www.colourpoint.co.uk

Cover pictures

Front: *Compound 2-4-2T No 111 departing from Ballymena with a train for Parkmore about 1930.*
A painting by Debra Wenlock.

Rear upper: *Beyer Peacock 2-4-0T No 64 leaves Moorfields with a Ballymena to Larne train in the mid-1890s.*
Courtesy David Francey; a painting by Norman Whitla

Rear lower: *The second Parkmore station when new in 1921 (from an illuminated book presented to Bowman Malcolm on his retirement).*
By kind permission of Tony Ragg

Contents

Appendices

Ballymena station in the 1930s, looking towards Belfast. In the foreground are the narrow gauge lines serving the engine shed (left) and yard (right). To the left, beyond the signal, is the broad gauge track serving the engine shed. To reach the shed, locomotives had to cross the narrow gauge tracks using the crossover visible in front of the cabin in this picture. Narrow gauge passenger trains departed from the east (left) face of the island platform. L&GRP

Prices and measurements

Prices are quoted in pre-1971 £sd without decimal equivalents (eg £4 8s 9d). There were 20 shillings (s) to the £, thus 1s 0d equals 5p. There were 12 old pence (d) to the shilling, 2d being roughly 1p. Even shillings are rendered 3s 0d, etc, and shillings and pence 3s 10d, etc. (In quotations shillings are sometimes rendered 3/-, 3s, etc, and shillings and pence 16/3, etc.)

Dr Patterson quotes distances in miles, furlongs, chains and yards. There are 8 furlongs to a mile, 10 chains to a furlong (thus 80 chains to a mile) and 22 yards in a chain. A chain is also 4 perches.

Chapter 1

Ballymena and the blue hills

The middle town

The Borough of Ballymena, the 'City of the Seven Towers', has a present population of 28,700 (in 2001) and, although a thriving town, it is one of comparatively recent development, as evidenced by its difference of name from that of the parish of Kilconriola, in which it is situated.

Three hundred years ago Ballymena was a village of 540 people. It was a less important place than Ballymoney, 17 miles to the north-west, where many years later the terminus of the Ballycastle Railway was to be situated. The history of Ballymena had begun early in the seventeenth century with the settlement of William Adair of Kinhilt. Kinhilt was a hamlet in Wigtownshire, and Adair brought with him a number of lowland Scots from that county and from Ayrshire, settling in what was known as the Manor of Kinhiltstown, lying between the Braidwater and Cloughwater rivers.

Ballymena was sited on the line of an ancient road that led from Tara to Dunseverick on the northern coast. The town was at the western end of the Braid valley, a mile or two from the confluence of the Braidwater and the larger River Maine. It was placed where the fall of the Braidwater made it convenient for the plantation owner, Adair, to erect his Manor Mill. In 1626, King Charles I granted Adair a Charter entitling him and his successors to hold two fairs annually, and a free market every Saturday for ever. This grant has been regularly maintained ever since.

While Ballymena possessed most of the stimuli that combine to produce prosperity, it had few of the disadvantages complained of in places less favourably situated. Its old name, *An Baile Meanach*, signified 'The Middle Town', as it was placed centrally in the County of Antrim. Belfast was too distant to interfere with its trade, and its location was at a natural focus for roads which led in from prosperous neighbouring villages. Even in times of agricultural or industrial depression the trade and commerce of Ballymena have been well maintained,

perhaps one of the best tributes to the business abilities of its inhabitants with their hard-headed Scottish ancestry.

The introduction of linen manufacture about 1732 by the Adair and Dickey families led to the metamorphosis of the insignificant village of the seventeenth century into a busy industrial centre. The Linen Hall, the property of the Adairs, was the last in the county to be devoted to its original use. It comprised a square of buildings two storeys high and an acre in extent, divided into offices for manufacturers and merchants.

In the early decades of the nineteenth century observers differed in their comments on the town. Thus in the Ordnance Survey Memoir of 1833 one of the places of worship is described as 'a substantial capacious building, very simple and similar in its exterior to a cotton factory'. A year later the writer of a guide book said, 'the town … is a very thriving place, more so than any inland town in the country; it is said to contain five hundred dwellings and about three thousand inhabitants. An excellent linen market is established here, and regular sales of butter for exportation. There are two fairs held in each year. There is one excellent and wide street of modern erection, and some very old-fashioned houses, having gabled fronts, like the old English cottages: near the centre of the town is a large and convenient market house, ornamented by a steeple sixty feet in height and behind is seen a rath or moat whose elevation is about fifty.' A steep hill in Church Street, between the old market house and Meeting House Lane, was stated to be a formidable obstacle to the progress of the mail coach as it went on its way from Belfast to Londonderry.

At the time of the 1841 census, Ballymena had 5,549 inhabitants. Thereafter the decennial census returns show an increase, apart from a slight drop in 1891, and this brought the number of people to over 10,000 by 1901. It is noteworthy how this population trend contrasts with that for the county of Antrim which, in common with nearly all the Irish counties, had its maximum population of 286,000 in the 1841 census. The Irish famine years in the later 1840s marked the start of a fall that went on for the next 80 years. By the 1926 census, Antrim's total was down to 192,000, but the 1951 census showed 231,000. There was thus a drift from rural life during the past century and a half, a feature common to many Ulster towns and due in part to industrialisation of the linen industry.

Mineral wealth

In contrast to the linen industry, based on the growing of flax, the district to the north-east of Ballymena became an important producer of iron ore, though its treatment was always a matter for cross-channel furnaces sited on the coalfields Ireland lacked. The rock that underlies much of the surface of Antrim is basalt, a black rock that was poured out as lava flows many millions of years ago. But not all of the rock is either black or basalt, and before the end of the eighteenth century the existence of red, iron-bearing strata between the basalt flows had been noticed by observant people. In 1784, the Rev William Hamilton, MA, in his book *Letters concerning the northern coast of the County of Antrim* noted that there were 'extensive layers of red ochre, varying in all degrees from a dull ferruginous colour, to a bright red, answering well for coarse paint … veins of iron ore, sometimes very rich, commonly of a brown or reddish cast …'

Two geologists, R Tate and JS Holden, gave the first detailed scientific description of the Antrim iron ore in 1870, and stated that while the first exploitation was begun in 1861 at Ballypalady by a Dr Ritchie, the industry expanded rapidly and, during 1869, 50,000 tons of ore was shipped to England from several ports along the Antrim coast.

Railway connections

With the rise of industry, railways were built. Although the first railway from Belfast, the Ulster Railway, went south-west towards Armagh in 1839, the Belfast and Ballymena Railway was not far behind it. The B&BR was started in 1845, and completed in 1848 to a station on the southern side of Ballymena, where the goods yard later stood and a short way south of the bank of the Braidwater. The extension of the railway to the north was accomplished by the ponderously titled Ballymena, Ballymoney, Coleraine and Portrush Junction Railway Company, which opened its line between Ballymena and Coleraine in 1855. The Belfast and Ballymena altered its name to the Belfast and Northern Counties Railway by an Act of Parliament dated 15 May 1860, the same statute giving it power to take possession of the BBC&PJR from 1 January 1861.

By the time iron-ore mining began, Ballymena had thus established railway connections which brought it into touch with the fast-growing city of Belfast to the south, and with the towns of Ballymoney and Coleraine and the city of Londonderry to the north. To the east of Ballymena, the topographical barrier of 'The Blue Hills of Antrim', both inspired the song of that name and prevented the easy establishment of branch lines from the main railway that ran the length of the county like a spine. For ten years or more the new mining industry in the Antrim hills took its product down to the Northern Counties Railway in horse-drawn carts, and saw it off in railway wagons on the next stage of its journey to the furnaces of England. Thereafter, in response to the growing demand of the mine owners and in search of honest profits, the first railways drove up the gentle valley slopes into the heart of the hills. The purpose of this book is to tell their story.

Chapter 2

The Glenariff Railway

Search in the glen

Glenariff trenches deeply through the eastern rim of the Antrim plateau and in five miles its river loses around a thousand feet of height. The upper sides of the glen are often extremely steep, and mural precipices carved out of a flow of basalt lava form striking features of the landscape. Streams entering the glen from north and south tumble over the cliffs on their way to the valley floor and the waterfalls in the Glenariff river have attracted tourists for many years.

The upper part of Glenariff was planted to woods during the middle of the nineteenth century but merges beyond into bare, peat-covered moors. In such a landscape the search for minerals of economic value was a comparatively simple matter. Mining surveyors were able to delineate the outcrop of the ore-bed with some accuracy and in Glenariff, as in other places, extraction was reasonably rewarding for a time. Though the work of the official geological survey of the area was published as a map and as a written description in 1886, mining had been in progress in the area 12 years before that date.

The mines are driven

In the Glenariff mining field, the outcrop of the ore bed lies high up on the south-west side of the glen, on the rim of the great shelf that reaches seaward to Garron Point. Because of the precipitous cliff faces, easy access to the ore bed was only possible at the head of the Inver Water, a tributary stream of the Glenariff river. In this area, the first systematic efforts at mining began in 1872 when, on 37 December, an agreement was signed between the landowner, the Rt Hon William Randal, Earl of Antrim, and certain gentlemen who were to become directors of a concern styled the Glenariff Iron Ore and Harbour Company. The company was formally incorporated with a capital of £130,000 on 25 March 1873 and in the following year, on 6 March, the Earl of Antrim granted it a lease of

work 'iron ore and ironstone' for a period of 19½ years. The lease, back-dated to 1 November 1873 since mining had already started, stated that a rent of one shilling per ton of ore was to be payable to the Earl, and went on to recite a list of 14 townlands, totalling 6,706 acres, in which mining might be done. Of these, Cloughcor was the most extensive, with an area of 2,942 acres. It should however be noted that the areas listed were those of the entire townland, and not the area of land under which mining might profitably be done.

Once mine adits had been driven, and the ore blasted loose and taken to the mine mouth in 'hutches', it had to be removed for shipment either to Cumberland or Scotland, for there were no furnaces anywhere in Ireland at the time. In 1874, the nearest railway line was that of the Belfast and Northern Counties at Ballymena, some 15 miles away by a rough mountain road. A narrow gauge railway line from Ballymena to Parkmore was then only in process of construction. To get a rail connection to Parkmore would have involved laying three miles of rather steeply-graded line from Cloughcor townland, and that would only have been the beginning. Transhipment would have been necessary to the main railway line at Ballymena and some 50 miles of railway haulage would have been required from the mine to Belfast, the nearest port.

The economics of inland movement of their ore did not appeal to the Glenariff Iron Ore and Harbour Company, whose directors had only to look down the glen to see the shore, four miles off and 610 feet below them. By laying a private railway to the coast on the south-east side of Red Bay, they could be independent of the two railway companies at Ballymena. Moreover, direct transfer of ore from wagon to ship then became possible.

Railway to the coast

Since the railway from the mines to the shore would be a private one and there was no intention of running passenger trains, parliamentary sanction was not required before the railway was made. It seems likely that the company used their own labour to build the line, for none of the well-known railway company's articles of association mention that two locomotive engines were on order for Messrs Robert Stephenson and Co, 40 wagons from Ashbury and 350 tons of rail from "copper mines of England"; the rails were, therefore, secondhand.

The company chose to site their pier in the townland of Carrivemurphy; deep water lay offshore but the pier was in an extremely exposed situation and safe berthing would have only been possible in calm weather. The existing harbour at the village of Waterfoot on the north-west side of Red Bay was no doubt considered, as it enjoys reasonable shelter, but its use would have involved making another two miles of railway. Apart from the extra expense, there were political considerations, for the Red Bay harbour at Waterfoot was already involved with the projected terminal facilities of the Ballymena, Cushendall and Red Bay Railway, incorporated in July 1872, and with the activities of the Antrim Wire Tramway Company (see Chapter 3),

both of which were, if not in opposition to the Glenariff company, certainly not well-disposed towards it. So the GIO&H chose, or had to be content with, independence of the existing harbour facilities.

Their railway began in Cloughcor townland, at an elevation of 609.8 feet above ordnance datum and near to where Glenariff merges into the treeless plateau. Its course ran north-east, and it descended towards the coast along a shelf cut in the valley side, at an even gradient of 1 in 40 for two miles, four and two-thirds furlongs. It passed, in turn, through the townlands of Diskirt, Callisnagh, Craignagat and Clonreagh and then, in the townlands of Greenaghan, 340 feet lower than at the start, it slackened in grade to 1 in 50.7 for about 120 yards. Here it crossed the deep gorge of the Altmore Burn on a two-span viaduct, supported on a masonry pillar 70 feet high and then resumed its 1 in 40 descent into the valley.

Four miles from its start the railway reached the foot of Glenariff and turned east along the coast. It was here than a stone-built engine house was erected and, close to it, a

The only known photograph of the Glenariff Railway, probably taken by Lawrence shortly after it was abandoned. It is taken looking up the valley towards Parkmore and the 1:40 gradient is very obvious.

National Library of Ireland

terrace of houses for employees. The gradient slackened to 1 in 71, and after a short level stretch the line crossed the coast road by the White Arch, whose name derived from the white limestone of the masonry abutments. The line then dropped at 1 in 60 for a couple of hundred yards and became level at the pier-head. The pier has long since been destroyed by storms, but a description of it in the *Ballymena Observer* of 10 May 1880 tells us that it was "built of concrete up to the high-water level, with a superstructure of timber … capable of exporting 200,000 tons per annum" and for easy berthing with "twenty-five feet of water alongside the greater part of the pier". The line had a total length of four miles and five furlongs.

At the head of the glen, the ore bed outcropped on both sides of the tributary valley of the Inver Water. On a large-scale map dated 1881, now in the office of the Antrim Estates company, four mine adits are shown on the south-eastern outcrop. These details are confirmed in the Geological Survey's written description of the area published in 1886. The railway line entered this upper part of the glen between the outcrops of ore and, at the termination of the line, an incline ran at right angles to it across the river to reach the north-west adits. On the south-east side, the ore bed was about 100 feet above the line, and access to it was gained by two reversing sidings, each about half a mile long. No buildings other than an explosives magazine are marked on this map, and it seems that permanent servicing facilities for the engine, other than water, were localised down at the White Arch. The only other buildings at Cloughcor were shelters or bothies for the miners.

The Field Club visit

Back in the city, the Belfast Naturalists' Field Club was a young and flourishing society whose members were always game for a field excursion in search of animal, vegetable or mineral matter. Nowadays, cars make such excursions easy but 90 years ago the members did not take their forays lightly. In July 1873, they visited the Glenravel mines, not far from Parkmore, and the description of that occasion in their journal mentions, incidentally, that "a regular railway is being laid down along the side of Glenariff". Someone mentally pigeon-holed that piece of news and two years later Glenariff and its iron ore mines were an obvious venue during a three-day excursion to the Antrim coast.

After an overnight stay at Cushendall, the party proceeded

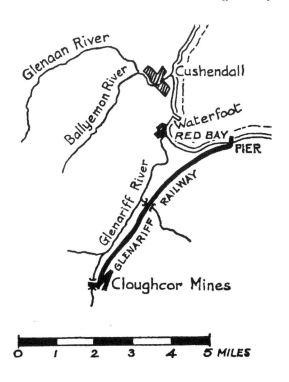

in wagonettes on Wednesday 21 July through the village of Waterfoot, until they reached the new pier of the GIO&H. Their journal tells us that, "Arrived at the pier, a special train, provided for the party by JJ Gardner, Esq, CE, the resident engineer of the company, was waiting" . . . and under his personal superintendence they were conveyed by the mineral railway up Glenariff, tracing the mountain side overlooking the valley. The train was made up of mining trucks, but they were so fitted up with seats under Mr Gardner's directions that "all were most comfortable and the steady motion of the wagons proved the superior construction of the line, over which thousands of tons of ore are intended to be conveyed to the pier at Red Bay."

This railway ride was one of the most interesting features of the excursion, and thus it happened that, in its earliest days, the Glenariff railway did convey passengers, albeit gratuitously and at their own risk.

The company dies

In spite of their large capital investment, the Glenariff Iron Ore and Harbour Company do not seem to have taken any steps to make sure that the quality of the ore persisted underground from the outcrop. This would have involved

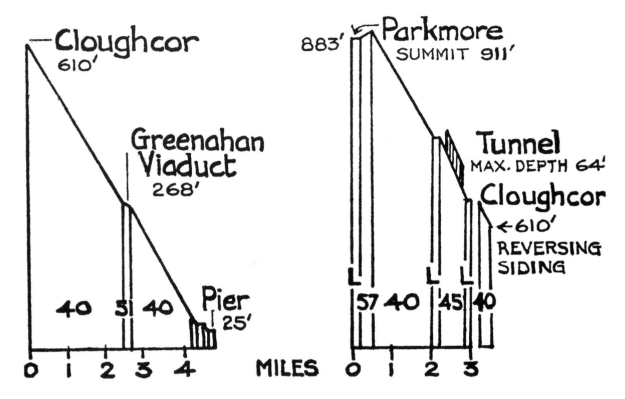

Gradient profiles of the Glenariff Mineral Railway (left) and the Glenariff Railway and Harbour Company's proposed link to Parkmore (right).

an expensive programme of drilling and, in their haste to extract ore and reap profits, it was not done. In the event, the high-grade ore seen at the outcrop thinned away as it was followed underground and the mines soon ceased to be economically viable. Any prosperity they may have enjoyed was short-lived, for mining lasted for only about three years and thereafter the railway in Glenariff lay derelict.

Traill's plan

The further story of the abandoned railway is linked with the name of William A Traill, who was prominent among those interested in railway development in County Antrim in the 1870s. The Traill family home was near Bushmills, and Traill himself was a graduate civil engineer. He had been on the staff of HM Geological Survey of Ireland, and had therefore a first-hand knowledge of the mineral resources of the district.

During 1876, Traill had attempted without success to get support for a narrow gauge railway between Ballymena

and the little town of Ballycastle on the northern coast. Though a small coalfield was there,* its best days were over and the output of coal was insufficient to justify the construction of a railway through such a thinly-populated region. Notwithstanding this reverse, Traill and his brother Dr Anthony Traill, were involved in 1879 in no less than three schemes. Two of these involved branches from the Ballycastle Railway, which was then being built by a separate company between Ballycastle and Ballymoney. The third scheme was aimed at a revival of the Glenriff line by linking it with the Ballymena, Cushendall and Red Bay Railway which, since 1875, had passed within three miles of the Glenariff railway at Parkmore.

During the autumn of 1879, Traill surveyed the course of a connecting line from the Cloughcor terminus of the Glenariff railway to the peat works at Cargan, two and a quarter miles below Parkmore. Preparations for the submission of a Bill to Parliament were begun. The BC&RBR directors became alarmed at this development,

* See pp 5–7 of The Ballycastle Railway

since Traill's scheme was potentially capable of diverting ore traffic from their own railway to the pier at White Arch. Nonetheless, Traill's scheme was widely publicised as one intended to relieve local unemployment and to open up the tourist trade in the Glens.

Winter 1879–80 saw Traill busily engaged in whipping up local enthusiasm for his connecting line and for the revival of the defunct Glenariff railway. On 8 May 1880 the *Ballymena Observer* reported a meeting he addressed in Cushendall, a village which had been waiting impatiently for four years for the BC&RBR to extend their line down from the top of the Glenballyemon, which was parallel to and a few miles north of Glenariff. Traill made it clear to his audience that the BC&RBR were unlikely ever to get their line beyond Retreat, down Glenballyemon and round by Cushendall to Red Bay, since the powers for construction had lapsed, capital was wanting, and the line would have been impossibly steep. His listeners realised there was much truth in his arguments and, thus encouraged, Traill proceeded to form a company and to draft a Bill for Parliament. By this time he had altered and shortened the projected course of his connecting line so that it had joined the BC&RBR at Parkmore rather than at Cargan.

A week after the notice of the Cushendall meeting, the *Ballymena Observer* published the prospectus of Traill's new venture, entitled 'The Glenariff Railway and Harbour Company'. There were to be four directors, two of them from the Glenariff Iron Ore and Harbour Company, and the Traill brothers, William and Anthony. The prospectus stated that the directors had arranged with the GIO&H to purchase their entire railway, rolling stock and pier. The connecting line from Cloughcor to Parkmore was to be three miles in length, with a maximum gradient of 1 in 40. Only one road bridge and one river bridge would have to be constructed, but a short tunnel, two furlongs in length, would be required to obtain the necessary gradient and to avoid the residence of Mr C Dobbs. The situation of the tunnel was to be in "the lithomarge bed, a rock comparatively easy to excavate". (Lithomarge is a red clay below the iron ore bed.) A station was proposed to give access to the rugged scenery of the upper part of the glen to the old mines, while two other stations would be at Parkmore, the termini of the combined lines, and at the pier.

The junction of Traill's connecting railway with the old Glenariff mineral railway would, in practice, have been particularly awkward. Due to the topography, trains coming from Parkmore would have had to sweep into the valley head and enter a reversing siding before they could proceed down Glenariff. A more direct route would have involved the expense of a viaduct across the river valley.

A company is incorporated

The company was now re-styled the Glenariff Railway and Pier Company but at the end of June 1880, the Bill was still being contested by the BC&RBR, and also by the Belfast and Northern Counties Railway. A few days later their opposition was withdrawn when the Glenariff company agreed to delete the requirements covering running powers over the Parkmore–Ballymena section of the BC&RBR's line. So it was that, in the summer of 1880, the GR&PC obtained their Act of Incorporation. All seemed set for the revival of the mineral line and it was confidently expected that the BC&RBR would take steps to secure powers to work passenger trains on their own railway.

Down at the White Arch, the engines of the Glenariff mining company had been shedded and silent, but in October 1880 the line came to life again. Traill, the enthusiast, was attempting to infuse his backers with some of his own zeal. On 9 October 1880 the *Ballymena Observer* reported a visit to the line by prospective supporters who, after a luncheon provided by Traill, gathered to listen to their host. They then "after Mr Traill's remarks … under his guidance proceeded to the terminus of the Glenariff line, which is situated just at the end of the valley and is surrounded on all sides by mines … having been comfortably seated in a van and a couple of trucks, a pleasant run of about half an hour brought the 'inspectors' to the pier, several stoppages being made on the way to view some of the prettiest scenery in Ireland. The return trip was made in less than 20 minutes, the incline being on a gradient of 1:40 and the terminus being 500 (sic) feet above sea level."

A meeting of the new company was held on 12 October 1880 in the Ballymena courthouse and it quickly became apparent that the BC&RBR's opposition had only been latent. The company now meant to prevent Traill's line from developing any worth-while mineral traffic by imposing a level of 1s 0d per ton-mile for any ore carried in the reverse direction, into Ballymena. The meeting appointed a local committee to further their affairs, consisting of Messrs

Martin, Gault, Crosbie, Kidd, Raphael, Chesney and Watson, with FA Williams as their local secretary. It was a gesture of defiance but it achieved nothing.

Abandonment

Thereafter, both because of the slow intake of capital and the resistance of the BC&RBR, Traill's scheme languished. The years passed without any construction being attempted and in 1885 formal steps were taken to obtain an abandoning Act. The old mineral railway was still *in situ* in Glenariff, unused since that train of two wagons and a brake van had rumbled over it in October five years before. The Earl of Antrim had neither received rent from the mining company nor tolls from traffic, and so on 8 November 1884 he secured a judgement in the London courts against the Glenariff Iron Ore and Harbour Company for arrears of rent. Under a writ, the Sheriff of Antrim seized all the chattels of the defendant and a sale took place at the Chamber of Commerce in Belfast on 18 March 1885. The *Belfast News Letter* advertised it on 15 March:

SHERIFF'S SALE

Earl of Antrim v Glenariff Iron Ore and Harbour Coy.

Valuable Mining Property

To Railway Companies, Contractors, Mining Engineers, Brokers and others. Wheatley, Kirk, Price and Goutly are instructed to sell by *Public Auction* at the *Chamber of Commerce*, Belfast on Wednesday 18th day of March at 3 o'clock in the afternoon prompt.

The following Goods comprising Two three foot gauge Six-Wheel Locomotive Engines (four wheels coupled) built by R. Stephenson and Co.; 40 iron side tip Iron-stone Wagons by the Ashbury Company Ltd.; Sundry Pile Driving Engines and Boilers; Side Lathe; about 500 tons of 40 lb and other lighter Flat Bottom Rails, Stores and other Effects of the Glenariff Iron Ore and Harbour Co Ltd, Glenariff, County Antrim, seized under a writ of *Fieri Facias* in the above cause to the Sheriff of the County of Antrim directed. The whole to be offered in Lots as per Catalogue to be obtained on application to the Sheriff's Office, Belfast or at the Auctioneers, Albert Square, Manchester or 52 Queen Victoria Street, London, W.C.

The rails were bought on behalf of the Earl of Antrim and left *in situ*. In June 1890, about three miles of the track were removed literally overnight by the owners of the land on which they stood, a 'midnight flit' that had a parallel in the disappearance of the Parsonstown and Portumna Bridge Railway in 1883. The sequel to this was the appearance of the landowner and Lord Antrim at the 1891 Spring Assizes in Belfast.

The Glenariff auction

An interesting sight of the final stages of the Glenariff railway is given in a series of letters exchanged between Basil McCrea and John McFarland, partners in the firm of civil engineering contractors that bore their names. They connect the fate of the Glenariff rolling stock with the growth of the Londonderry and Lough Swilly Railway, which was then working a line from the City of Derry to the town of Buncrana in County Donegal. At the time, the regauging of the Swilly line was under discussion, but the directors were not over-anxious to incur the expense of bringing in their gauge from 5ft 3 in to 3ft, and thus having to replace their rolling stock. However, the completion of the 3ft-gauge Letterkenny Railway, which was to meet the Swilly's line at Tooban, was making the change expedient and the commonsense of the decision was being pressed upon the directors by John McFarland. He had joined the board of the LLSR only in 1884, but he and McCrea held many shares in the company and were able to exert a powerful influence on its affairs.

Basil McCrea and John McFarland saw in the sale of the Glenariff rolling stock a unique opportunity to acquire dependable vehicles at a low price for the regauged Swilly line. Though a decision to regauge had not been taken by the date of the sale, it followed within a few days. Meanwhile, McCrea and McFarland were prepared to purchase the machinery on chance, perhaps with a view to using it on their own contracting work if the Swilly remained a standard-gauge line. Basil McCrea was in Belfast, and wrote to his partner in Derry from their city office:

> 10 Donegall Street
> 17 March 1885
>
> Dear McFarland,
>
> *Glengariffe (sic) Rolling Stock.* I only saw Malcolm* this morning and he says he was sent by his own Coy. to value the stock and report on it some time since – and he consequently knows all about it. The lathe is he says good and will turn wheels. The Engines are in good order and cost £1800 – are better than any

* Bowman Malcolm, Locomotive Engineer of the BNCR

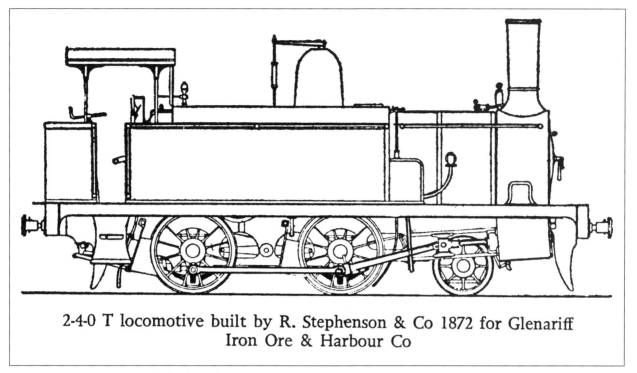

2-4-0 T locomotive built by R. Stephenson & Co 1872 for Glenariff Iron Ore & Harbour Co

N.G. Engines now wrought by themselves. I sent you his report by 11.25 train and hope you have got it before now. If you think good you might send Dawson here to-morrow morning. I am meantime sending for McCoy who went to view the Plant on Monday and will hear what he thinks of it. Malcolm thinks it will go very cheap and engines could run on Buncrana line when regauged, the present rails being heavy enough. Collins concurs about Engines.

and on the following day, McCrea wrote again:

. . . Auction at 3 o.c. to-day – I say McCoy who wants to buy a good many articles himself and demanded 5% on all he would buy, he is to call on me at 2.30 to-day and I believe he'll acct at 5% up to purchases amtg. To £500, above that sum 2½%. Lathe old-fashioned, will turn wheels, told him £20 to £25 might be gone for it. Engines £400 each. Wagons £10 each and Brake Van with scrap iron in it £25. The lot in which Diver's Suit is he will give £70 for himself, he might I told him buy for us at up to £50 – the suit he considers worthy £40 by itself, he thinks he may buy himself some of the Rails at 13s a ton, but this is nonsense. McCoy thinks the whole will go cheap unless the party selling them buy them in (The Earl of Antrim? I think is selling) . . .

On the day after the sale, McCrea reported to his partner:

I attended at sale yesterday. McCoy bought the Two Engines at £450 each, £900-0-0, 40 wagons at £10 each £400, Springs for Engines £4, Brake Van, weighted with about 10 tons Iron for £25 – in all £1329. McCoy's Commn. 2½% £33-4-6. We must set about bringing these away at once, where should they be taken to? I presume Derry, and what means do you recommend? I fancy we must charter a vessel, they must be cleared away from where they are. McCoy has the lot with the diving suit which he'll sell us at a price if we want it – should I buy it and for how much – I cannot tell you what it cost as it went among a lot of other things … John Gault went in for the Engines, I think he got the lathe at £36. . .

Shipment to the Swilly

Writing to McFarland on 20 March 1885, McCrea continued the discussion of the means by which their purchases should be removed:

Glengariff stock. I cannot find McCoy today but presume I must pay for all in a day or two – then we want all removed very shortly. I have asked Cumming for a quotation from Retreat station to L'Derry, it will take a good deal to bring the Plant to the Cushendall line. Malcolm thinks we got them wonderfully cheap (Silas Evans who was present at the sale appears to have told him), and he says the only way to get them away will be by chartering a vessel – either steamer or sailing – also he thinks the Pier won't carry engines unless strutted and strengthened . . .

A week passed, during which McFarland made arrangements to send a fitter to Glenariff to start dismantling the engines. McCrea wrote on 27 March, obviously pleased with the bargain:

> . . . You will see he (Dawson) expresses a moderate approval of the Rolling Stock at Genariffe. Young McCoy writes they were delighted with it and said the Engines were worth £1,000 each.

The shipping arrangements took some further time to settle, for the Glenariff pier, after ten years of neglect, was indeed too weak to carry the engines. On 11 April, McCrea informed his partner of the decision:

> . . . I had McCoy with me and we consulted as to what should be done to strengthen the Glenariffe Pier. We came to the conclusion that we could not with safety bring the Engines over the Pier, unless by making extensive repairs which would be too costly. We arranged to bring them from Cushendall Pier 1½ miles distant over a good level road. I am in communication with Tate as to depth of water &c at Cushendall, afterwards I must write Black and Jackson re steamer calling on a Saturday afternoon on way from L'pool to Derry.

Final arrangements for removal of the stock were placed in the hands of Philip Ellis, the locomotive superintendent of the LLSR, and the shipment was made about the end of May from Red Bay pier, which McCrea regarded as 'Cushendall Pier'.

On the Swilly's line, the two Glenariff engines became Nos 5 and 6 and had a life there of only 14 years, surprisingly short for engines which had received such lavish praise when they were bought.

To judge by the Board of Trade railway returns, the 40 wagons and the brake van were not taken into LLSR stock until 1886, the delay no doubt being dictated by the amount of money the Swilly were prepared to spend on new purchases. Unfortunately, detailed records of the Swilly's wagon stock do not seem to exist for these early days.

Chapter 3

The Ballymena, Cushendall and Red Bay Railway

Iron in the blue hills

In the uplands east of Ballymena, the existence of iron ore was first recognised in 1843 by Mr Crommelin of Newtown Crommelin, but it was not until 23 years later that mining was started in the Glenravel tract by Mr James Fisher of Barrow-in-Furness. Fisher rented land from Mr Edward Benn at a rate of £10 for the first year and, so efficient was he as a mine manager, that in his first half-year of tenancy he was able to ship 18,000 tons of ore to England. Thereafter mining activity increased, and in the 1870s ore was being extracted on both sides of the upper part of the valley between Martinstown and Parkmore.

Lack of local coal supplies made smelting out of the question and, from the start, the mining companies were faced with the problem of getting the ore away from this remote part of Antrim. The nearest railway was the main line of the Belfast and Northern Counties Railway at Ballymena, eight to ten miles from the nearest outcrop of ore. Transport by horse-drawn carts was not attractive, as an output of 100–200 tons a day was envisaged, but the roads were rough in a dry summer and nearly impassable in winter. Moreover, the distance to Ballymena from the Parkmore mines and back was around 30 miles and there would be practically no return traffic. The alternative was a steep descent of the Glenballyemon road to Cushendall near which, as we have noted, the sheltered harbour of Red Bat was available for shipping.

Haulage of ore by road was therefore replaced by a mechanical substitute and, in May 1871, the Wire Tramway Company Ltd was incorporated in London to build and operate overhead bucket haulage on Hodgson's principle. This company owned a subsidiary, the Antrim Wire Tramway Co, and by March 1872 it was laying out the course of an eight mile route between the Cargan mines and Red Bay harbour. The Antrim Iron Ore Company had agreed to pass 55,000 tones of ore over the tramway in six years, or to buy it at £13,000 cash, or £7,000 for the section between Cargan and Retreat.

A railway is planned

More or less simultaneously with the Wire Tramway scheme, an orthodox railway was planned, with much the same aims as those of the Wire Tramway Company. The promoters of the railway first met in 1871, and the Parliamentary Bill for the Ballymena, Cushendall and Red Bay Railway was first deposited on 30 November of that year.* Of these early dealings we have no official record, for the first entry in the company's minute book is dated 10 January 1872. On that day the promoters met at 9 Victoria Chambers, Belfast to discuss progress; their names were William, Thomas and James Valentine, John Skelly and James Hind. The venue of their meeting was the city office of one Silas Evans, a gentleman best described as a professional railway manager, who had already been employed by the Belfast and County Down Railway and who was later to become the secretary of the Ballymena, Cushendall and Red Bay Railway, and also for a time, secretary and manager of the Ballycastle Railway.

The BC&RBR had appointed as their engineer, William Lewis, MICE, of 43 Dame Street, Dublin. He had surveyed the course of the line from Ballymena, up the valley of the Glenravel Water, past Cargan, Parkmore and Retreat Castle and down Glenballyemon to the coast at Red Bay, where the harbour was situated, one and a half miles south of the village of Cushendall. As planned, the railway line passed completely through the iron-ore mining district and was capable of moving ore either to the existing BNCR line at Ballymena, or to the coast for direct shipment.

Lewis's map accompanying the Bill submitted to Parliament in November 1871 illustrates vividly the problem which the topography of the district presented to the company, especially in bringing their line down to the coast; something akin to climbing from the centre of a saucer towards its rim and then getting safely down to the table. From a pass between the mountains of Trostan and Crockanlough – the rim of the saucer – the line had to be brought from an

Concurrently, a survey was made for a roadside tramway between Ballymena and Broughshane but the scheme did not reach the stage of being submitted to Parliament (PRONI, Record D662/17)

altitude of around 1,000 feet down almost to sea level at Red Bay pier, in only four miles as the crow flies.

Lewis's map shows a brief summit level at 1,071ft above ordnance datum, from which the line descended Glenballyemon, past Retreat Castle, on a gradient of 1 in 33 for a distance of about one and a quarter miles. It then entered a level catch siding or reversing road at 839ft OD in Altmore Upper townland. After reversal, the line dropped at 1 in 48 to a second catch siding at 787ft OD, not far from the south bank of the Ballyemon River. Having thus lost almost 300 feet of height, a second reversal brought the line down the slopes for two miles at 1 in 34 into the townland or Knockans North. Here a third catch siding necessitated another reversal. The line then went to Red Bay pier, but to lose the remaining 400 feet of height it was to have performed an almost complete circle, followed by a drop at 1 in 36/31 to a level crossing with the coast road. It would have had much in common with the Darjeeling railway in the Himalayas.

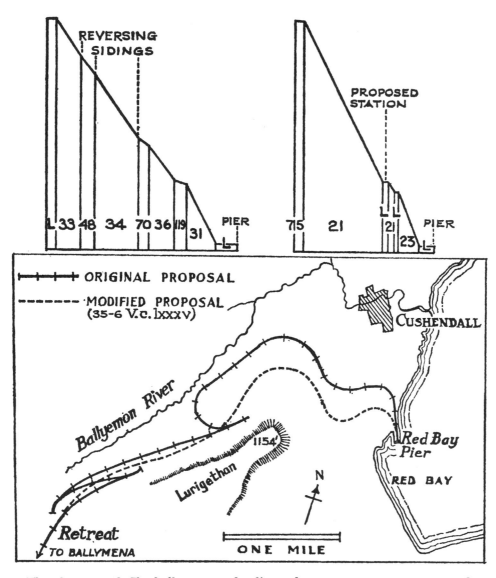

The descent of Glenballyemon—the lines that were never constructed

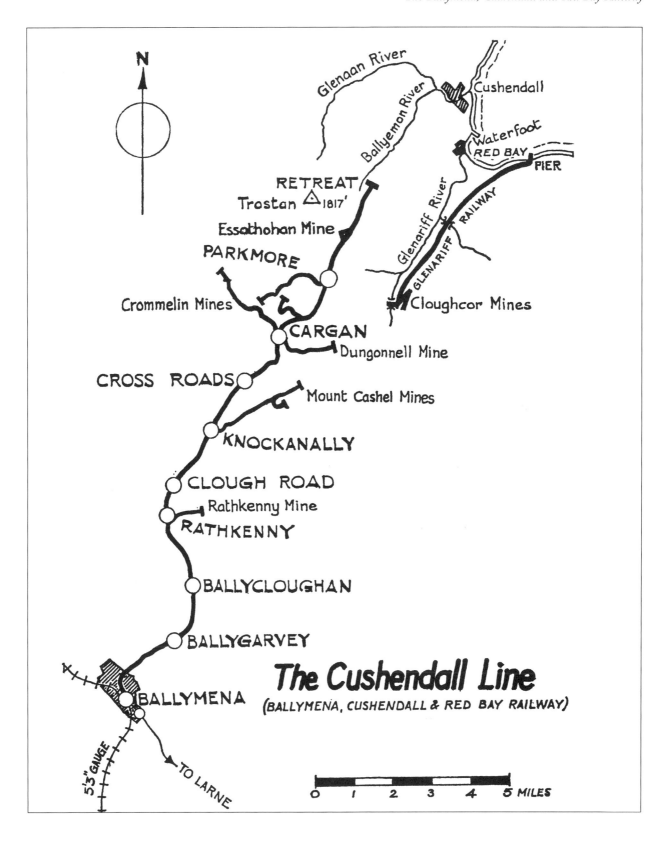

N

Glenaan River

Ballyemon River

Cushendall

Waterfoot
RED BAY
PIER

RETREAT

Trostan △ 1817'

Essathohan Mine

PARKMORE

Glenariff River

GLENARIFF RAILWAY

Crommelin Mines

Cloughcor Mines

CARGAN

Dungonnell Mine

CROSS ROADS

Mount Cashel Mines

KNOCKANALLY

CLOUGH ROAD

Rathkenny Mine

RATHKENNY

BALLYCLOUGHAN

BALLYGARVEY

5'3" GAUGE

BALLYMENA

TO LARNE

The Cushendall Line
(BALLYMENA, CUSHENDALL & RED BAY RAILWAY)

0   1   2   3   4   5 MILES

By the use of reversing sidings and sharp curves, Lewis managed to avoid anything steeper than 1 in 31. However, second thoughts prevailed and, on 5 April 1872, a revised plan was submitted with the Bill. The alterations were to begin at 14 miles and seven chains out of Ballymena and from the summit a short fall at 1 in 715 brought the line down to a height of 1,069 ft OD. There then was to follow a terrifying descent into Ballynahaville townland, where a station is shown on the parliamentary plan on a short level stretch at 309ft OD. There was then to follow a further half mile at 1 in 21, a short level stretch, and a drop at 1 in 23 to a bridge across the coast road, whence the line would have run in towards the pier on the level. It is difficult to see what advantage was gained by the alteration, apart from obviating the operating complication of the reversals and the replacement of the level crossing by an underbridge at the coast road. The prospect of a drop of four and a half miles at 1 in 21 would have daunted many a driver, to say the least.

Incorporation

Having deposited their Bill for the second time on 5 April 1872, the BC&RBR promoters had to sit back while parliamentary procedure ran its course. After passing the examiners, it survived the committee stage without opposition, went to the House of Commons on 24 June and received the Royal Assent on 18 July.

The Act of Incorporation of the BC&RBR authorised the company to build 22 miles 22 chains of railway from Ballymena to Red Bay pier. The directors named were William Valentine and Andrew Currall. Of particular interest is the reference to the gauge, for the BC&RBR happened to be the first Irish company to build their line on a gauge smaller than the standard 5ft 3in. The actual wording runs:

> Notwithstanding anything in the Act of 9th and 10th Victoria, chapter 57 contained, the company may construct the railway of such gauge as they think fit, provided that it be not wider than 3 feet or narrower than 2 feet.

From this elastic specification arose the Irish narrow gauge of three feet.

The 1872 BC&RBR Act further stipulated that the pier at Red Bay should be under the control of the Grand Jury of Antrim – forerunners of the present Antrim County Council – and the Commissioners of Public Works. It was not to carry passengers "without the consent of the Board of Trade". The maximum authorised capital was fixed at £120,000, made up of £90,000 in shares and £30,000 in loans. The BNCR was permitted to subscribe up to £25,000.

An offer from Hodgson

Waiting for their Bill to become law, the promoters of the BC&RBR met on 4 March 1872 and were addressed by Charles Hodgson, the patentee of the Wire Tramway. He was aware that the railway company intended to make their line down to the coast, but since he spoke of the *proposed tramway*, his aerial ropeway cannot have been actually built. He then went on to describe the tramway – four sections each two miles in length, each section containing four miles of 2³⁄₈in steel wire rope supported on 50 standards and powered by a 20hp steam engine. The ore would travel in 200 buckets, each holding 2½ cwt and the entire contraption would be able to deliver 280 tons of ore per day at the pier. Having sought to impress the assembled BC&RBR promoters with these statistics, Hodgson asked if they would agree to buy the wire tramway in three years time for £13,000. He reckoned that by making his contract with the mine owners he would forestall the descent of the Glenballyemon by the railway.

Fully conscious of the operating difficulties presented by their steep line, the railway promoters were more than a little interested in Hodgson's offer. They suggested a sum of £10,000, which Hodgson refused to accept. As events turned out, he would have been wise to have clinched the deal. Meanwhile construction of the wire tramway proceeded and by about the end of 1872 it was in place between Cargan mines and somewhere near to Red Bay pier.

Railway events move slowly

A week after their Act had received the Royal Assent, the BC&RBR directors met in Silas Evans' office, made him their secretary at a salary of £150 a year and ordered the first calls to be made upon the shares. For the next 11 months the company apparently went into hibernation, for no meetings of the board were held, and Evans managed affairs from his Belfast office.

Before the next board meeting there was some reshuffling among the members. They met on 24 June 1873 under the chairmanship of John Skelly, who had been among the original promoters but had not been named as a director in the Act of Parliament. In the interim, Evans had found a contractor to build the line, but the minutes tell nothing of how the contract was advertised, nor who tendered for it. Neither do they tell how or when it was decided that the gauge of the line should be three feet, though it is likely that the experience of the Isle of Man Railway guided them.

A provisional contract was made in June 1873 with James Connor to construct eleven and a quarter miles of line from Ballymena to Cargan, and to supply rails, sleepers, signals and stations for £5,500 per mile. This did not include the purchase price of the land. The contract was sealed on 7 November 1873. The decision to build only to Cargan was forced upon the company by the disappointingly slow intake of capital. Less than a third of the share capital had been subscribed and the company had been forced to raise money by resource to their loan authorisation, and to pay five per cent interest on it.

At the next meeting of the board, on 22 September, James Hind and Thomas Valentine reported that they had visited locomotive and wagon builders in England. The locomotive builders – the minutes do not state which – had pressed the company to adopt a gauge of 3ft 6in rather than the maximum of 3ft allowed by the Act. Clearly their opinion weighed heavily with some members of the board in spite of the fact that such a change would have needed further Parliamentary authority and added expense. They were brought to their senses by their engineer, Lewis, who pointed out that the bridge clearances were only suitable for a three foot gauge line. That settled the matter.

In spite of the directors' visit to England it is clear that the matter of locomotive supply was already more or less settled, since later in the meeting Silas Evans read letters he had received dated 3 July and 16 September, from Black, Hawthorn and Co of Gateshead. This firm had already furnished the BC&RBR with a specification for locomotives with 12 inch cylinders, and offered to supply three at a cost of £1,470 each. The directors decided to accept their offer, stipulating that delivery of the three engines was to be staggered; the first was to arrive after four and half months, the second after six and a half months and the third after eight months.

Up in the air once more

The BC&RBR board again assembled on the last day of 1873. Wagon supply was debated and the directors then went on to consider the use of wire tramways as *feeders* to their line. Some months before, the Antrim Wire Tramway's line had connected Cargan with Red Bay. Negotiations were already in hand with the Mountcashel Iron Ore Company and the Knockbuoy Mining Company with a view to carrying ore from a station at Quarrytown, once the railway was built. But no firm decision had yet been taken as to how the ore would be transported from the mines in the hillsides down to the railway in the valley, whether by horse-drawn carts, by branch lines, by hutch lines, or by overhead wire tramway. So Silas Evans was asked to arrange for a Mr Howell to make surveys for a line of wire tramway "from a point on the railway near Quarrytown to the Knockbuoy and Carreen mines, and to find from the Wire Tramway company the cost of putting it up".

But, by the end of 1873, 21 months after rejecting the BC&RBR's offer of £10,000, the Wire Tramway company was bankrupt. On 5 January 1874, Mr SC Fox, as liquidator of the Wire Tramway company, attended a meeting of the BC&RBR directors and asked them to consider subscribing towards the formation of a new company to take over the existing wire tramway. But the directors, understandably wary of committing themselves, deferred a decision and left Fox to try and make the best he could out of the ruins. A bankruptcy sale was advertised in the local press on 29 May 1875.

Contact was renewed in September 1875 between the Cushendall company and the liquidator who, by then, was ready to accept the Cushendall's offer of £360 for "the whole of the timber, rails, engine houses, buckets etc" and £140 for the "ten-house engine at Grand Junction station at Evishacrow. The driving grear, shunt rails, belts &c at Lime Kilns station. The pulleys &c of the line from Lime Kilns stations to Red Bay terminal, the patent rights of this tramway and the wayleave of the entire from Red Bay to the mines." Since nobody seems to have photographed the wire tramway, this description from the Cushendall minute book gives us as good a picture of it as we are likely to get. Whether the tramway ever conveyed any appreciable amount of ore seems doubtful.

The railway is opened

Having seen something of the wire tramway, we must now return to the Cushendall's own railway which Connor was building between Ballymena and Cargan. The country through which it passed offered no obstacles and the line lacked any noteworthy engineering features. Land purchase inevitably caused some trouble, owners suddenly attaching great value to land that had neither carried good crops nor fattened good beasts, but being vociferous in protests over severances. In July 1874, the minute book referred particularly to difficulty being experienced in acquiring land from the McCarts at Kinbally, a townland on the Ballymena side of Ballycloughan.

Connor took about 15 months to complete the laying of the line. On 5 January 1875 the company wrote to the Mountcashel Mining Company saying that they would shortly be in a position to carry iron-ore traffic for them. There was no siding below the mines and Lewis was urged to complete a "siding or station for iron ore at the Cross Roads at Carrycowan". Only the simplest of accommodation would have been needed.

The shareholders' minute book records that the line was partially opened, at the request of the mining companies, for ore traffic on 26 March 1875 and 'completely opened' to Cargan for general merchandise as well as ore on 1 July. During the later weeks of the summer, Connor was employing 400 men on the still unfinished parts of the line above Cargan.

Soon after the opening, it was evident that the line was taking much of the output of the mines in the lower part of the iron-ore field. Up to the end of June 1875, 11,336 tons of ore had been carried and the resulting income of the company was £1,271, an average of about £100 per week. During July and August 1875, the weekly tonnage rose to about 1,500 and the weekly receipts to above £130. On these results, the *Railway Times* commented that this was nearly £11 per mile per week "an amount unprecedented … in this history of Irish railways". And this in spite of the iron trade being in 'a depressed state'.

Advance to Retreat

The extension of the line beyond Cargan was delayed for lack of capital. Only about half the authorised £90,000 of ordinary share capital had been subscribed when Lewis submitted his plans for the Cargan–Retreat portion of the line to the board on 26 April 1875. The BNCR had been approached for financial backing and had agreed to lend the Cushendall company £7,500 if the line were extended to Retreat and made suitable for goods traffic throughout.

So a contract was signed with Connor to construct the Cargan–Retreat section for the sum of £10,600, or just over £2,000 per mile. The unfinished state of the works becomes evident when we read in the minutes of the same meeting that a contract was sealed with John Gault of Ballymena to erect a goods shed at Cargan for £68 11s 2d.

By the end of the year the line had been pushed well towards Parkmore. On 1 January 1876 a connection had been established with the Evishacrow mines over a short and steeply-graded branch trailing towards Parkmore and on the north side of the valley.

Steps to insure the company's buildings against fire damage were not taken until February 1876. The board's minute book lists the items for which cover was obtained and sketches a picture of a simply furnished railway, carrying most mineral traffic:

BALLYMENA: engine shed, coal store, smith's and carpenter's shop, office and weigh house.

CROSS ROADS STATION: goods store.

It seems strange that no mention is made of the Cargan goods store.

During the summer of 1876 Connor and his men were extending the line towards the watershed. They crossed the 900ft contour a mile north of Evishacrow and a short way beyond Parkmore they had reached 1,000ft above sea level. The summit level was 45 feet higher, between Parkmore and Retreat, and was followed by a 1 in 31 descent towards the terminus. This section of the railway was laid along the course of a disused road whose course can still be seen below Retreat. No attempt was made to accept the revised line shown in the plans accompanying the parliamentary bill, Retreat had become the accepted terminus. The line was opened to there on 8 October 1876.

Thoughts on the wire tramway

Having secured their bargain at a time when Connor was bringing the railway towards Retreat, the BC&RBR had to think seriously about what use they were going to make of their acquisition. Clearly, its existence in Glenballyemon relieved its owners of any urgent necessity to extend to Cushendall and Red Bay pier as their parliamentary powers allowed them to do.

So the Cushendall company considered use of the idle tramway to carry ore from Retreat down to Red Bay. In the course of a lengthy discussion at the board meeting on 7 October 1875, the practicability of eventually extending their railway a little way beyond Retreat to meet the tramway was argued, as was the alteration of the tramway to carry ore *on to* Red Bay pier. At the meeting, an estimate was tabled of the wages of the men who would be needed to work the tramway:

1 engineer	£1 10s	per week
1 fireman	15s	
8 fillers at top @ 15s	£6 0s	
4 emptiers at Red Bay @ 15s	£3 0s	
2 walkers @ 15s	£1 10s	
2 station men to pass buckets	£1 10s	
1 foreman	£3 0s	
1 clerk	£1 10s	
1 extra man	15s	
Total wages	£19 0s	per week
For 1,200 tons of ore per week	3¾d per ton	

At the board meeting on 15 October it was reported that it would cost £4,000 to alter the railway line to meet the wire tramway and, after some discussion, Silas Evans was told to visit the site. He reported favourably a week later, but action was deferred. In the following month a site for an eventual junction between railway and tramway in the townland or Altmore Upper was agreed upon, but nothing further happened.

Upon completion of the line to Retreat during the autumn of 1876 the section of wire tramway between Cargan and Retreat was redundant and the railway company started dismantling it. They loaded the materials on to their own wagons and took them to storage at Ballymena, the remainder of the wire tramway from Retreat to Red Bay being left in the care of Mr Reilly, the shipping agent at Red Bay.

Further dispersal of the wire tramway took place in March 1877, when some of the buckets were sold for three shillings each. The remaining portion lay derelict for the rest of that year, though the company apparently decided to retain it for, when a Mr Hilliard asked whether he could buy the steam engine situated at Knockans, two miles from Cushendall, it was resolved not to sell it. Then the inevitable happened, and by the summer of 1879 parts of the tramway were being stolen. A request by one of the mine owners earlier in the year that the company reconsider the linkage or railway and tramway near Retreat had brought no response, for the Cushendall company preferred to concentrate upon conveying ore inland to Ballymena rather than towards the coast.

On 28 August 1879 the board resolved to sell such of the tramway as was still standing but rescinded that decision a month later when they found that, by leaving it in place, they might use it to bargain against Traill's scheme to join the Glenariff railway with their own. As we have seen in the previous chapter, although Traill's scheme gained parliamentary sanction,

The abandoned summit at Retreat on 26 June 1940.
W Robb

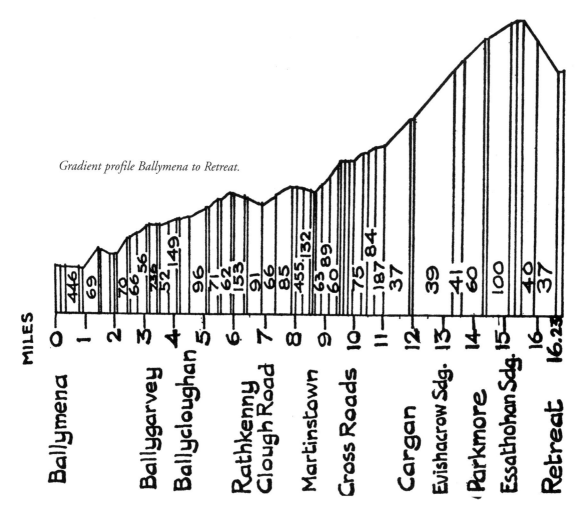

Gradient profile Ballymena to Retreat.

it failed to gain financial support from shareholders. Once Traill's railway scheme was safely out of the way, the Cushendall directors, at their meeting on 25 March 1881, again decided to dispose of their tramway. Though it had been lying unused for some eight years, they still thought highly of their steam engine at Knockans and placed a reserve price of £225 on it. It failed to sell and remained on the company's hands until the following July when they accepted £167 10s for it at Belfast.

The Course of the Cushendall Line

From the Ballymena terminus, which had merely an office, a goods store, interchange sidings and a small engine shed, the 'Cushendall line' as it was locally known, circled the perimeter of the town in a cutting that passed under the roads radiating from Ballymena to the north and north-east. Adverse gradients of 1 in 69/72/70/66 were encountered. The surrounding country was intensively farmed, with small fields, each with its massive, whitewashed gateposts of rubble stone and conical cap, so typical of the Ulster scene.

After covering a mile to the north-east, the line neared the woods around Ballygarvey House and turned towards the north. Four miles out, after traversing the townland of Ballycloughan, the country assumed a more rocky aspect and the first of the iron-ore mines was seen along an escarpment in Eglish townland on the 400 foot contour. The climb continued until, six miles from Ballymena, a short downgrade gave relief and the train ran freely into Rathkenny townland, a place to become well known in later years for its creamery. On the hill slopes to the east, the Rathkenny iron-ore mine worked by the Antrim Iron Ore Company was served by a siding which trailed towards Ballymena.

The line was now entering much poorer agricultural country. Hedges were replaced by stone walls or 'dykes' and, to the right, the ground rose towards rounded hills whose summits were above the 1,000 foot contour. To the left, the meandering Clough Water made its way towards its confluence with the River Maine at Glarryford. The village of Clough, whose name means 'the stony place', lay three miles away to the north.

Some eight miles from Ballymena and on a rising grade, the line crossed the Clough Water by a stone bridge, a few yards from the meeting of the smaller Skerry and Glenravel Waters. There was a cross-roads nearby, and a long branch line ran off in an easterly direction towards the Mount Cashel ironstone mines. These adits were located 800 feet above sea level on the north-facing slope of a hill named Carncormick, in the townland of Evishnablay. Colloquial abbreviation of the name of the townland resulted in the workings being referred to as the 'Bleagh' mines.

From the junction with the Bleagh branch, the railway now climbed into the upland region at an average gradient of 1 in 60, keeping the Glenravel Water in company on the right. At a level crossing, nine and three-quarter miles from Ballymena, in Carrowcowan townland, the company built their only intermediate station and for some years named it after the townland, later changing the name to 'Cross Roads'. The cross roads was not far distant, where the main Ballymena–Cushendall road was intersected by another road that rose to the bleak mining village of Newton Crommelin a mile away. Along the narrowing valley, the railway held its north-west course for a mile before skirting the grounds of Glenravel House, an oasis of trees in an otherwise bare landscape. Then, as the line turned towards the north, it steepened markedly and, at 1 in 37, entered a deep and damp cutting to pass below the main road near the small mining hamlet of Cargan.

Around Cargan, iron ore was mined on both sides of the valley at various times. To the east, a branch line crossed the main road on the level and went up the valley of the Ballsallagh Water for one and a half miles into the Dungonnell mining tract. Four adits were driven here on the north side of the stream, nearly 800 feet above sea level, and for a time the Antrim Iron Ore Company extracted a quantity of good-quality ore. Activity then ceased and the mines were closed, not through exhaustion of the ore bed but because of difficulties in meeting the requirements of the landowners.

After the closure of the Dungonnell mines, the branch railway was cut back to a length of about a quarter of a mile, serving the British Aluminium Company's Cargan bauxite mine. It was at Cargan that the association of the aluminium ore bauxite with the iron ore was first discovered by Mr JFW Hodges, JP, in about 1871.

On the west side of the Cushendall railway at Cargan an interesting branch line went off. Called the Crommelin Mineral Railway, it crossed the Cargan Water and ascended the steep slope towards the ore outcrop by means of a rope-worked incline with a gradient of about 1 in 11. Having climbed from about 700ft at Cargan to nearly 1,000ft, the line became more or less level and went curving around the hill slope, first west and then north, passing first an engine house that served the incline and then, in turn, the Tuftarney Mines, the Crommelin Mines, Walker's Drift and Salmon's Drift, until it finally reached Herd's Drift. The last was remotely situated in bleak moorland on the banks of the Skerry Water at a height of about 1,100ft above sea level.

Back on the main Cushendall line, the

The abandoned and dismantled bridge over the Clough Water river at Martinstown on 19 June 1940.   W Robb

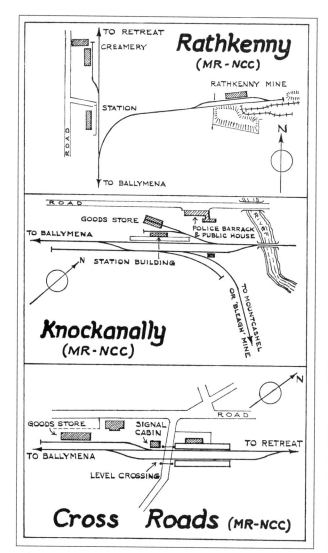

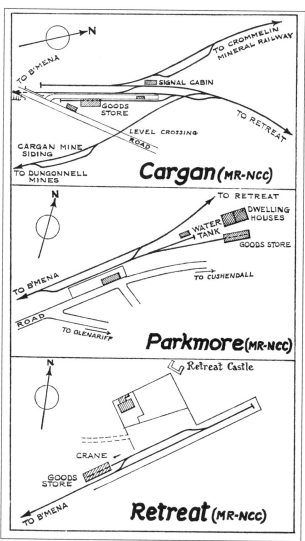

The track diagrams above show the BC&RBR stations as they were in BNCR days, after passenger services had been introduced in 1886 (to Knockanally) and 1888 (to Parkmore). Before 1886, the only stations were goods facilities at Cross Roads and Retreat. Knockanally is better known as Martinstown, its name after 1920. Retreat never had passenger facilities.

gradient of 1 in 39 continued for over a mile beyond Cargan, the line keeping close to the east bank of the Cargan Water. On the ascent, a steep siding curved in from the Evishacrow Mine and Chambers' Mine, which were opened about 1870 for iron ore and then, after being closed for many years, reopened for bauxite. On Ordnance maps, the Evishacrow siding is shown as ending not far to the north of the river crossing, but a later extension seems to have been continued around the hill into a valley occupied by the Binvore Burn, where mining trials were carried out.

Above the Evishacrow junction, the gradient eased to 1 in 41 and then to 1 in 60 as the line reached a treeless wind-swept plateau, seamed with peat hags, and neared the road fork to Retreat and Glenballyemon on the left, to Glenariff on the right. Here, in later years, the BNCR built Parkmore station, but in the days of the BC&RBR the location was noteworthy for the long Parkmore siding which trailed in towards Retreat, giving access from the Ballynahavla Mine and other mine adits close to the Tuftarney mines.

The railway left Parkmore on a rise of 1 in 100 and

The site of Martinstown station (Knockanally) on 2 June 1963, looking north. The station building is in the foreground and the station house beside the water tower.
Richard Whitford

was soon 1,000 feet above sea level. To the left Trostan mountain rose, smoothly rounded, with a summit altitude of 1,817 feet, which made it the highest hill in County Antrim. The ore outcrop ran parallel with the railway along the southern slopes of Trostan and was worked in a number of small adits, notably those at Essathohan, where the railway reached its summit level of 1,045 feet above sea level and where there was a siding to serve the mine.

From the summit, the railway continued across grassy moorland, partly in cutting, a warning of the steep glen ahead as the gradient dipped from 1 in 40 to 1 in 37. This slope was maintained down to Retreat, a terminus made for the goods traffic offered by the farmers in the lower part of the glen and by the small coastal communities of Waterfoot, Cushendall and Cushendun. The station was named after the ruins of nearby Retreat Castle. The massive white limestone, that forms a basement to the great sheets of black basalt, outcropped a short way from the railway terminus where it was quarried beside the Glenballyemon road and burned to lime in kilns. For many years the coal to fire the kilns was brought by road from near Ballycastle.

Ballymena and the Northern Counties line

Under the ownership of the BC&RBR, their railway was a simple affair with facilities at Ballymena, Cross Roads, and Retreat solely for goods. In Ballymena, the company's yard and workshops lay to the east of the BNCR's main line, and a short way north of that company's passenger station. The Northern Counties goods station and yard had always been sited half a mile to the south, where the main-line passenger station of the Belfast and Ballymena Railway had been. Thus, although the Cushendall brought in trains from Retreat with mineral or merchandise, and chiefly the former, the broad gauge facilities were half a mile away. So, from the start, to get their massive tonnages of iron ore away, the Cushendall adopted the simple means of having a number of their own broad gauge wagons, doing the transhipment by a gantry at their own terminus, where narrow gauge wagons dropped their loads into broad gauge wagons below, and then handing the loaded broad gauge wagons to the BNCR to be taken to Belfast.

After September 1880 a connection was provided across

the Braid Water bridge to the narrow gauge line of the Ballymena and Larne Railway at Harryville station. From then, the Cushendall company had the choice of either narrow gauge movement of their goods to the port of Larne, or transhipment to the broad gauge as before.

Extensions are Planned

After two years of operation, the Cushendall directors were acutely aware that their line was not able to serve the market yard at Ballymena, and considered how best this might be done. The Ballymena market precinct was older than the railways and stood on the north-east side of the town, between Ballymoney Street and Broughshane Street. When the Belfast and Ballymena Railway had entered the town, they had chosen to keep to the west side, since access to the market would have involved expensive demolition of existing property. In its turn, the BC&RBR was attracted to the west side of the town because the broad gauge railway artery was established there and because it was over its metals that forwarding traffic would have to be sent.

But Ballymena's market place, neglected by the railways, remained nonetheless a busy centre of commerce, and since its situation was hallowed by tradition it was up to the railways to go to it, rather than for the Fair Green and Market House to migrate to the railway. Indeed, the problem of access to the market was exercising not only the Cushendall management, but also those of the Northern Counties and the Ballymena and Larne companies. The Cusdendall company's solution was to draw up a Bill in 1877 proposing the construction of no less than five 'railways', two of which related to the market and the others to the mining areas of the Braid valley. The relevant Act became law on 4 July 1878.

Had the Cushendall's plans for market connections been realised, a triangle of narrow gauge lines would have been created on the north side of the town. Railway No 1, as defined in the Act of Parliament, was a short one, its junction with the existing Cushendall railway trailing towards the terminus, and with a length of 5 furlongs 4 chains and 8 yards.

The second railway in the 1878 Act was to be 4 furlongs 4¼ chains in length, running from a point 370 yards east of the east side of the old Ballymoney road to the market place. It formed the third side of the triangle.

The estimated costs of these two railways were £12,000

and £9,000, so that, although only single-track affairs, they would have cost about £18,000 per mile, which illustrates the expensive demolitions and land purchase which would have been involved. It is noteworthy that the Act authorised the gauge of these lines to be not more than 5ft 3in and not less than 2ft, so that either standard or narrow gauge could have been laid. It was probably the promoters' intention to lay the first of the market branches in mixed gauge, so that vehicles of both companies could reach the market.

The other three railways (Nos 3, 4 and 5) authorised by the 1878 Act were to give the Cushendall company access to the Braid Valley, along the north side of which iron-ore mining had been started at Clonetrace, in a district not served by the Parkmore line or its branches.*

Railway No 3 was to diverge from the existing railway about two miles from Ballymena and run for 2 miles, 2 furlongs and 3 chains in a generally ENE direction to terminate near the village of Broughshane. It was estimated to cost £13,000, including £1,800 for stations and £1,313 for sidings. No engineering works of any consequence were required and the gradient for part of the way would have been 1 in 80. Railways Nos 4 and 5 were to start from its terminus.

Railway No 4 was to extend along the Braid Valley for 4 miles 4 furlongs and 14 yards to Aughfatten townland, near Cleggan Lodge. It would have resembled the Parkmore line in following a through route between the interior of the county and the east coast and would have served the farms of the Braid Valley, rather than any mines.

Railway No 5 was to be 2 miles 2 furlongs 7 chains in length, and to provide access to the Clontrace mining tract. After rising at 1 in 55/45, it was to end at Dougherty's Bridge, whence tramways could have connected the line to mines worked in Elginny, Clonetrace and Ballylig townlands.

With its chronic shortage of capital, the BC&RBR was never able to build any of these five branches. In 1880, when the authorised time for their completion lapsed, a further Act of Parliament was obtained, this being a financial precaution to ensure that capital authorised under the 1878 Act could be used to complete some of the works detailed in the 1872 Act of Incorporation. Three years later, and still hopeful that money might flow in, the company went to the expense of yet another Act, the purpose of which was to revive the extinct powers of the 1878 Act. But

---

* The Ballymena and Larne Co was promoting an Act at the same time, along the same lines.

in spite of all this, no construction was ever started.

Even though they lacked railway transport, the mines in the area around Clontrace were able to maintain production, and even continued to do so after many of the other mines had closed down. This seems to have been due to an fortunate combination of good quality ore occurring as a thicker bed than usual, and at Ballylig, the ability to drain the mine easily since the adit was driven on a rise. Around 1885, when government geologists visited the area, ore was being carted to Ballymena at a price of 2s 6d per 20–25cwt. In 1912, when they again reported on the mineral resources, it was stated that the haulage of the ore to Ballymena railway station was being done "by light traction engines and wagons". After being closed for many years, the Ballylig mine was reopened during the Second World War.

Storm clouds gather

After their adventurous 1878 Act, the Cushendall company remained an independent concern for only six more years. Their dividend during 1878 was five per cent and represented the peak of their earnings, though in that year mineral and general merchandise tonnages were both less than in 1877. The chief cause of concern was the iron trade depression and, pressed by the mining companies, the railway had to reduce its charges for ore freight and hope for better times. They were not to come.

In spite of the gathering clouds, the company contracted in February 1878 with one Blayney Adair, who had built a railway house at Retreat, to erect two cottages at the level crossings at Islandtown and Ballygarvey. Then, in the autumn of the year, a courageous gesture was the decision to get Lanyon, the consulting engineer, to survey the course of a line from Cleggan to Carnlough, a distance of around seven miles, for which he was to be paid £25 per mile. This would have been an extension of 'Railway No 4' of their 1878 Act and would have been given access to a good harbour, which their original scheme via Retreat had failed to do. A Bill was prepared for Parliament, but in February 1879 it was decided to withdraw it.

A serious matter now facing the board was deterioration of their permanent way and here, as on many another small railway, early parsimony was catching up. Robert Collins told the board on 3 February 1879 that renewals were becoming an urgent necessity and estimated that £940 a year would have to be spent over the next ten years, much

of it in replacing 45 lb iron rails with 54 lb steel rails, and home grown larch sleepers with larger ones of imported red pine. The wooden tops of the bridges also needed to be replaced by iron. Bowman Malcolm deepened the gloom by reporting that the engines would need heavy repairs before long, and estimated the cost of this at £79 per engine per annum spread over ten years.

The dangers inherent in the company's over-reliance on mineral traffic were now fully evident, and though it was still the major source of their income, it was rapidly diminishing. At the board meeting in March 1879 there was a long discussion on the advisability of carrying passengers, which would have required a host of changes in the method of working. The board asked Collins to estimate the cost of 'making the line suitable', and it was arranged that Cotton of the Northern Counties would estimate the cost of running passenger trains, while Donaghey (the locomotive superintendent) would estimate the extra locomotive costs involved. In total, they presented such a formidable picture that no action was taken. In the first half of the year the dividend fell to 4¼ per cent, and in the ensuing half it dropped to 2½ per cent. That winter the board were stalked by the spectre of Traill's Glenariff Railway.

Unemployment was increasing throughout the district, and in January 1880 the Glens of Antrim Relief Committee had tried to focus attention on the depressed state of the area by drawing the Board of Trade's attention to the fact that the Cushendall line did not carry passengers. This the Board of Trade were well aware of, since they published the information in their annual railway returns, but they had no powers to force the owning company to change their way of working. In the following year the Cushendall directors again discussed whether their line could be made 'suitable for passengers'. They thought it could be managed for £6,000, but when the Northern Counties, who knew better, spoke of £9,000, nothing further was done.

The year 1880 began in dull fashion, the ordinary shareholders receiving no dividend in the first half. But events brightened and in the second half of the year they reaped 3½ per cent. Eventually, the year turned out to be the busiest the company had ever had, with train mileage up to a record 43,522 from 26,613 in the year before, and the mineral tonnage 118,721 compared with 79,663 in 1879. Even general merchandise, which in terms of tons carried amounted to only around 3% of the weight of minerals, showed a healthy increase, though the 3,272 tons only earned £553 as against the £11,561 received for ore haulage.

Beginning of the End

During 1881, both mineral traffic and general merchandise fell away sharply and by the end of the year the gross receipts were only £8,528, a poor figure beside the £12,133 of the previous year. Total working expenditure had increased by £192.

From May 1882, secretarial administration of the company seems to have become lax, as the minute book contains no record of board meetings. The directors' reports to the shareholders refer repeatedly to falling traffic in ore, and to the mine owners' assertion that unless the railway reduced their rates they could not keep the mines open. Depression in the iron trade continued to be the primary cause. By the end of 1882, resignations had reduced the number of directors to three – Thomas and William Valentine and James Hind. They then resigned, but were reappointed and the board strengthened by the advent of Sir Charles Lanyon Kt and John Young, chairman of the BNCR.

At the half-yearly meeting held on 29 February 1884, the directors stated that "the results of the working of the line for the past half year have not been satisfactory in consequence of the continued depression prevailing in the iron-ore trade." No solution was sought, no cure was offered. The statutory meeting was followed by an extraordinary meeting at which the chairman read to the shareholders the title of a parliamentary Bill:

> . . . to authorise the Belfast and Northern Counties Railway to construct tramways from Broughshane to Clonetrace and from Retreat to Cushendall *and to vest the undertaking of the Ballymena, Cushendall and Red Bay Railway in the Belfast and Northern Counties Railway* . . .

On the motion of Thomas Valentine, seconded by James Hind, the meeting unanimously approved the contents of the Bill. It was the beginning of the end of the Cushendall company. On 14 July 1884 the Bill became law, and took effect three months from that day.

Ex-Ballymena Cushendal and Red Bay Railway 0-4-2ST No 61 at Parkmore after passenger services had commenced.

L&GRP

Chapter 4

The Ballymena and Larne Railway

The Port of Larne

Though Larne became well known later as the Irish terminus of the cross-channel sailings from Stranraer in south-west Scotland, its port facilities were developed comparatively recently and a century and a half ago it was merely a small fishing village. In the early nineteenth century the Post Office mails largely dictated the existence of organised transport services between Scotland and Ireland, and they were then being run between Donaghadee in Co Down and Portpatrick in Wigtownshire. These particular sailings ceased in the late 1840s but were revived in the 1860s, after railways had been built to the two ports. Largely because of the exposed situation of Portpatrick harbour, they lasted for only ten years.

They very existence of the Portpatrick Railway depended on the continuation of cross-channel services from the south-west of Scotland, and once the Donaghadee sailings were seen to have no assured future, the organisation of an alternative became imperative. Stranraer and Larne offered alternatives to Portpatrick and Donaghadee, the more sheltered harbours at each side compensating for the somewhat longer journey.

When the Carrickfergus and Larne Railway (C&LR) opened in 1862, Larne was graduating from a small fishing village to a town. About 2,800 people lived there, and their number was increasing steadily. The SS *Briton* operated a short-lived service to Stranraer from 1862 to 1864, but this languished for a time in deference to the Donaghadee sailings. By the end of the 1860s, however, Larne was ready to displace Donaghadee as the Irish port for the 'short sea route'.

Prominent in forwarding the emergence of Larne, his home town, was James Chaine, a businessman who had been instrumental in improving the harbour at Larne. Chaine enlisted the support of the C&LR, the BNCR and the Portpatrick Railway, and together they formed the Larne and Stranraer Steamboat Company in 1871. A new paddle-steamer, the *Princess Louise*, was ordered and, on 1 July 1872, the service which the SS *Briton* had started ten years before was revived. In 1875, the PS *Princess Beatrice* joined the *Louise* ensured the success of the enterprise. These two paddlers maintained the service until 1890, when the first of a series of larger steamers began to succeed them.

At the outset, only a small proportion of the mails went through Larne and it was not until after 1892 that the amount of mail assumed substantial proportions. Essentially railway-owned, but never becoming a train ferry because of the different gauges at the terminals, the service was continued up to recent times. Nowadays, the service has been replaced by Larne–Cairnryan and the proportion of travellers arriving by rail has greatly diminished, the transport of road vehicles determining the design of all modern vessels.

Of Larne, a guide book published in 1875 said, "This is quiet little town, beautifully situated but in no way distinguished from others of its class in the north of Ireland … The export trade is principally in rock salt and limestone. Cotton goods and canvas are pretty extensively manufactured in the town". Twenty years later, the population had doubled and *Boyd's Pictorial Guide* devoted six pages to a description of the town. Lime, Irish tweeds, woollen fabrics and bricks were listed as the local manufactures, while exports were catalogued as lime, limestone, whiting, iron ore, bauxite, paper, linen, flour, grain, cattle, sheep, horses, pork and butter. The imports were stated to be coal, timber, esparto grass and general goods. For the size of the place, Larne was indeed a busy port.

Boyd's 1895 guide book gives due credit to …

the late Mr James Chaine, MP for Co Antrim and owner of Larne harbour who, believing in its great possibilities, set about its development with extraordinary activity and enterprise. The pier, which is over 1,000 feet long, was nearly all constructed by him at very considerable cost, and through his efforts Ballymena and all the towns lying between, were brought into direct communication with its harbour by a narrow gauge railway.

The erection of the Olderfleet Hotel . . . was largely due to the enterprise of the same gentleman. He died in 1885, in the prime of life, from pneumonia induced by a chill which he caught while superintending arrangements for the departure from Larne Harbour of their Royal Highnesses, the Prince and Princess of Wales.

The memory of James Chaine was perpetuated by the erection of a round tower, a little to the north of the harbour which he did so much to form. It was built in 1886 of Irish granite, to a height of 92 feet, and is a prominent landmark for travellers. On the tower is the inscription *'Si monumentum requiris circumspice'* ('If you seek a monument, look about you').

Railways to Larne

The opening of the standard gauge line from Carrickfergus to Larne in October 1862 came 14 years after the Belfast and Ballymena Railway had built their line from the city along the shore of Belfast Lough to Carrickfergus and inland from Greenisland to Antrim and Ballymena. From 1848 until 1862, 15 miles of road separated Larne from the railhead at Carrickfergus.

The Carrickfergus and Larne Railway Company (CLR) was incorporated by an Act of 15 May 1860, with an authorised capital of £125,000. On the same day, the name of the Belfast and Ballymena Railway was changed to that of the Belfast and Northern Counties Railway, and the company was authorised to subscribe £20,000 to the share capital of the CLR. Though nominally separate, the two companies were closely linked. Some directors held seats on both boards, the same secretary served both companies, and arrangements were made for the Northern Counties to work the CLR. The latter company remained independent until July 1890, but its close association with its parent was evidenced even in the annual returns of the Board of Trade, which quoted the two sets of returns together.

With both the CLR and the 'short sea route' firmly established, the growth off Larne continued. By the 1870s, as we have seen in a previous chapter, exploitation of iron-ore beds had begun among the Antrim hills and a large tonnage was being exported to the English and to a lesser extent to the Scottish furnaces. By 1873, ore was spilling

down Glenariff to the rickety pier on the open coast east of Red Bay. Concurrently, the Antrim Wire Tramway Company was planning to convey ore in buckets by their aerial ropeway along the far face of Lurigethan from Glenariff and down to the sea at Red Bay pier. From the same Glenravel orefield, the BC&RBR were building their line down to the waiting broad gauge wagons at Ballymena, whence it would go to Belfast. As yet, the expanding port of Larne took no part in this new export trade, and James Chaine set out to see that it did.

West of Larne, the valley of the Inver, or Larne river, cuts a narrow glen down to the sea from the basaltic upland. Though the Inver Glen is short and less spectacular than the great glens to the north, it nevertheless provided a shorter access route to Larne from the city of Belfast than did the coast road by Carrickfergus and Whitehead. A dozen miles from Larne, and half way to Belfast, there was Ballyclare, a thriving little place lying three and a half miles off the BNCR's main railway line towards the Antrim, but deriving little benefit from the railway other than sharing a station name-board along with the name of the village of Doagh.

In Ballyclare, paper-making had been carried on for so long that its early history was obscure. By 1740, a paper mill was in full production, and a local newspaper dated April of that year carried an advertisement asking for supplies of rag and straw, and inviting applications to the trade of paper making. A new and larger corn and paper mill was erected to the south-west of the town in 1836. Apparently corn-milling did not prove as successful as paper-making for some years later the business, owned by the Ballyclare Paper Mill Company, was concentrating on paper made from rags and straw, and was producing about 50 tons a week.* With its thriving paper-making industry, the town offered a promising target for a new railway from Larne.

The Larne and Antrim Railway

The first proposal to make a railway from Larne by the inland route up the Inver valley came in 1872, when the promoters of the Larne and Antrim Railway (LAR) put forward a scheme for constructing a standard gauge

---

* In 1875 the mill was acquired by the North of Ireland Paper Mill Co Ltd, owned by a group of businessmen from Lancashire. With the influx of extra capital and fresh ideas, the mill made rapid progress. During the next 20 years, while Ballyclare flourished, various other small paper mills throughout Ulster closed down, until in 1896 the Ballyclare mill and another mill at Larne were the only paper-making plants left in Ulster. The Ballclare mill closed in 1950 due to high freight charges.

line between the two towns of its title. The route was the obvious one, commencing from Larne Harbour, passing through the town and gaining height up the Inver valley. Once on the upland, 400 feet higher than the start, the line was to continue to the south-west over the watershed into the valley of the Six Mile Water, a mile north of the village of Ballynure. Keeping on the north bank of the Six Mile Water, the line was to pass Ballyclare and three miles beyond, the village of Doagh. To Antrim town, the route then followed the broadening valley, the line flexing towards the west near the terminus. Only the hamlet of Parkgate would have been on that section of line, which for the last eight miles would have run almost parallel to the existing main line of the BNCR.

The LAR promoters employed William Lewis, CE, to survey the course of their line and submitted their Bill to Parliament early in 1873, Lewis's plans and sections were drawn with his characteristic care and show that, for the purposes of the Act, three railways were proposed. Railway No 1 was the major project, 21 miles and half a furlong in length, and connecting Larne with Antrim. Railway No 2 and Railway No 3 were merely short spurs connecting Railway No 1 to the CLR at Larne and to the BNCR at Antrim respectively. Though separate terminal stations are shown, the fact that Railways 2 and 3 were to join the existing 5ft 3in gauge lines, proves that the LAR was to have been standard gauge.

Lewis's 'Estimate of Expense' which accompanied the Bill reads as follows:

The House of Lords,
Session 1873.

LARNE AND ANTRIM RAILWAY
Estimate of Expense

I estimate the expense of the Undertakings comprised in the Bill under the above Short Title, according to the deposited plans and sections including the purchase of the necessary property and contingencies at the sum of seventy-five thousand six hundred and thirty-three pounds nineteen shillings.

As to Railway no 1	£73,845	0s
As to Railway No 2	850	0s
As to Railway No 3	938	19s
	£75,633	19s

Dated this 26th day of Decmber 1872
(signed) William Lewis, Engineer

Witness (signed)
Chas. H. Brett,
Solr. Belfast.

Once deposited with the Clerk of Parliaments, the Bill began its normal course. It received the examiner's certificate on St Patrick's Day 1873, but the sequence of parliamentary events was then interrupted, as the promoters withdrew their Bill.

The Larne and Ballyclare Railway

It is clear that the promoters of the LAR had second thoughts, for their abortive scheme was immediately followed by another, less ambitious perhaps, certainly smaller in more senses than one, but following the same course as had been proposed for its defunct predecessor.

For James Chaine of Larne, enlistment of support for a railway to Ballyclare was not difficult. The promoters of the Larne and Ballyclare Railway (LBR) had William Lewis prepare plans and sections of the line which, since it had already been surveyed for the LAR scheme, was largely a repetition of what had already been submitted.

The Larne and Ballyclare Railway Bill was read a first time on 23 May 1873. The second reading was on 19 June, the remaining stages went through during July, and on

5 August 1873 the Royal Assent was given to the company's Act of Incorporation. The Act named Lord AEH Trevor, James Chaine, WR Anketell, WB Glenny and W Eccles as the first directors, and authorised the building of a line of railway from the quay at Larne to the town of Ballyclare, a total length of 11 miles 7 furlongs and 2 chains.

The LBR differed in one important feature from the Larne and Antrim, and that was in the matter of its gauge. The LAR would have been on the standard Irish gauge of 5ft 3in – broad by English standards. But by 1873 the BC&RBR had already been incorporated for a year and, as we have seen Chapter 3, had been empowered to build to a gauge of "not wider than three feet or narrower than two feet". The Glenariff mineral line was preparing to work on a gauge of three feet.

The fashion was set, the novelty of the narrow gauge was much discussed, and for the Larne and Ballyclare Railway, a gauge of three feet was aimed at. The Act was more explicit than in the case of the Cushendall, for while the company might make its line to "a gauge of three feet", it insisted that sufficient land be taken and all bridges constructed for a 5ft 3in gauge line "except between the commencement of the railway and a point in Larne 1 mile 1 furlong away".

To Ballymena and a change of name

Six miles to the west of Larne, behind the basalt buttresses of Agnew's Hill and Shane's Hill, were the gathering grounds of streamlets that fed the Glenwhirry river which, after 15 miles of westward flow, joined the River Maine only four miles to the south of Ballymena. Glenwhirry, that broad quiet strath with a Scottish-sounding name, full of the bubbling call of whaups and farmed since Plantation times by thrifty Scots settlers, pointed the way to James Chaine and his friends when they were planning an extension.

Surveys in the hills to the north of Glenwhirry had found iron ore, and although the area was never to attain the importance or the output of Glenravel, there was certainly promise that ore traffic from mines would make a

Ballyclare narrow gauge station in 1936, looking west. The overbridge in the background carried the Main Street and a second bridge to the left of the lifting gantry carries it over the Sixmilewater which then turns sharply to cross under the railway by bridge 621 in the foreground. The site of the platform is now occupied by an Asda store.

L&GRP

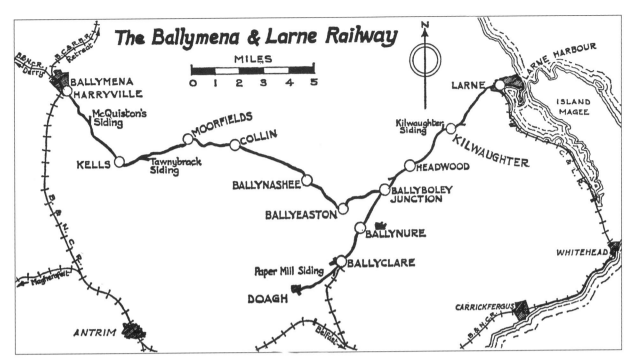

significant contribution towards the profits of the railway.

The company promoters hastened with their extension. Six weeks after they had obtained their Act, a meeting of the provisional committee of the LBR was held on 29 September 1873. OB Graham took the chair, WR Anketell acted as secretary *pro tem*, and William Ellis J Magill and James Chaine were also there. They decided that Mr Lewis should proceed "without delay" to survey the line from Ballynure to Ballymena "and be offered £300 for the work".

Ballynure was a village of a few dozen houses, nine miles from Larne on the road to Ballyclare. Sited on the watershed, at about 400 feet OD between the valleys of the Inver Water and the Six Mile Water, the neighbourhood was a suitable junction point for a drive past Ballynashee, north-west to the head of Glenwhirry.

On 4 November 1873, Mr Anketell's office at 3 Custom House Square, Belfast, was the venue for the first ordinary meeting of shareholders of the Larne and Ballyclare Railway Company. Five persons attended, James Chaine heading them since he had been the principal subscriber with a share of £5,000. William Eccles, who had put down £500, followed, and with them where Thomas Patterson, WB Glenny and WR Anketell. At a directors' meeting held immediately afterwards, Chaine was elected chairman, while Anketell remained the temporary secretary. A month

later, the design of the company's seal was submitted by Mr Magill and approved.

The company's minute book relates little of what took place during the next seven months, but promoters and staff were by no means idle. Plans for the authorisation of the Ballynure–Ballymena section were in progress, a Bill was submitted to Parliament and an Act obtained on 7 August 1874 which incorporated the Ballymena and Larne Railway Company (B&LR) as a replacement for the Larne and Ballyclare Company, and authorised it to construct two railways, each of three foot gauge. The first of these was the longest, 17 miles from near Harryville national schoolhouse to a junction with the LBR in the townland of Ballybracken, 7 miles 3 furlongs from Larne. The estimated cost was £62,469.

The second railway authorised by the Ballymena and Larne Act of 1874 was to have been a short one, 2 miles 5 furlongs 7½ chains, and although it was never constructed, it is of great interest as the earliest attempt to bridge the gap between the BC&RBR and the B&LR. It was to leave the B&LR 6 furlongs 133 yards from its terminus at Harryville and sweep around the eastern side of the town to a junction with the Cushendall line in Drumclog townland. Its estimated cost was £13,902, or about £5,000 per mile.

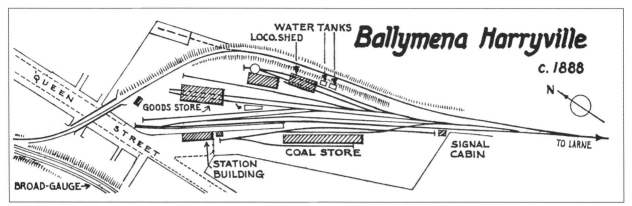

Ballybracken, Ballyboley and Ballymena

Ballybracken townland lies one and a half miles north-east of the village of Ballynure. It is on the south side of the Six Mile Water, at that point a very small stream forming the boundary between Ballybracken and the next townland of Ballyboley. Although the junction and station buildings were actually in Ballybracken townland, the place became known as Ballyboley Junction, probably because that townland was much more extensive and populous. Indeed, a short way south-west of the junction, the line crossed the Six Mile Water and ran in Ballyboley townland for some distance.

The intake of capital after the 1874 Act was slow, and this effectively prevented any progress during the whole of 1875. A board meeting was held on 9 December 1875, when it was decided that when the total subscription of capital reached £50,000, the shares would be allotted. The chief applicant was James Chaine, who had asked for 1,000 £10 shares. At the next board meeting, held on 19 January 1876, it was ordered that William Lewis was to be paid £300 on account for his survey work and that he was to be appointed engineer-in-charge of the construction. His fee for this would be £4,000, a quarter of which would be taken in shares.

The B&LR shareholders were summoned on 5 February 1876 and heard a reassuring report by Lewis that

> … the centre line is marked on the ground and pegged throughout its entire length. The works being of a very easy and ordinary character, there is no reason why the entire cannot be completed within eighteen month from the time of getting possession of the necessary lands.

Progress had been tardy, and it was to continue thus as capital still came in slowly. The 1874 Act had authorised the company to raise £136,000 in stocks and shares and £45,000 in loans and debentures. Even by the end of 1877, only £80,592 had been subscribed. Lewis's encouraging report had failed to loosen the local purse strings.

The directors held two meetings in February 1876 and at the first of them asked their solicitor, Mr Brett, to advertise for a secretary. It was decided to keep the work within the family and offer the position to Mr George Brett at a salary of £100 a year, while the company's offices were to be in a room in Messrs L'Estrange and Brett's city office at 7 Chichester Street, Belfast.

Tenders for construction had been asked for and were opened at the board meeting on St Patrick's Day 1876. They had come in from five contractors: Connor and Manisty, 65 Great George's Street, Belfast; Thomas J Dixon, Celbridge, County Kildare; James Kent, 156 York Street, Belfast; TH Falkiner and JW Stanford, 17 Upper Gloucester Street, Dublin; William Oughterson, Kilkenny Junction Railway, Kilkenny.

Unfortunately the minute book does not detail what their offers were, but they must have been debated at some length as it was not until the board's next meeting on 23 May that it was decided to award the contract to Dixon. At the same meeting, a call of £2 per share was authorised, and the secretary was told to mention in his circular "that the works were being energetically proceeded with". Work started very soon after the contract was placed and was initially concentrated on the Larne–Ballyclare portion, which had been authorised by Parliament nearly three years earlier. However, the main objective was followed up when, on 5 June 1875, the directors told Mr Brett to proceed to take land on the Ballymena section.

Dixon made good progress at first, and at the half-yearly meeting Lewis stated:

I beg leave to report that the works of this line of Railway are being carried on with energy by your contractor, Mr T.L. Dixon. The fine weather (so singularly favourable to their construction) has been fully taken advantage of by him and considerable progress made in the formation of the works in progress, consisting of earthworks, fencing, masonry &c. between the towns of Ballymena and Larne. The principal river bridges have been raised above flood levels, and will soon be completed, a large amount of culverts built; and I have no doubt, from the arrangements made by this Contractor for the quick completion of the work, that this Railway may confidently be expected to be ready for traffic within the specified contract period.

In September, orders were placed for 1,000 tons of steel rails from the Barrow Haematite Steel Company at £7 10s per ton, delivered in Larne, while a second 1,000 tons was to be an open offer until the end of the year at the same price. Larch sleepers were also bought, 3,000 from Dixon the contractor, 10,000 from Gault of Ballymena and 15,000 from T Dixon and Sons of Corporation Street, Belfast. In each case, the price was to be 1s 6d per sleeper. Being short of ready cash, the company tried to persuade the suppliers to take 10 per cent of their money in the form of shares.

By the beginning of November bad weather was slowing down the work and the directors, becoming concerned, pressed Dixon to hasten. He promised to have the Larne–Ballyclare section complete by 1 March 1877, but was over-optimistic by a matter of five months.

The half-yearly meeting was held at the beginning of February 1877, and Lewis then stated:

> Since my last Report, I beg leave to say that, notwithstanding the unusual severity of the past weather, your Contractor, Mr Dixon, has made very considerable progress towards the completion of his Contract; the works have not, in any way, been injured by the constant floods and storms which have so injuriously affected many other Railways and public works; and our river and road bridges, earthworks, fencing &c (though recently formed) have proved, in every respect, sound and substantial. The line from Larne to Ballyclare (for which section our Act was first obtained) will, if the weather prove at all favourable, be ready for goods traffic early in the spring, and the remainder of the line to Ballymena during the autumn of this year.

The greater part of the rails and materials for the Permanent Way has arrived, thus enabling the Contractor, with the opening fine weather and long working day before him, to bring his works to a quick and satisfactory completion.

Power and rolling stock

During 1876, the first moves were made towards a decision on engine stock and, after approaches to RF Fairlie, maker of the double-boiler engines, and to the Baldwin Company of Philadelphia, the wise decision was made on 20 October 1876 to place an order for one engine with Beyer, Peacock and Co of Gorton, Manchester.

On 2 February 1877 the chairman was empowered to order two more 'engines with breaks' from Beyers, and carriages and wagons from the Bristol, Carriage and Wagon Co. Delivery of the first engine was made in March 1877, and a week after its arrival Dixon applied for its hire, so that he could start ballasting. Six wagons were hired to Dixon in May.

Improvements at Ballymena

Reference has already been made to the 1874 Act which authorised the railway to terminate at Harryville. The choice of that site was not altogether happy, for the station was on the southern margin of the town, in the fork between Larne Street, leading to Larne, and Queen Street, leading to Antrim. In the vicinity, streets of red-brick terrace houses were springing up, but the business premises mostly lay across the Braid Water. The expense of bridging the river would have been considerable. The 1874 Act had authorised the construction of two and a half miles of railway around the eastern perimeter of Ballymena, but no attempt had been made to construct it because of the shortage of money.

Harryville was most certainly not going to be convenient, either for the town market place, or for passengers. The only point in its favour was its proximity to the BNCR's goods station, which was on the opposite side of Queen Street. Even passengers had deserted that station, which had been the original terminus of the Belfast and Ballymena Railway. By the time the B&LR was being built, the BNCR had linked up with the erstwhile BBC&PJR, had bridged the river in the process and resited their passenger station half a mile further north.

The B&LR directors were fully aware of the shortcomings

Ballymena and Larne Railway 2-4-0T No 1, built by Beyer, Peacock of Manchester in 1877. The design was closely modelled on that of Isle of Man Railway No 6 Peveril *of 1875. A second of the type, No 4, arrived in 1878 (see page 87).*

L&GRP

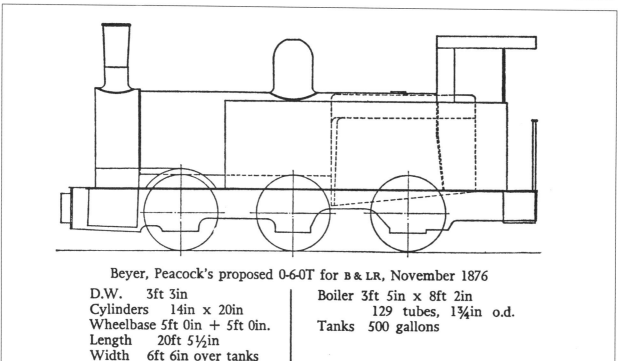

Beyer, Peacock's proposed 0-6-0T for B & LR, November 1876

D.W.   3ft 3in
Cylinders   14in x 20in
Wheelbase 5ft 0in + 5ft 0in.
Length   20ft 5½in
Width   6ft 6in over tanks

Boiler 3ft 5in x 8ft 2in
    129 tubes, 1¾in o.d.
Tanks   500 gallons

The end result of the Beyer, Peacock proposal – 0-6-0T No 3, one of two delivered in 1877. A similar locomotive, No 6, was delivered in 1883.
L&GRP

of Harryville, and of the advantages to be gained by joining their line to that of the Cushendall company, which beckoned to them from their terminus just north of the Northern Counties passenger station. Between the two narrow gauge termini was the mainline bridge over the Braid Water, fully occupied with two lines of 5ft 3in gauge, but nevertheless an inviting route to the elysium of the north-east part of the town. The matter was discussed at the board meeting on 13 October 1876 and Lewis was asked to report "on the possibility of getting from Ballymena station to the Cushendall line along the Northern Counties line". However, to accommodate the B&LR on the Braid Water bridge mixed gauge would have been needed. The project got no encouragement from the BNCR, and went no further. The B&LR had to concentrate on what they had begun, rather than start on new ventures.

Completion Piecemeal

With Dixon ballasting with borrowed engine and wagons, completion of the line seems to have become rather frantic. In January 1877, a deal was made with the York Street Flax Spinning Company of Belfast for the purchase of some second-hand timber. It cost the B&LR £12 10s and was used to knock up a temporary engine shed at Larne.

As forecast, the Larne to Ballyclare section was finished first, and to whip up enthusiasm and coax more share

purchases from the populace, the company persuaded the Lord Lieutenant of Ireland to allow himself to be conveyed over the line on 30 July 1877, a morale-booster for the half-yearly meeting. On 17 August George Brett penned the directors' report:

The Directors have much pleasure in reporting that since the last half-yearly meeting the construction of the line from Larne Harbour to Ballyclare mills has been so far advanced as to admit of his Excellency the Lord Lieutenant of Ireland being conveyed over it on 30th July last.

Rapid progress is being made towards the completion of this Section as well as with the Works of the Main Line from the Junction to Ballymena, and the Directors anticipate that each will be finished within the specified period.

Then William Lewis contributed his portion:

I beg leave to report that one section of your Railway, namely – from the Quay at Larne to the Paper Mills at Ballyclare – is now nearly completed and ready for Traffic; and that the Works of the Line to Ballymena are so far advanced that little will remain to be done to complete same by the end of the present year. Over the first Section, upon which a locomotive has been working for some months past, the line is sound and in safe running order, and the motion of the engines and carriages both smooth and steady.

On 1 September the Ballyclare section was opened for

goods traffic, though still only semi-finished. Three days *later* the signals were ordered from Messrs Courtney and Stephens!

The autumn of 1877 drew into winter and Colonel Rich, one of the railway inspecting officers of the Board of Trade, came to view what had been achieved. The company had been confident that he would pass their line as fit for use, and his unfavourable report, including objection to the state of the fencing, came as a rude awakening. It was now mid-November, and the short daylight and bad weather were combining to slow the contractor's efforts. On 15 November, Dixon again borrowed a locomotive, for ballasting was still far from complete between Ballyboley and Ballymena. A further supply of gravel ballast was required and in December about an acre of suitable land was leased from a Mr JJ Kirkpatrick at an annual rent of £3. It was a gloomy Christmas for the shareholders.

At the next half-yearly meeting on 15 February 1878, Lewis tried to cheer the audience by reporting that "a few weeks at the most" would see the completion of the Ballyboley–Ballymena part, although admitting that no buildings were yet erected. Dixon was stated to have two engines at work on the line. Shortage of capital was fundamentally the cause of the delays and, in an effort to speed matters, a loan of £26,000 had been negotiated with the Irish Board of Works at the end of 1877.

On 15 March, Lewis conferred with the directors, bringing with him plans of the signalling system and of the goods stores and stations. He was given authority to spend £580 on the erection of a goods shed, coal store, office and weighbridge at Ballymena, and £150 on approaches and sidings at Kells, and was requested to urge the work on. At the same meeting the board received the resignation of George Brett, their secretary. His work was taken over by FW Rew, who was the company's manager.

Judging by the minute book, heavy weather was being made of the signalling, and layout plans were sent to Messrs Courtney and Stephens as late as April 1878. At the board meeting on 18 June, Rew was asked to try and speed up delivery, since "the date for opening the line being fixed for 1st August, the directors expect the signals to be ready on 20th July."

Even by the spring of 1878 passenger-station buildings were still non-existent. On 21 May plans were confirmed with Lewis for buildings at Ballyclare, Kells and Ballymena

"and a small waiting room and ticket office at Larne on the platform". On 3 June it was decided to erect a station at Ballymena, but a week later the decision was reversed and Collins, the consultant engineer, was asked to advise regarding an alternative site. The minute book does not detail this change of plan but it seems likely it was considered that Harryville should merely have temporary passenger accommodation, in view of the possibility of a link up with the Cushendall line and the repositioning of the town station that would ensue.

At Larne Harbour there was still no accommodation for passengers. At the board meeting on 9 July, after it had been reported that "work on Kells and all the other stations" was "being proceeded with", it was decided to leave the question of temporary accommodation for passengers at the harbour in Rew's hands, which rather suggests that the directors were washing *their* hands of the matter.

Inspection

By the end of June 1878 the management considered they were ready to open their line, the Board of Trade was asked to arrange for its formal inspection and on 28 July Colonel Rich penned his 1,600 word report. Having described the railway in general terms, the Colonel then gave a lengthy catalogue of incompletion. Every station was inadequately furnished in some respect or other, and none of the buildings was finished.

The two level crossings came in for particular criticism. These were at Curran Road in Larne, and at Headwood, six and a half miles inland. There were no gates at either place, and neither lamp signals nor house for a gatekeeper. Perhaps the company had thought that a resident gate-keeper was not needed at Curran Road, but attendance was essential at Headwood where the line crossed the main public road.

Just outside Ballyclare station, the Six Mile Water passed below the railway. The river bridge caught Colonel Rich's eye, and he demanded that the bridge parapet should be raised "to prevent passengers stepping from the carriages into the river in case any portion of the train should stop outside the station." He found Ballyclare station in the same unfinished state as the rest, and left the company with the unpalatable news that their railway could not be opened for passenger traffic until it was properly finished.

The directors took urgent steps to comply with the

A posed photograph of 2-4-0T No 4 on a passenger train at Larne Harbour, taken from the Curran Road bridge about 1878. Harbour Road is visible behind the train and the distant hill is on Islandmagee. Behind the third carriage is the wheat store for McAuley's Flour Mill. The British Aluminium Company's works were built later in the area of the left background. The man looking out of the engine is William Pinkerton, the first Engineer of the B&LR and later Town Surveyor for Larne.

Nelson Poots collection

Board of Trade requirements. At the board meeting on 5 August, it was minuted that Lewis was to put up "a gate with lights etc." at Curran Road and to erect a wooden shed on the harbour platform "at a cost of about £20". A fortnight later the company gave written undertakings regarding the two crossings.

Eleven years were to pass before the legislature were to be shocked by the Armagh collision on the Great Northern Railway, and traffic control by time interval was still commonplace. Colonel Rich's report referred to "the means of keeping an interval or space between following trains", and the company chose to work their line using the train staff and ticket system.

During the first half of August 1878 the stations were busy places, the contractors being constantly goaded by Lewis to fulfil the inspector's demands. But it was a case of shutting the stable door, for the summer passenger traffic had already been lost for that year. Colonel Rich made a

second inspection and on the evening of 20 August wrote his second report in James Chaine's hostelry, the Olderfleet Hotel at Larne Harbour. Most of the unfinished items mentioned in his first survey had now been attended to and, apart form the lack of platform facing boards at three places, the stations were as required.

But the two level crossings still failed to satisfy the critic. The Headwood one was either to be 'legalised', which meant going to the expense of a further Act of Parliament to get authority for its existence, or else the company were to carry the road over the railway by a bridge within the next year. The company undertook to do one or the other. At Curran Road crossing they undertook to build either a 'lodge' or a bridge. The Colonel had evidently done some research, for he went on to point out that while the Curran Road level crossing was authorised for the B&LR, the parallel line of the CLR had been laid over the road without any such statutory authority. Perhaps the comforts of the Olderfleet Hotel had

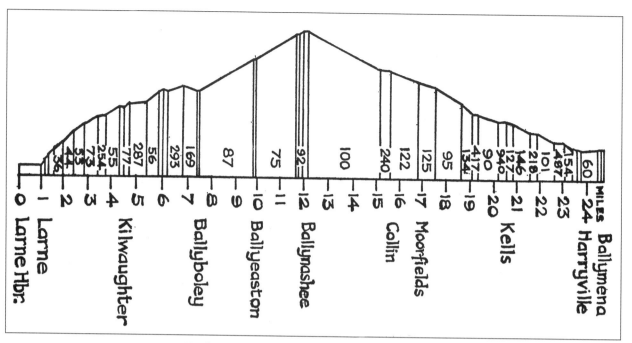

Gradients on the Larne Harbour to Ballymena section.

The start of the Inver bank out of Larne, looking east, photographed on 12 June 1948 from the Bridge Street bridge. In the distance the locomotive shed, Works and signal cabin can be seen. The passenger station is out of sight to the left of the cabin.

John Meredith

mollified the Colonel, for he ended his criticism of the nearby crossing with the observation that he had been told that the two railway companies and the county were together going to build a road bridge over the railway, and so do away with the crossing. On the flat reclaimed land near the harbour, the cost of an overbridge with its long approach ramps would have been a heavy burden for the impoverished company to bear. The affair recalls the Pennyburn road crossing on the Londonderry and Lough Swilly Railway at Derry, which was a thorn in the flesh of Board of Trade inspectors for years. The two were similarly situated.

By now, Colonel Rich had seen enough of the B&LR to convince him of their good intentions, and he recommended that sanction be given to the company to open their line for passenger traffic. The B&LR were not slow to go into action and services began on Saturday 24 August 1878. The reckoning came the following January, when the company settled the Olderfleet Hotel's bill for £77 9s 6d, to which the board minute refers as "for luncheons etc, etc. on occasion of the Shareholders' Trip and Inspection of Line by Government Inspector." The bill was almost four times as much as had been spent on the passenger shelter at the harbour.

Improvements

The stations in use at first were Larne Harbour, Larne, Ballyclare Junction, Ballyclare, Kells and Ballymena. The section from the junction to Kells was twelve and three-quarter miles in length. Within weeks, requests came in for stations within that long stretch of line.

On 27 September 1878 the board decided to invite tenders for a station at Moorfields, a convenient site for Glenwhirry folk and where the main Larne–Ballymena road was joined by a secondary road from Kells. Butler, the Ballymena contractor, offered to build a station there for £220, including a access road to it and a siding. This sum did not cover the provision of signals, for which he offered separately, whereupon the board decided to see whether they could get signals more cheaply through the Gloucester Wagon Co. Seemingly, the firm who had done the signalling elsewhere was out of favour. The outcome is not recorded, but Moorfields station was opened on 14 December 1878 for both passenger and goods traffic.*

At the September board meeting a request was read for a station at Ballynashee, a townland at the summit of the line, between the valley of the Six Mile Water and Glenwhirry.

There was no village there, but the country was sufficiently populous for the demand to appear reasonable and Rew was asked to report. On 11 October he recommended "a cheap passenger station and goods siding" and Lewis estimated the cost at £180. Although tenders were invited from Butler and from Dixon, action was deferred. The request was renewed in July 1879, Rew reported favourably on the site, and on 17 October the directors authorised the building of a platform and the erection of a shed for coal and goods at a total cost of £30. The establishment of the station at Ballynashee yielded block sections of four and a quarter and eight and a half miles between the junction and Kells.

In April 1880, a further station was requested at Ballyalbana Bridge, near the village of Ballyeaston, which was about half way between the junction and Ballynashee. Again, Rew inspected and reported, and at the next director's meeting it was agreed to level the ground and spend £10 on an approach road. The work was completed by June and trains stopped there on market days. The halt was officially referred to as Ballyeaston Bridge and had a short life. On 24 May 1882, Rew told the board that the profits from the halt for 1881 were less than five shillings a week and he had therefore decided to discontinue stopping trains there as from 1 June. It was not revived until 30 years later.

On the same day as it was decided to close Ballymena, Rew arranged to stop some trains at Headwood level crossing from 1 June. No platform seems to have been provided then, though one was built later, and the Headwood stop conveniently broke the lengthy seven and three quarter mile section from Larne. It was a 'flag station' at which trains could be flagged to a halt by the crossing keeper.

The last of the new halts came in 1887, when a halt and siding were made at Collin, where a secondary road linking Broughshane and Doagh crossed the line. It lay three and a quarter miles from Ballynashee and two and a quarter miles from Moorfields, and was never a block post. The halt was looked after by Katie and Joe Wicklow for many years. Joe was employed on the permanent way, Katie was his wife. There was never a station house at 'The Collin', as everyone called it, and the Wicklows lived a few hundred yards away in a cottage. Collin was a flag station, like Headwood, but more often than not Katie ran out at the last minute to attend the train, leaving her red flag at home. However,

---

* As Moorfields signal cabin has a plague saying it was built by the Gloucester Wagon Co, presumably they did get the contract.

she wore a red petticoat and had only to lift her skirt to accomplish what the flag was intended to do.

Ballymena link

The abortive attempt in late 1876 to share the BNCR bridge into Ballymena did not end the affair. After further debate, the B&LR submitted a parliamentary Bill in November 1877 in which they attempted to secure authority to build no less than eight separate sections of new railway. Largely because of current opposition from the Cushendall company, only three sections were eventually authorised, but the projects set out in the Bill are of great interest since they illustrate the ambitious ventures into which the B&LR were being led by the vision of vast tonnages of iron ore. The eight railways of the Bill were:

1 *Doagh extension,* 1 mile 3 furlongs 4 chains. Estimated cost, £6,042 15s.

2 *Branch N of Headwood*, ¾ mile, to an end-on junction with a tramway, 7 furlongs 1 chain 5 yards. The latter was to rise steeply from 474ft OD to 107ft OD on Agnew's Hill, to serve iron-ore mines there. The incline is shown on the Parliamentary Plan with rising gradients: Hor/1 in 7/10.7/14/9/8.8/12/6/7.3/5/Hor. No doubt it was intended to work it by rope haulage.

3 *Kilwaughter branch*, 1 mile 1 furlong 4 chains 8 yards.

4 A short line in *Larne town*, to the quay.

5 *Clonetrace branch*, 7 miles 2 furlongs 8 yards, from Ballymena via Broughshane. Estimated cost, £31,714.

6 *Ballylig branch*, 4 furlongs 1 chain 10 yards, from the Clonetrace branch. Estimated cost £2,124 10s.

7 *Spur at Ballymena*, 6 chains 11 yards. Estimated cost, £838.

8 *Spur at Ballymena*, 2 furlongs 2 chains 6 yards. Estimated cost, £1,755.

Nos 7 and 8 were intended to link Railway No 2 of the B&LR Act 1874 with Railway No 5 of the present Bill.

The resulting Act of Parliament, dated 8 August 1878 (41–42 V cap ccxxvii) only authorised three of the lines. These were:

(i) *Doagh extension,* from Ballyclare townland to a point 120 yards S of the post office in Doagh.

(ii) *Kilwaughter branch*, reduced in length to 1 mile 8 chains. Starting in Lowtown townland, 4 miles 3 furlongs from the terminus at Larne quay and terminating at Rory's Glen, 100 yards E of the NE quoin of Hugh Baillie's house.

(iii) *A junction line to the Ballymena, Cushendall and Red Bay Railway*, 5 furlongs 9 chains in length, parallel to the main line of the BNCR.

In addition, the Act allowed the company to abandon Railway No 2 of their 1874 Act, which was superseded by the line defined in the third section of the new Act. In formulating the 1878 Act, the schemes for the Headwood branch and its attendant tramway and the short line in the Larne Harbour area were cast aside. The lengthy Broughshane branch and its little Ballylig offshoot were catered for by the BC&RBR Act of 1878, which had been passed a month previously (see Chapter 3). Finally, since a direct connection to the Cushendall line was now authorised, the need for the two short spurs at Ballymena disappeared.

The B&LR Act of 1878 stated that the company could use "in perpetuity" the line and embankment of the BNCR for making their Railway No 3 and "shall pay for the use thereof a rent of £50 per annum".

In compensation for their failure to reach into the Clonetrace mining area, the B&LR received the promise of full co-operation from the Cushendall company under two sections of their Act. The Cushendall company was to give the B&LR "full working facilities with respect to all traffic from or to any place upon or near the Cushendall Railway". Moreover, if and when the Cushendall completed their railways to Clonetrace and Broughshane (Nos and 5 of the BC&RBR Act, 1878) the B&LR could "run over and use …, with their engines *and carriages of every description*". The B&LR thought that they had come out of the struggle very well. It was unfortunate for them, that as the Cushendall was only a mineral line and had no Board of Trade authority to run passenger-carrying vehicles, no B&LR carriage could go on to their line.

Although the directors authorised Lewis to advertise for tenders for the Ballymena link in February 1879, there was a long delay due to lack of capital, and not until 1 January 1880 were four tenders opened. The lowest offer was from Messrs Butler and Fry of Ballymena at £5,850 and the work was given to them. Other bids came from Mr R. Relf of Okehampton, Devon, Messrs Westray, Copeland and Co of Barrow-on Furness and J Gault and W Kane of Ballymena.

The permanent way for the Ballymena link was supplied to Butler and Fry by the railway company. Construction involved the demolition of two terrace houses in Queen Street, between the road crossing and the Northern Counties

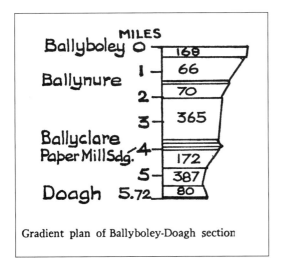

Gradient plan of Ballyboley-Doagh section

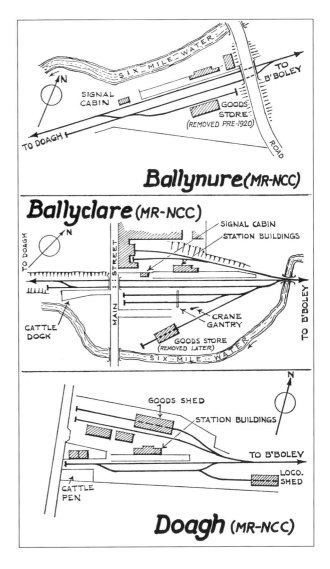

line. The street was crossed on the skew by a 45ft span girder bridge and the line was opened on 22 September 1880, for passenger, mineral and goods traffic.

The Doagh Extension

Although the 1878 Act gave the necessary authority to build this one and a half mile extension, work on it was postponed until the summer of 1883, again through lack of money. At the half-yearly meeting in February 1882, Mr Chaine stated that potential income was being lost, mentioning particularly coal traffic to Doagh. The decision to start making the line was not taken until July 1883. Work on it began on 7 August.

On 27 November 1883, the board authorised expenditure for the terminal buildings: the passenger station, £200; the platform, £25; the goods shed, coal shed and weighbridge house, £220. Construction involved no engineering difficulties and, after the Board of Trade inspection by Major General Hutchinson on 24 April 1884, he was reported to the shareholders as having said that "the line has been well finished, the works appear to have been substantially constructed and to be standing well". The line had been open for goods traffic since 8 February 1884. To comply with the Board of Trade requirements, a further £190 had to be spent before passenger traffic could begin, which it did on 1 May.

On 5 June 1884, Rew told members of the board that the cost of the Doagh extension, including land, law expenses and engineering, had totalled £3,921. The station and works at Doagh had exceeded the original estimate and came to £1,473. The total cost was equal to £3,827 per mile.

At the Ballyclare paper mill, a new siding had been made at a cost of £171 10s "to compensate for the portion of the main line previously used as a siding …" Part of the cost of the extension involved the purchase off a piece of land from OB Graham, the deputy-chairman. He was due £278 19s 5d for it, but to show his confidence in the future of the B&LR he was content to accept £270 in debenture stock and £8 19s 5d in cash.

The Course of the Line

From Ballymena station, shared after 1880 with the BNCR and consisting of one through platform, the line to Larne went in a south-easterly direction, with the twin lines of the broad gauge Northern Counties line alongside. The line crossed the Braid Water on a stone-built, three-arch viaduct, parallel to that carrying the broad gauge. The back of terrace houses in Queen Street lay to the left below the embankment. A short way out and the narrow gauge line curved to the left, passed through a gap in the houses and crossed over the busy thoroughfare of Queen Street to enter Harryville station.

Curving to the right, the line passed in turn behind the weighbridge, goods store, turntable and engine shed to regain the course of the original line about 200 yards beyond the old platform. According to the Clearing House mileages, the distance from Ballymena to Harryville

Miss Janieson poses with driver James McCart and fireman William Hunter beside No 103 at Kells about 1925.

J Jamieson collection

was nominally 46 chains. Passenger accommodation at Harryville was of the simplest, consisting of a single platform with a wooden office-cum-waiting room.

Making for the country on a 1 in 145 rise, the railway crossed two small streams, tributary to the Braid Water, and about a mile out curved to right and left to avoid two rounded hills. Near mile post 23 (measured from Larne Harbour) and two miles from Ballymena, a siding on the left and trailing towards Larne served a brick works. In the working timetable the siding was named 'McQuiston's' and from it the line steepened to 1 in 101 for nearly a mile, followed by 1 in 218/146 into the valley of the Kellswater.

Kells station, which served the neighbouring villages of Kells and Connor, was four and three-quarter miles from Ballymena and approached along an embankment. Sited above the north bank of the river, it had one platform on the north side, brick buildings with a wooden framework which gave it some resemblance to half-timbering, a crossing loop and two headshunts. The local industries consisted of a bleach works and two dyeworks owned by the Dinsmore family. One of the factories obtained its coal from the railway yard via a private bogie line of 2ft 6in gauge. The coal was shovelled from railway wagons into a storage bunker, from which it was loaded into small wagons like the Scottish miner's 'hutches'. These were pushed across the river on a bridge by man-power to a coal store at the mill boiler station.

From Kells, the line climbed into Glenwhirry and at the platform end met with a 1 in 90 bank which lasted for nearly a mile. Shorter stretches at 1 in 417/134 gave an easing, before a mile and a half of 1 in 95 brought the line to Moorfields. Over this stretch, and within a mile of Kells, there were two features of interest, a siding and a bridge over the river. The siding, named on Ordnance maps as 'Kirk siding', as called 'Tannybrake' by the men. Sited in the townland of Tawnybrake, it was at an overbridge and trailed towards Larne. It served a nearby dyeworks.

The Kells Water bridge was a single-span girder structure. From there to Moorfields the distance was two miles, during which the railway kept close to the south bank of the river. The river was fast flowing, and a succession of mill races were taken off it to supply water power to beetling mills. These mills, now vanished from the Ulster landscape, carried out an important finishing process in linen manufacture.

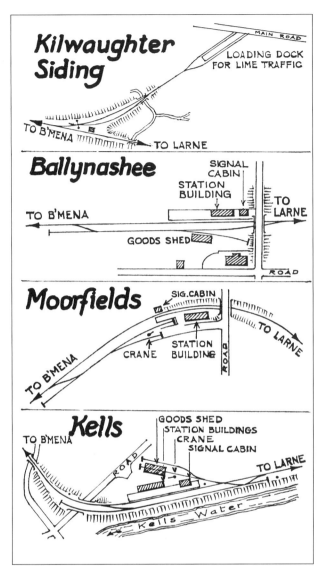

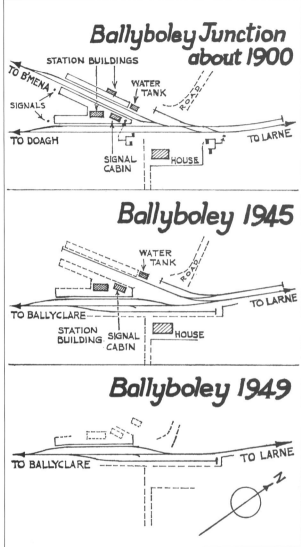

Moorfields itself was little more than a few houses near to Moorfields House. A beetling mill and a dyeworks provided employment, and a post office, store and dispensary catered for the other needs of the neighbourhood. The station was in a cutting, just before a road over-bridge, and had a siding trailing towards Ballymena and a headshunt. The two storey, brick-built station house was on the right hand side, the little signal box on the left.

Between Moorfields and Collin, the line rose at 1 in 122/125, all the time keeping within sight of the stream, which was here named the Glenwhirry river. The last of the mills, with their pervading rumble of water wheel and beetles, had been left behind and the river banks were flat and liable to flooding.

Nearing Collin halt, an open platform serving scattered farms and cottages in the rather bleak upper part of Glenwhirry, the line had reached 500 feet above sea level. Arable land was becoming sparse, and on both sides of the line the hills swelled, the rounded mass of Big Collin blocking the view to the south, while farther to the north the black basalt crags of Slemish reared spectacularly to over 1,400 feet, "stickin' up like a hard hat" as one driver graphically described it.

Once beyond 'The Collin', the line parted from the stream and climbed steadily at 1 in 100, south-east along Tildarg Hill. Rather empty, sheep-grazing land lay on both sides, until near mile-post 13 there was a cluster of houses called 'Back of the Hill'. The heavy gradient persisted, the line ran on to an embankment, curved to the south and reached the summit at mile post 12. The fireman's work was done and the train ran breathlessly into Ballynashee, 660 feet above the sea.

Ballynashee was placed at a road overbridge near a crossroads, and was on an ill-defined pass or 'col' between Tildarg Hill and Wee Collin. There was a passing loop and a headshunt on the short summit level. The ascent had brought the train to the limit of arable cultivation and great areas of peat bog now stretched towards the surrounding hills. The station buildings were on the left, the agent's house on the right.

Leaving Ballynashee, the line started down a steep and sustained grade, dropping at 1 in 75 for two miles to Ballyeaston halt, and then at 1 in 87 all the way to Ballyboley, a total distance of 4 miles 29 chains and a formidable obstacle to a heavily-laden coal train coming up from Larne. Ballyeaston halt was placed just west of an overbridge in the middle of a long curve; it probably had no accommodation for passengers other than a platform.

Ballyboley ('Ballyclare Junction' in B&LR parlance) had three platform faces and most of the appurtenances of an important junction station. Two of the platforms served the 'main line' while the third platform looked after the Doagh trains. The station building and the signal box were on the platform between the main line and the branch. Both roads had crossing loops and long headshunts. The layout of the station in B&LR days is not known, but it was undoubtedly spartan, for the sidings and permanent buildings were of BNCR construction, during the 1900–10 period.

From the junction, the run to Headwood level crossing measured just over a mile, with a rise at 1 in 169, followed by a fall at 1 in 293. In this stretch there was a short iron-ore siding serving the Shane's Hill mines laid in 1882 and probably lifted about 1890. Trains did not call at Headwood until 1882, and a waiting shed was not provided until 1896.

A short way towards Larne, the train encountered the steep descent to the sea, during which 408 feet of height were lost over a distance of six and a half miles. A fall at 1 in 66/56 took the line into the valley of the Larne (Inver) river. It was normal for goods trains to stop hereabouts to pin down wagon brakes, but on occasions this was no done, the train 'got away' and the seaward journey became somewhat terrifying for all concerned. However, the Larne signalman was always ready to give a clear road when he heard frantic warning whistles from the bank.

Two miles and a quarter from Headwood, Kilwaughter siding went off to the left, sandwiched between downgrades of 1 in 77 and 1 in 55. On the latter slope, a quarter mile past the siding, Kilwaughter halt was opened beside a level

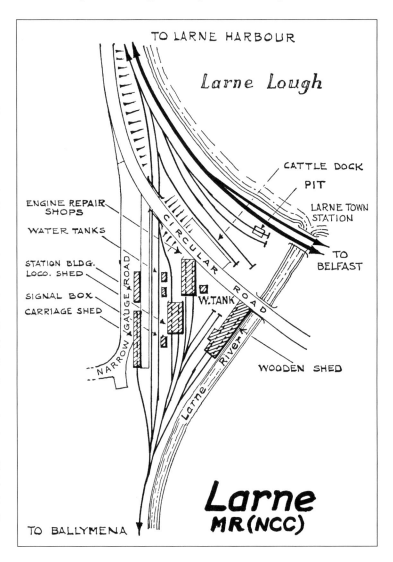

crossing. It provided a convenient stop for local people but was a headache for enginemen who were trying to start away up the bank on a wet rail. A short siding to Ballyrickard Quarry was opened for a time, a quarter of a mile below the halt.

After short stretches at 1 in 264/73, the steepest part of the Inver bank, or of the whole line for that matter, faced the train. First a mile of 1 in 44 in a sheltered glen where the rails were slow to dry, and where Millbrook Bank siding was situated. Winding on down, the houses of Larne came in view and then, as a grand finale, a quarter mile of 1 in 36. The river was over a wall to the right, Larne town station was in front, single-storey brick offices on the platform on the left, engine shed and towering signal box and yard to the right.

The final stretch to the harbour was a mile in length and was almost level. The Circular Road overbridge was passed at the platform end and then the broad gauge CLR (BNCR worked) line from Belfast came in on the right. The two lines ran in close company along the shore. Two-thirds of the way to the harbour, just before passing below the bridge carrying the Olderfleet Road, the narrow gauge line split, the line to the left leading to a complex of sidings which flanked Curran Road (later renamed Harbour Road). The line to the right divided again, one branch running in to one face of the passenger platform, while the other joined

with a broad gauge line to run as mixed gauge track to sidings at the south of the quays.

The branch line from Ballyboley Junction to Doagh followed a more subdued course. Beginning on the divide between the valleys of the Larne River and the Six Mile Water, it followed the latter stream, losing almost 200 feet of height over six miles. At Ballyboley, as the main line began its vigorous climb at 1 in 87, the Doagh road dropped quietly away from it, falling at 1 in 168 for a short way. There followed over a mile of 1 in 66 to Ballynure station where there was a single platform.

From Ballynure to Ballyclare the line dropped gently at 1 in 365, passing two beetling mills. Entering Ballyclare station, the Six Mile Water passed under the railway. On the bridge, sidings ran off the right and left, the former to a coal yard and the latter to goods sidings. The station buildings and signal box were on the right hand side of the line, the platform ending up against the Main Street overbridge, while the cattle dock and pens were through the arch.

Ballyclare had a foundry, a bleach works and a beetling mill, but for many years the main employer of labour was the paper mill. This mill was on the north bank of the river half a mile west of the town and was served by a narrow gauge siding. From August 1877 to February 1884 the branch ended there; thereafter, the extended line passed it on the way to Doagh. Across the river from the mill, the BNCR's

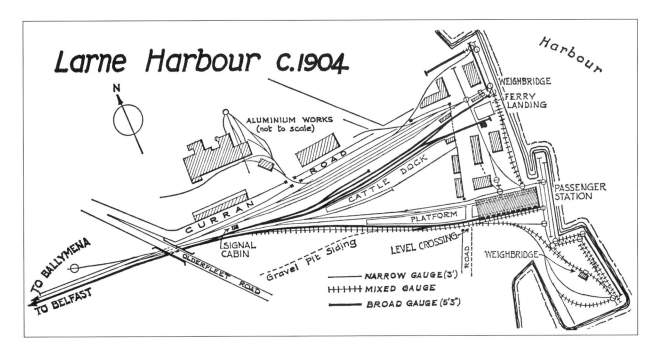

broad gauge branch ran in from Kingsbog Junction, but had no connection with the lines at the paper mill.

Coal for Kirkpatrick's bleach works was loaded into specially designed containers at Larne Harbour. At Ballyclare, there was a gantry to transfer the containers to road lorries for delivery to the bleach works, probably one of the few instances of container traffic in coal, and

certainly a pioneer example of the technique. The gantry was later transferred to Ballymoney for general use, serving both narrow and broad gauge sidings in the goods yard there.

The rest of the branch was largely taken at 1 in 72/387 to the lowest point. Then, turning away from the river, the line ended in a steepish half mile at 1 in 80, which brought it to Doagh station platform where it ran level to the buffer stop, at the south end of the village street. The goods yard was to the south of the station, and a spur to the south ran off the loop to the engine shed.

Chapter 5

The B&L faces the facts

Excursions and alarums

A few years before the Doagh extension was built, exciting projects had been afoot in the Ballymena and Larne's territory. The company itself promoted an extension which, had it been built, would have taken it into the valley of the River Bann, towards the Derry Central Railway's ground. The scheme was that of the Ballymena and Portglenone Railway, a concern which obtained its Act of Incorporation on 11 August 1879 (42–3 V cap ccxx) in spite of opposition from the BNCR.

The Ballymena and Portglenone Railway was planned as a three foot gauge line, leaving the B&LR 190 yards south of the Harryville station, passing south of the village of Ahoghill, rising to a summit at 404ft OD and then descending to 1 in 51 to Portglenone on the River Bann, just over ten miles from Ballymena. There were to be stations at Ahoghill and Gracehill. The Act authorised £60,000 of share capital but by 1881, when only £1,566 had been subscribed, the project was overtaken by a far more ambitious scheme which would have extended the narrow gauge railway across the entire county of Londonderry.

An eventual extension to Londonderry had been foreseen by the Northern Counties company, who had offered financial help to the Portglenone scheme if it were made broad gauge and a branch off their own line, rather than off the Ballymena and Larne. By so doing, the BNCR would have gained control of the scheme and been able to inhibit its potential growth towards Londonderry, which would have been directly opposed to their own main line. But in spite of the BNCR's efforts, the Portglenone project remained a narrow gauge child of the B&LR.

The greater scheme which overtook the Ballymena and Portglenone was that of the Londonderry and Larne Railway. Promoted by James Chaine and his friends, it would have been 48½ miles in length and the course as far as Portglenone was as already planned. The River Bann was to be crossed by five arches of 35ft span, and one opening 20ft span. Thereafter it would have gone by Swatragh, and Bovevagh, south of Dungiven, Feeny and Claudy, eventually reaching the bank of the River Foyle at Newbuildings. The more formidable obstacle of the Foyle was to be crossed by a viaduct of 44 spans, each of 35 feet. Once over the Foyle, the line would have accompanied the Great Northern Railway into the city of Londonderry. How it was expected to earn its keep one can only wonder, for Dungiven was the one sizeable town on its course, much of which would have been through sparsely populated moorlands of the north part of the Sperrin range. There the line would have climbed to two summit levels, 536 feet near mile post 18 and 879 feet near mile post 29¾. The Londonderry and Larne Railway Bill was duly submitted to Parliament, but was withdrawn after its second reading. It was a grandiose scheme, opposed by the Derry Central Railway Company and discussed at various public meetings,

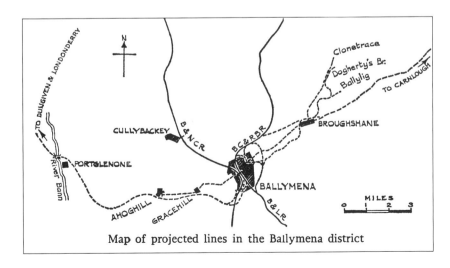

Map of projected lines in the Ballymena district

and neither it nor the Ballymena and Portglenone project ever became more than plans on paper.

A minor echo of the B&LR's 1878 Act was heard in 1879, when the company obtained powers (42–3 V cap cixxiv) to make a branch 3 furlongs 9½ chains in length, north of their line, a short way on the Larne side of Ballyboley Junction. It was to trail towards Larne and, with much of its course rising at 1 in 13, presumably rope-worked, Lewis estimated its cost at £1,800. The branch would have served an iron ore mine but was not built.

In 1885 a scheme for a three foot gauge roadside tramway from Ballymena to Ahoghill (48–9 V cap cxciii) arose, perhaps from the memory of the abortive Portglenone project. According to the *Ballymena Observer* of 21 March 1885, a census of traffic on the Ahoghill road taken during the week ending 7 March revealed that 1,589 carts, 646 cars, and 2,145 pedestrians had passed. The company, whose chief promoter was Robert Morton of Ballymena, was authorised to raise £14,000 of share capital and £6,000 in loans, but the scheme advanced no further.

Shortly before the excitement of the line to Londonderry, contact with the B&LR from quite another direction might have been established had a scheme promoted by the Belfast Central Railway come to fruition. The Belfast Central was a struggling little concern, favoured only in being located centrally in the city. It had four miles of broad gauge track which linked the Great Northern, the Belfast and County Down and the dockside lines. The directorate were English businessmen, and though they were never able to pay their shareholders any dividend, they did not lack ambition.

In 1880 they obtained an Act (43–4 V cap clxxxiv) which, among other matters, gave them powers to build a narrow gauge line to Ardoyne, in the west of the city. They followed this by promoting in 1881 a separate company, styled the Ballyclare, Ligoniel and Belfast Junction Railway (44–5 V cap ccxv), which was to have built a three foot gauge railway from Ardoyne, sweeping round the northern perimeter of Belfast to Skegoniel and then heading towards the village of Glengormley on a rising gradient of 1 in 40. At Glengormley, it was planned to curve towards the west, reach a summit at 484ft OD and then pass below the BNCR, two miles north-east of Templepatrick. Having crossed the Six Mile Water, the line was to rise at 1 in 70 into Doagh, there to end against the B&LR, which already had powers to extend there. The BL&BJR was backed by

the Belfast Central, but encountered vigorous opposition from the BNCR who were intending to make their own branch in Ballyclare. The BNCR already followed a better graded course on their main line, but they had the operating disadvantage of a reversal at Greenisland. Although the Northern Counties were not able to prevent the BL&BJR from obtaining their Act, no capital was subscribed and the parent Belfast Central itself was gobbled up four years later by the Great Northern.

Consolidation

With their connection made to the Cushendall line and the Doagh extension finished, the Ballymena and Larne was complete. By rights, it should have been able to look forward to a prosperous future with reasonable confidence. Further extensions were virtually impossible for, in spite of the flighty schemes towards Derry and from Ligoniel, the bounds of the company were circumscribed: by the sea coast on the east, by the hills of Antrim and the Cushendall line to the north, and by the broad gauge territory of the Northern Counties system to the south and the west. Indeed by November 1884 the Northern Counties was dangerously close, for the branch from Kingsbog to Ballyclare was then opened.

During 1880 and 1881 satisfactory arrangements were made with the various mining companies who were being persuaded to route their ore over the narrow gauge into Larne. By the middle 1880s iron-ore mining had been in operation in Antrim for around 20 years and thousands of wagon loads of the red-brown ore were being railed annually to Belfast and Larne, *en route* to English furnaces. The Antrim Iron Ore Company was sending a large tonnage of a low-grade ore, lithomarge, from Parkmore, Cargan and Rathkenny, and a rate of 1s a ton was negotiated for the haul from Ballymena to Larne. The traffic in bauxite was extending, too.

On the face of the hills north of Ballyboley, mining was extending nearer the B&LR's line, though the railway there was in the valley, whereas the adits were some 500 feet higher. In January 1881, a Mr Coventry submitted plans and estimates for a wire tramway to obviate the tiresome business of bringing the ore down from the hill by horse and cart. The inducement was not sufficient, and no construction was undertaken. Then, in June 1881, a proposed siding at Ballyboley, to cost £600, was discussed with the mine-owner, Dr Ritchie. This was opened on 1 September 1882 and replaced the siding at Moss Bridge, 630 yards from Headwood crossing.

The Ballymena and Larne depended for much of its continued success upon the prosperity of the Antrim iron-ore industry. The growth of mining had been phenomenal and nowhere else in Ireland had such a tremendous tonnage of minerals been extracted in so few years. But the prosperity of the mining industry depended in turn upon the demand from the cross-channel smelters, and the writing was already on the wall by the early 1880s.

At the meeting of shareholders on 22 August 1881 no dividend was declared on the ordinary shares. The chairman referred to a hard winter with much snow, which had had to be cleared away by hand, and to frost damage to lead piping in the stations which had put the company to further expense. Coal prices, he said, had increased, but the volume of general goods traffic and the number of first class passenger had both declined. There were as yet no through bookings with the Stranraer steamers, and therefore no profits from that source.

Even more ominous was the disappointing volume of iron-ore traffic which, although it had shown an increase over the previous year as a result of the direct connection with the Cushendall line, had been less than forecast. To add to the pervading gloom among the management, there was vociferous criticism of Sunday trains from a few who objected to the Ballymena and Ballyclare mill workers enjoying themselves by the sea on their only day off work. Mr Moffett of the York Street Flax Spinning Company rose to ask whether the company had run any goods trains on the Sabbath, probably having heard of one. He was assured that only one such train had been worked on a Sunday during the previous six months, and had conveyed iron ore required urgently for a ship that was under demurrage.

Depression

During 1880 and 1881 the Cushendall line carried around 100,000 tons of mineral traffic each year, while the Ballymena and Larne's tonnages were 53,000 and 62,000. It is doubtful whether more than a quarter of the Glenravel and Parkmore ore went over the B&LR; the rest continued to be transhipped at Ballymena into broad gauge wagons. In February 1882, the meeting of shareholders was given the dismal news by James Chaine that "the iron-ore traffic had

not come up, and never had come up, to the expectation of the directors'. His gloom was based on forecasts and the unjustified hopes that the B&LR would capture the bulk of the output of the iron-ore mines of the whole of Antrim. Actually, 1882 turned out to be the best year for mineral traffic in the company's history, with a total tonnage of 75,844, which brought in £7,250. But it was still far less than had been hoped for and, over the year, the ordinary shares paid only 2¼ per cent.

After 1883, mineral traffic began to be affected by the continued depression in the cross-channel iron trade, and during 1884/1885 the tonnages carried fell to 74,445 and 65,833. The directors now realised that their hopes of a rising tonnage were never likely to be fulfilled as, apart from a reduction in the amount of iron being smelted, a cheaper, high-grade Spanish ore had become available.

The meeting of shareholders on 25 August 1884 was an unhappy one. Of the directors, only James Chaine and William Ellis attended and they faced 31 shareholders. There was to be no ordinary dividend, but loans ad preference and debenture stocks were swallowing up their 4% to 4½%. The directors' reports was read, but when the chairman proposed its adoption, an amendment, moved by Samuel Curry and seconded by William McMeekin, urged that it be not adopted and that a dividend of 2% be paid on the ordinary shares. Where the money was to come from was not mentioned and a little arithmetic would have shown the objectors that £2,700 would have been needed to pay the proposed 2%. When a vote was taken, 14 shareholders, representing 420 votes, were for the resolution and 18 for the amendment, but since the latter held only 94 votes between them, the amendment was lost.

At the end of 1884 it was minuted that "owing to the continued depression in the iron trade" the rates for the carriage of ore were to be reduced by agreement. The old 3s 4d rate from Parkmore was reduced to 2s 5d per ton, while that from Ballyboley dropped from 1s to 10d. With the falling tonnages, these necessary reductions reacted badly on the company's income from mineral traffic:

Year	Tonnage	Receipts
1880	52,794	£4,934
1881	62,211	£5,891
1882	75,844	£7,250
1883	74,266	£6,741
1884	74,445	£6,353

| 1885 | 65,833 | £5,188 |
| 1886 | 62,043 | £4,784 |

It was apparent to those shareholders who had studied the successive half-yearly reports that the basic cause of the company's difficulties was the common one of over-capitalisation. A secondary cause was the high proportion of capital in the form of loans, preference and debenture stock. The position at the end of 1884 was as follows:

Authorised Capital –	stocks and shares	£186,000
	loans and debentures	£65,100
	Total	**£251,100**
Paid Up Capital –	ordinary shares	£135,552
	4½% preference stock	£31,980
	Total	**£167,532**
Loans –	at 4%	£40,450
	at 4½%	£10,780
Debenture Stock –	at 4%	£700
	at 4¼%	£9,120
	Total	**£61,050**

Against this weight of loan and debenture charges, were net earnings of £6,091 in 1884, which was insufficient to

Moorfields station in railway days, looking west.

Courtesy David Francey

provide payments to the ordinary shareholders after the priority demands had been met.

Personal relationships

In a company history derived largely from formal written records, the assessment of personalities is not always an easy task. But there is no doubt that James Chaine, the first chairman, was the mainstay of the company, and was held in respect and affection by those around him. At the meeting of 20 February 1882, in the course of his re-election as chairman, it was claimed that "the railway without Mr Chaine would be like a ship without a rudder". Three years later, after his sudden death, his place as chairman was taken by OB Graham of Larchfield, Lisburn, while William Eccles succeeded Graham as deputy chairman.

No complete list of B&LR stationmasters is known to exist and many of the appointments and transfers were not chronicled in the minute books, indicating that the directors delegated these matters to their manager. We do not know, for example, if the same person was stationmaster at Moorfields in 1880 and in 1882, but in the absence of contrary evidence he may well have been. The first reference to the Moorfields stationmaster in the Board Minutes is dated 2 June 1880, when Rew reported to his directors that he had received a threatening letter signed 'Rory of the Hills' and vowing injury to the line "if the stationmaster at Moorfields was not removed". Who Rory may have been we do not know, nor do Rew's minutes tell the reader how or whether the threat was countered. But an intriguing sequel did follow. On 31 May 1882, Rew reported that James Logan, stationmaster at Moorfields, had absconded and that his accounts were deficient by £6 13s 9d. Another startling piece of news was that Rew had suspended John Wilkinson, the Larne agent, for having made irregular passenger returns and for having accounts that were £3 15s 2d deficient. Wilkinson found the money, paid it on 9 June and then emigrated.

Moorfields station in 1986, looking west towards the bridge.　　Leslie Cooper

The Larne stationmasters seem to have been less dependable than their inland colleagues who, apart from the Moorfields man, are never mentioned. Between Christmas Day 1885 and New Years' Day 1886, the Larne man, by name Fielding, "had not been attending to his duties". Rew could not countenance such a magnificent spree and duly reported the matter to his board, saying that he "attributed the cause to drink, for which he had replaced him". Six months later, another Larne stationmaster was suspended for being £23 1s 9d short in cash.

William Pinkerton became the company's locomotive superintendent

Larne Town station on 13 June 1945, looking west towards Ballymena. The former station is on the left and the shed, with 4-4-2T No 113 in the centre.

DG Coakham

in March 1877 and for the next three years signed the 'Certificate respecting the Rolling Stock' that accompanied the half-yearly reports. Then, although he remained in office, Rew's name replaced his, whereupon Pinkerton, annoyed and humiliated, wrote a letter of complaint to Rew, as secretary. The letter was read to the directors on 17 October 1880, but Pinkerton was merely told that the directors regarded Rew as 'generally responsible'.

Pinkerton seems to have been of an inventive nature and an 'apparatus for locking sidings' which he patented later became well known as 'Pinkerton's Box'. Deciding to try and capitalise his brain child, the inventor wrote to his directors in June 1881 offering to grant the company the right to use his device "in consideration of their giving him £30" – and he got his money.

Pinkerton also tried to get better repair facilities during 1882, and his request that they should be made available either at Larne or at Larne Harbour, suggests that they must have been virtually non-existent. His request was accompanied by a recommendation for the adoption of Rowan's 'Patent Piston Rings' on the engines, and he obtained sanction for their use on two of the five. He also asked for another engine, for which he had to wait a year, and for a set of engine wheels, which were ordered at once.

During 1886, Pinkerton's position with the company became difficult and one senses that it must have been due to differences with his general manager. On 4 January, Rew submitted for the board's approval, a proposed new agreement with Pinkerton who, after being demoted from locomotive superintendent to foreman, was to act under the general manager and "to make himself generally useful about the works". Pinkerton was also "to drive in cases of emergency and to reduce the expenses to the lowest point consistent with safety." Finally, his appointment was to be subject to one month's notice. Surprisingly, Pinkerton's acceptance of the new terms was reported to the board on 13 January but his stay with the company ended only eight months later. The minute book refers to 'dismissal', though the secretary was told to write to him "stating that his dismissal was not on account of any neglect on his part, but was rendered necessary by a rearrangement in the management, and that the earnings of the line would

not admit of the directors being generous and they could not therefore give him more than one month's salary". That may have been the case, yet by December 1886 a Mr Horner was the company's engineer and locomotive superintendent! *

Economy drive

At the shareholders' gathering in February 1885, the chairman's address was as depressing as ever. Trade had been unusually bad. And the *Belfast News Letter* reported him as saying:

> This was more or less an agricultural line running through an agricultural country and although they had been blessed with a very good harvest in this country, other countries had been similarly blessed and consequently there was no great movement of agricultural produce from this country, nor any great demand for foreign produce coming into the country, because of people feeding off the stuffs they grew.

There had also been a good turf (peat) harvest and because of this the local demand for domestic coal was less. There had also been a decrease in the iron ore traffic, and in Cumberland, their chief market in ore, 23 out of 56 furnaces were idle. Then again, nearer home:

> The Ballyclare Paper Mill had changed hands and instead of esparto grass, which they had brought over the line in large quantities in previous years, they had substituted straw. They were of course carrying straw over the line, but it was not such a paying article.

He had some consolation to offer, for the third class traffic had shown "a marvellous increase", During 1884, there had been 166,494 third class passengers, compared with 146,455 in 1883 and 138,297 in 1882. The improvement, he claimed, was unforeseen and was taxing their coaching stock to capacity.

Turning to the Doagh extension which had been working for nine months, the chairman was reasonably hopeful, claiming that it "would pay very well, as even at present it was making what might be termed a good shape at opening up a country."

The shareholders then had their say. A Mr Kirkpatrick moved that the balance of £343 that was to be put to reserve should be applied instead to ballasting and otherwise

Though it has not been possible to establish identity, it is noteworthy that a William Pinkerton died at Barleith, Kilmarnock, on 8 Dec 1915 at the age of 61. His father had been foreman boilermaker at the Kilmarnock works of the Glasgow and South Western Railway. William was his eldest son and, according to the obituary notice in the Kilmarnock Standard, *he had had practical training as an engineer, displayed a gift for clerical work and a faculty for organising. He became foreman of the carriages department at Kilmarnock station and in 1901 was made locomotive superintendent at the Hurlford running sheds.*

improving the line. A sound idea, perhaps, but he failed to get a seconder. He also read, but did not move that, firstly, more carriages be attached to the 9am goods train from Larne on every Ballyclare monthly cattle market day and on Fair Days; second, that greater economy be used in every department of the line; third, that no free travel be allowed to anyone unless they were employees of the railway company and, fourth, that all special trains were to be paid for. Unlike some of the shareholders, Kirkpatrick's criticisms were at least constructive, and six months previously he had drawn the management's attention to the lack of thorn quicks in the hedges, and to the fact that many of the fence posts were rotten.

Kirkpatrick was followed by a Mr Watson, who for years had been a severe critic of Sunday travel, and who now moved "that the Sunday traffic on the line be discontinued". William Wilson seconded this, but an amendment to the effect that the Sunday traffic continue, proposed by James McAllister and seconded by William Agnew, was carried by 20 votes to eight. Wasson's voice was a regular feature of the shareholders' meetings, but he never achieved his object.

Doagh on 10 August 1937, after the withdrawal of passenger services. We are looking from the station towards Ballyclare and the brick building is the stationmaster's house, still occupied today. CP Friel collection

2-4-2T No 42 near Kilwaughter siding with the Ballyclare goods, on 28 July 1949.

DG Coakham

Outside advice

In an attempt to ease their acute financial worries the company promoted a parliamentary Bill which became law on 16 July 1885. It gave the company powers to raise £30,000 of additional capital by the issue of preference stocks and by borrowing on mortgage. Less important was permission to "abandon and relinquish the construction"{ of that part of the Kilwaughter branch authorised by the 1878 Act which had not been built, from the main road to Rory's Glen.

With OB Graham in the chair and ruin staring the company in the face after only seven years of operation, it was decided to seek the advice of an independent expert on what economies could be made. For this they turned to George Henry Wood, manager and secretary of the Isle of Man Railway since its opening in 1876. The choice was eminently sound, for the two concerns had much in common, the island one being the senior by a few years.

Ex-Ballycastle Railway 4-4-2T No 113 shunting near the Paper Mill siding at Ballyclare on 13 June 1945. The train is sitting on the stub of the Doagh branch and the Mill siding swings left through the gate.

DG Coakham

The contents of Wood's report were communicated to Rew in a letter from the chairman:

> We have now received the report from Mr Wood, manager of the Isle of Man Railway and it will be handed to you for perusal. In it he recommends certain economies and as it is absolutely necessary that everything that can be done should be done in this direction, we have decided to have his suggestions and recommendations carried into effect with all possible speed and rely on you to give the fullest effect to our wishes. He suggests a rearrangement of the Head Office which would necessitate our dispensing with the services of Mr Brown.
>
> He also suggests that you put one engine out of steam and yet do the present work.
>
> The results of the suggestions and recommendations is that you can reduce your staff as follows:

1 engine driver	1 pumper	1 smith
1 fireman	1 carpenter	5 porters
2 cleaners	1 storekeeper	1 collector
1 guard	1 covermaker	

> Please let me know the wages saved by these reductions.

Mr Eccles can go over the report with you and show you where they arise.

Already, in early November, it had been decided to save rent by vacating the company's office at 2 Royal Terrace, Larne as from May 1886, and to manage the line from premises available in Ballymena.

At the shareholders' meeting in December, it was stated that owing to the continued depression of trade, the company had been obliged to withdraw the special passenger and mail trains connecting with the Stranraer steamer, and to use the ordinary train service for passengers by that route. So, from 1 January 1886, the mid-day train from Larne and the 3.45pm train from Ballymena were taken off.

Friction and failure

Since October 1884 the Cushendall line had become the property of the BNCR. The new owners were developing the tourist potential of the Antrim coast and glens and they made arrangements to run passenger trains from the spring of 1886. Discussions were held regarding the signalling needed at the end-on junction between the two narrow gauge lines. Then, wretchedly poor and feeling that they owed the BNCR nothing so long as that company bled away the Glenravel ore down their own line, the B&LR agreed to allow Cushendall passenger trains to run from the junction into Ballymena station in return for a payment of £25 a year. Incensed by this, the mainline company threatened to force the B&LR to lift their rails from Ballymena station, which was Northern Counties ground in any case, but the matter was resolved without any such action being needed.

On 23 December 1885 it was decided to use the powers of the 1885 Act and issue £30,000 of 4½% perpetual preference shares of £10 each, but at a discount of 10% to encourage investors. The entire amount was soon taken up. Equally good support was given in May 1886 to an issue of 4¼% debentures and no less than £22,000 was taken up by three applicants: William McCalmont of London, William McDonald of Larne and the chairman. While these issues eased the immediate peril, they also increased the company's dividend commitments.

The cuts in services brought the inevitable complaints, in particular one from the clerk of the Ballymena town commissioners who, in July 1886, suggested alterations to the new services. In reply, he was told that it would merely result in a special train having to be put on "which the company cannot afford." It was as bad as that.

Rew resigns

Probably seeing no secure future ahead of him, FW Rew tendered his resignation as manager and secretary at the board meeting on 14 May 1886. The directors treated him more generously than they had Pinkerton and his salary was paid to the end of the year. In the minute of that meeting, reference is made to Mr Wheatley "the new manager" who was to come on 1 July, while Rew was "to remain at Mr Wheatley's option for some time … but having liberty to leave for another situation after 1 July."

The Mr Wheatley mentioned was William Thomas Wheatley, son of Thomas Wheatley. He succeeded his father as the lessee and manager of the Wigtownshire Railway at some date in 1883. The Wigtownshire Railway was taken over in the Portpatrick and Wigtownshire amalgamation of 1885, when Wheatley was appointed locomotive foreman

at Stranraer. In fact, Wheatley never did take up his duties at Larne, for in May 1886 he became general manager of the Girvan and Portpatrick Junction Railway.

Rew made his departure during July 1886. He was present at the board meeting on 5 July, but the minutes were written by his successor, JD Nott, who remained with the company until it was wound up.

Eclipse

In November 1886 the Ballyclare paper mill was also feeling the pinch. Its management wrote requesting a reduction in the special rates that had been agreed between the parties, and suggesting what they might be: coal down from 1s 7d to 1s 3d per ton, esparto grass from 3s to 2s, chemicals 2s 6d to 2s, wood pulp 2s to 1s 3d, china clay 2s to 1s 3d, lime 1s 6d to 1s. All that the railway company could agree to was the lower figure for esparto and a penny off the rate for coal.

The venue for the board meetings was next discussed. It had generally been in 'Brett's office' in Chichester Street, Belfast since 1884, or occasionally in the chairman's office in the York Street spinning mill in Belfast. Mr Brett offered to make no charge for the continued use of his office, but merely to charge for his time as the company's solicitor.

During 1886, economies reduced the total working expenditure to just over £9,000, a saving of £500 on the previous year. But total receipts fell heavily from £15,112 to £14,377, so that net receipts were down over the year. Mineral traffic was the lightest for seven years, and the number of passengers in both classes was down. Effort was maintained during 1887, at the end of which a decided improvement could be reported in all classes of traffic. Net receipts were almost £1,000 higher than in 1886, but no dividend could yet be justified for holders of ordinary shares. A dividend did, however, reappear in 1888, when ¾% was paid over the year.

The nadir of economy reached on 9 January 1889 when the board decided to try to make a modest profit on the 'yard sweepings' at Ballymena which, until then, had been taken away "by Mr Gault without payment". At one time the company were glad to get the horse droppings removed; now things were so bad that it was resolved that "they should be collected and disposed of by auction".

The inevitable could not be long delayed and at the board meeting on 4 March 1889 it was decided to sell the railway.

It spite of all the efforts made over the previous five years, it had become clear that the Ballymena and Larne could not continue to function as an independent unit. OB Graham moved, and W McDonald, seconded a resolution that the line be sold to the Northern Counties company under terms which had been already the subject of discussion:

(a) BNCR to pay off all loan capital of the B&LR, £23,720 in cash in full when matured.

(b) BNCR to issue debenture stock (3¼%) and exchange it at par for the first charge on the B&LR stock of £40,300.

(c) BNCR to issue 3½% debenture stock and exchange it for the remaining balance of the B&LR debenture stock of £22,800.

(d) BNCR to issue debenture stock (3½%) and exchange it for the entire preference stock of £63,820 of the B&LR, or pay off this sum in cash at seller's option.

(e) BNCR to give 40% of their ordinary stock at par in exchange for ordinary B&LR stock, or pay off in cash at £4 10s per £10 share. If the former is done, then the dividend can be withheld for three years while the permanent way and rolling stock are made more efficient.

(f) BNCR to pay off £3,000 to £4,000 due to sundry creditors of the B&LR.

(g) The rates to Ballyclare paper mill not be increased in any way.

(h) A representative of the B&LR board to have a seat on the BNCR board.

(i) The cost of the Bill to be borne by the BNCR.

On 1 May 1889, a special general meeting of the shareholders was held at Larne Harbour. Seventy shareholders were present and they were asked to approve the terms of the parliamentary Bill which would end the brief life of their little company. The minutes list the holdings of those who attended and those who voted by proxy. Much the largest holding was owned by D McDonald, who held 753 preference shares personally, and the votes of 1,890 ordinary shares by proxy. The other chief shareholders were OB Graham and William Chaine. The vociferous Wasson, whose contribution over the years had been to fulminate against Sunday trains, held five shares. When the vote was taken, 30 shareholders carrying 2,009 votes were for the Bill, 38 shareholders carrying 383 votes were against it. So the Bill went forward for parliamentary consideration, and became law on 16 July 1889 (52–3 V cxcvii).

On Wednesday 19 March 1890, the last meeting of the Ballymena and Larne directors were held in Mr Brett's office. The railway was no longer theirs, they could only deliberate on the disposal of some rails that were lying at Larne Harbour. It was a pathetic finale to a brave undertaking.

Ex-Ballymena and Larne Railway 0-6-0T No 107 on a train of mineral hoppers at Martinstown about 1925. The staff are James Swan (permanent way man), W Wilson (guard), John Johnston (stationmaster), Roddy Millar (driver) and W Gourley (fireman).

H Herron collection

Chapter 6

Life under the Northern Counties

Two-stage takeover

Assimilation of the Ballymena lines by the Belfast and Northern Counties Railway was a piecemeal process. The Ballymena, Cushendall and Red Bay Railway had been absorbed in October 1884, but the Ballymena and Larne did not lose its identity until August 1889.

The Cushendall company had handled only mineral and goods traffic during the nine years of its independent existence. Mineral traffic had always formed the bulk of this, while on a tonnage basis, general merchandise averaged only 3% of the total, and brought in from 4– 6% of the income. For the first 18 months under the Northern Counties this pattern was perpetuated.

One-sided traffic

The new owners of the Cushendall line saw that its earning capacity was capable of development and were stimulated to follow this up by the obvious decline in iron-ore traffic. The railway could not reactivate the mineral workings, but they did have the capital to undertake the refurbishing that would enable them to start passenger traffic. Under independent ownership, a few passengers probably had been carried unofficially, either to oblige local residents or to assist mine officials in their administration, but nothing could be organised in the absence of Board of Trade authorisation. There were no stations, only loading banks at Carrowcowan and at Retreat. There was no signalling. But Ballymena was the expanding centre of industry in County Antrim, and as it drew an increasing number of workers from the surrounding country, so the same workers bemoaned the lack of passenger trains on the Cushendall line.

Tramway schemes

By the middle 1880s roadside tramways were becoming deservedly popular in County Antrim. The little steam tramway at Portstewart first ran in 1882, in the next year the

Portrush–Bushmills–Giant's Causeway tramway joined it, being operated at first by steam, later by electricity generated by hydro-power from the River Bush. With these two systems at work, it was no surprise that the Act of Parliament authorising the BNCR to take over the Cushendall company gave permission for the construction of two 3ft gauge roadside tramways. One of these was to have linked Retreat station to a point near the Cushendall Hotel, the other was from the terminus of Railway No 3 of the 1878 Act to Dougherty's Bridge at Clontrace. Neither was constructed.

The Retreat–Cushendall tramway would have been on the east side of the public road in Glenballyemon, losing 886 feet in height over 3 miles, 4 furlongs, 9.8 chains. The minimum gradient would have been 1 in 30, the maximum 1 in 16.4. Permission was given to use … "animal power … and with the consent of the Board of Trade … steam or any mechanical or electrical power …." Being a roadside tramway, the Act took care to specify the behaviour of "every locomotive propelled by steam" and insisted that "the whistle of such locomotive shall not be sounded for any purpose whatever, nor shall the cylinder taps be opened within sight of any person riding, driving, leading or in charge of a horse upon the road, nor shall the steam be allowed to attain a pressure such as to exceed the limit fixed by the safety valves so that no steam shall blow off when the locomotive is upon the tramway". Moreover, speed was limited to 12 miles an hour in the open country and to six miles an hour in "any city town or village". It was as well it was never built, for there would have been little chance for the engine to 'take a race' at the 1 in 16.4 which faced it on leaving Cushendall.

Conversion

During 1885, the BNCR put in hand the first of the necessary improvements to the Cushendall line, on the eight and a half miles from Ballymena to Knockanally. The permanent way – it could scarcely be called 'old' for it had been laid ten years before – was not good enough for passenger traffic, in which a derailment could not be tolerated. The 45lb wrought-iron rails were considerably worn, especially near Ballymena where traffic had been heaviest, and a programme of systematic replacement with 50lb steel rails was undertaken. Damp had decayed many of the original sleepers, and while they were being replaced by creosoted larch, opportunity was taken to increase their width from six to eight inches.

At Ballymena, use was made of the existing station, already shared between the Belfast–Londonderry broad gauge and the narrow gauge link line between the Cushendall and the Larne roads. New stations were made at Ballycloughan, Rathkenny and Knockanally (later Martinstown), with platforms nine inches above rail level.

Ballycloughan station, four miles from Ballymena, was built at a level crossing with a secondary road that linked the hamlet of Quarrytown with the main Ballymena–Cushendall road. It had no siding at first, but one was made later.

Rathkenny station was sited two miles beyond Ballycloughan, where the mine siding joined the railway, and about 300 yards to the south of the creamery.

Knockanally station was two and a half miles north of Rathkenny and eight miles from Ballymena, where the 'Bleagh' iron-ore siding ran in. The station was named after the townland of Knockanully (as the Ordnance Survey spelt it) but was actually in the adjacent Martinstown townland, and it was renamed after the latter in April 1920. Knockanally achieved some importance as a temporary passenger terminus and, to control the resulting evolutions from the conflict of passenger and mineral trains, the BNCR erected a modest ten-lever signal cabin, leaving three levers spare.

Board of Trade inspection

The improvements to the Ballymena–Knockanally section were judged complete by March 1885 and towards the end of the month it was formally inspected on behalf of the Board of Trade by Major-General Hutchinson. He wrote his report on 31 March on his return to London, noted the improvements that had been made and listed various matters which still needed attention, including the lack of name boards at the stations. Two of the level crossings had defective gates and none of them had any lamps.

The General then turned his eagle eye on the new tramcar carriages. He had been called to County Donegal

in January of the previous year and there he had seen the damage that a high wind could wreak on narrow gauge carriages. Both the West Donegal and Lough Swilly railway companies had suffered derailments on a night of high wind, and although in the first instance there was evidence that excessive super-evaluation of the track had contributed, the General was firmly of the opinion that the length of the carriages had presented too great an obstacle to the wind. As the Cushendall carriages were the same length as those of the Donegal lines, the General said that future purchases should be shorter but, as on the Donegal lines, his recommendations were ignored.

A final recommendation was that a speed limit of 20mph should be imposed until all defective rails had been replaced, and that it should be 25mph thereafter.

The BNCR promptly attended to the requirements and on 5 April were able to start a passenger service to Knockanally. It was their first venture at the conveyance of passengers of the narrow gauge. To make sure they had done as they had been told, they received a second visit of inspection from General Hutchinson later in the year, and were no doubt relieved to learn that this time his keen eye had seen nothing out of order.

Passengers to Parkmore

Knockanally was a terminus for passengers for only two years and five months, for as fast as available resources allowed, the five miles towards Parkmore were rehabilitated. Stations were made at Cross Roads, Cargan and Parkmore.

The genesis of Cross Roads had been the Carrowcowan ironstone mining siding. The new station and its crossing loop straddled the roadway, with signal box and goods store on the down side of the crossing gates, platforms and waiting room across the road.

Cargan station served a small mining community and was placed one and three-quarter miles beyond Cross Roads, but its completion was delayed because of difficulty in buying the necessary land. There was a crossing loop, with the platform and goods store placed between the railway line and the main road.

On a windswept and unpicturesque site stood Parkmore station, two miles above Cargan. It was strategically placed at a road fork where one branch led to Glenariff and the other over the pass to Glenballyemon and Cushendall.

The Board of Trade inspection was arranged in August

An excursion train, bound for Parkmore, is shunted by 0-4-2ST No 102 at the Cushendal yard at Ballymena, prior to departure, probably about 1900. Note the two clerestory coaches at the rear. L&GRP

The same train is seen some time later, heading north, probably approaching the Ballymoney Road, Ballymena. The four coaches and van would have been quite a challenge for this small engine in the long climb towards Parkmore.

L&GRP

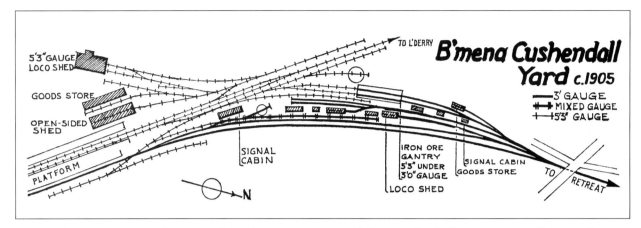

1888, and was again entrusted to General Hutchinson. He noted that there were still a number of the old wrought-iron rails "failing at the joints" and asked for them to be replaced. He then discovered that the level crossing at Cross Roads had never been authorised by Act of Parliament, and that three other level crossings, between Ballymena and Knockanally were similarly illegal. But, wisely, he reckoned that it would be expensive for the Northern Counties to cure the omission by civil engineering, and tolerantly suggested that they be allowed to deal with the matter in their next application to Parliament.

Once permission was given, the Northern Counties lost no time in starting passenger trains up the steep grades to Parkmore. According to their next half-yearly report, this was done on 27 August 1888, which might have been a little early as General Hutchinson's report to the Board of Trade is dated 31 August, though it was not unknown for a line to be opened on the inspector's verbal permission. But in a director's copy of the half-yearly report, a marginal manuscript note gives the date as 1 September, which seems more appropriate but, whichever date it was, it unfortunately failed to catch the summer excursion traffic.

The final section of the railway, from Parkmore to Retreat, offered practically no inducement for tourist traffic, the bulk of which gravitated into Glenariff. So the last two and a quarter miles were never provided with passenger facilities, nor was the Glenballyemon tramway ever built, for the good reason that regular commuter traffic would have been too light to warrant the capital outlay. The Board of Trade were never asked to give approval for the use of the Parkmore–Retreat section for passenger services, and no passenger trains ever ran over it.

Closely dating the opening to Parkmore was the establishment of a further station at Ballygarvey, between Ballymena and Ballycloughan. It was more in the nature of a halt, with only a short platform and a shed at a level crossing. General Hutchinson's reports do not mention it, so it is unlikely to have been open in August 1888, but it is recorded in a timetable two months later.

'The wild and desolate basaltic vale'

The opening up of Glenariff to tourists took place over two decades and is mentioned in contemporary guide books. Previously, Black's *Guide Book for Tourists to Belfast and the North* in 1875 devoted some 20 pages to the Antrim coast, yet dismissed Glenariff in only a few lines merely saying:

> . . . further south, at the head of Red Bay, is Cushendall, one of the sweetest villages in Ulster. Between it, and the last-named town, the wild and desolate basaltic vale of Glenariff, the valley of caverns, is passed.

Yet 20 years later, *Boyd's Pictorial Guide* spread three pages on a eulogy of the glen, describing it as:

> the most beautiful and enchanting of all the Antrim glens … easily reached from Cushendall by public cars, which run several times a day to Parkmore railway station.

Such was the difference that organised public transport made.

The BNCR followed up their provision of passenger trains to Parkmore by turning their attention to Glenariff itself, renting the glen, making footpaths through it, and opening it to the public during the summer of 1889. Before the railway company took over the glen, it was already heavily forested but access was difficult to the river, and to the succession of fine waterfalls. The glen was pretty much as nature had made it, uncommercialised and

An ex-BC&RBR 0-4-2ST, probably No 101, at the original wooden Parkmore station, probably in the late 1890s (compare with the rear cover). The woman and boy leaning from the first coach are probably the photographer's family.

Rev WG Davis collection

No 102 shunting at Parkmore in the late 1890s with a clerestory coach in the formation, while the passengers wait for the operation to be completed. The house in the background survived until recently. Today this area is heavily wooded.

L&GRP

unsuited to the passage of large numbers of people or all ages and dimensions keeping to a timetable and eager for refreshment in the heat of summer. So *Boyd's Guide* further regaled its readers:

> We leave the conveyance on the main road, and enter a path leading into the glen, where an excellent path extending the entire way has been made by the Railway Company who have also, for the convenience of visitors, erected at the foot of the glen a commodious and artistic Tea House, situate on a little plateau, commanding an artistic view of surpassing loveliness. For a small charge, visitors are supplied with tea, cake, butter, preserves, lemonade, etc; and those who prefer taking their own provisions with them, can have the use of the tea house for the nominal fee of one penny each person, and be supplied with hot water and the necessary delf etc for a repast, for one additional penny. A photographic dark room has been fitted up in the tea house, and a charge of six pence is made for the use of same.

The tourists came over the hill from Parkmore station in their wagonettes, left them at the lonely post-office at the top of the glen, allowed gravity to assist them along the new paths, drank tea and ate to their heart's content, took photographs of each other, and then set off again in Henry McNeill's conveyances towards Larne. Glenariff had arrived and the railway had made it possible.

Along with the seasonal excursion traffic, the general traffic also developed. A goods shed was erected at Parkmore in 1896, and some small dwelling-houses were built for the station staff the following year. Additional land was acquired in 1899 and a waiting-room built at a cost of £116 to shelter excursionists from the wild weather that could sweep down from the hills. Knockanally got a goods store in the same year, a modest edifice costing £23, and in 1900 Ballycloughan acquired a siding that cost £52 to lay. Cattle docks were built at Parkmore, Retreat and Ballymena, and Cargan's passenger accommodation was improved.

By the turn of the century the process was complete, the Cushendall line had been fully equipped with the accommodation for man and beast, though both came second to the indispensable minerals.

The Larne line joins in

The assimilation of the Ballymena and Larne line was more straightforward than that of the Cushendall. Whatever the financial plight of the company, it was

running both passenger and goods trains and there was no ordeal by Board of Trade examination. Nevertheless, there was much the BNCR had to do before they could accept the line as fit for the traffic it carried.

During the first year of their ownership, the Northern Counties spent £1,534 on what the half-yearly report termed 'Improvements to Way and Works', and a further £967 on rolling stock. Ballymena coal traffic was also considered. Very little coal was mined in Ireland and all supplies for Ballymena and neighbourhood were shipped into Larne from cross-channel sources. Ballymena's requirements had represented a steady traffic for the B&LR, but handling conditions were primitive and coal for domestic use was stored in a yard on the south side of Harryville station, between the platform and the signal cabin.

During 1889, the BNCR built a siding and coal store for the Ballymena gas company on the north side of Harryville and on railway-owned land. This building, strategically placed at the back of Wilson's laundry, was capable of holding about 300 tons of coal and had a floor for carts at road level, while the rails were carried in from Harryville yard on a gantry supported on columns. Inside, the store had room for seven or eight wagons at a time, but the engine was not permitted to enter because of the risk of fire. The depot was completed in 1890 and cost £625.

During 1892, a start was made on improving the station buildings on the B&LR line. 'Way and works' still accounted for over £300 that year, but more than £1,300 was laid out to provide a house for the Ballynashee agent, sheds at

*0-6-0T No 108 (ex-B&LR No 6)
poses with her crew at Larne Harbour
turntable on 3 August 1902.*

Ken Nunn collection, LCGB

Opposite: *The coat of arms of the
Belfast and Northern Counties Railway.*

Right: *Ex-B&LR 2-6-0ST No 5 (as
BNCR No 109) outside Larne shed
around 1902. In BNCR days the narrow
gauge engines seem to have carried
no decals to denote ownership, the
numberplate serving this function.*

Real Photographs Ltd

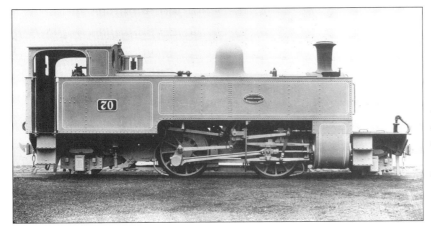

*Builder's photograph of compound
2-4-2T No 70. This engine and sister
No 69 were built by Beyer Peacock in
1892 for the B&LR section. They were
renumbered 110 and 111 in 1897.*

Beyer Peacock

Compound 2-4-2T No 110 (originally No 69) arriving at Ballymena from Larne sometime between 1897 and 1904.

Real photographs Ltd

Doagh, and various gatekeepers' houses. In the following year, expenditure on new buildings at stations amounted to £1,636. The wretched little engine shed at Larne, about which Pinkterton had complained, was demolished and replaced, and workshops were added at a cost of around £500.

Improvements continued at Larne and in 1896 a reliable water supply was installed and £276 spent on a cattle dock. During the same year, Headwood crossing got a waiting shed, Ballyclare a goods shed and an additional siding, while Moorfields rose in status by the acquisition of a fine, brick-built, two-storey station house – £591 worth and still very much lived in 110 years later.

In 1892, the rolling stock was strengthened by the purchase of two compound side-tank locomotives. They were built by Beyer, Peacock and Co to the design of Bowman Malcolm and were the forerunners of a successful class of six engines, the last of which was built in Belfast 27 years later. With these acquisitions, the Northern Counties brought the operation of their B&LR section to a high pitch of efficiency.

The original terminus of Harryville remained in use for passenger traffic after the line had been taken past it and over the river in 1880. For almost ten years the town enjoyed the luxury of two narrow gauge stations, though most of the passengers went through the main station. The new owners withdrew Harryville's passenger facilities, as from 1 January 1890, though it remained in use as a goods station.

Joie de vivre

The running of narrow gauge trains seems to have been done with a certain amount of exuberance. Perhaps the prospect of a more secure future under the BNCR was exhilarating, but the locomotive engineer disapproved and sought to stop the practice in a 'Notice to Enginemen' dated 18 June 1891:

RACING ON PARALLEL LINES

I am informed that some Drivers – both Broad and Narrow Gauge – are in the habit of racing between Ballymena Passenger Station to the point where the Broad and Narrow Gauge diverge, and from Larne

Station to the Harbour. It must be clearly understood that such a practice is most objectionable and will, under no circumstances, be tolerated.

His warning seems to have had little effect, for he renewed it on 26 July 1892:

SPEED ON Narrow gauge SECTION

Strong complaints have been made to me of Drivers on B&LR Section running at excessive speeds, and I wish now to caution all concerned to be careful in future to avoid anything of the kind.
I have been told of cases of very high speeds when there was absolutely no excuse, as the train had to wait for time at Stations.

Racing between Ballymena and Harryville was a not a pastime that any careful driver pursued, for the bridge over Queen Street was entered on a sharp left-hander, and followed by a right-hander, and had a speed limit of 20mph.

The Larne Aluminium Works lines

In 1900, a factory was built at Larne by the British Aluminium Company to treat bauxite chemically and remove impurities before shipment as alumina for conversion to aluminium metal. The works were built to the north of Curran (later Harbour) Road and were provided with quite an extensive 3ft gauge private railway system. Between the Harbour station and the Olderfleet Road overbridge, two level crossings connecting the works with the BNCR lines.

The aluminium works railway was operated by three small Peckett 0-4-0 tank locomotives, Nos 1, 2 and 3, built in 1904, 1906 and 1914. No 3 was dismantled in 1953 and, to take its place, a four-wheel Planet diesel engine was acquired from the company's Kinlochleven factory. No 2 engine was sold in 1955, leaving No 1 and the diesel to work the railway until the factory closed in 1960. No 1 is now preserved on the modern Giant's Causeway Railway. More information on the BAC line is on pages 154–58.

The waste product from the works, red iron oxide, was dumped in extensive ponds built on the foreshore, which was to the south-west of the factory, across the Olderfleet Road and the railway lines. Access to the ponds was obtained by a long siding which passed over the broad and narrow gauge BNCR lines just west of the Olderfleet Road overbridge.

Profit and loss

Until the two narrow gauge concerns were absorbed by the BNCR, their financial and operating statistics were shown in the half-yearly reports and were reissued in the annual Board of Trade Returns. After amalgamation, the narrow gauge results of the BNCR were not publicised. Of particular interest, therefore, are some breakdowns of statistics for the Cushendall and Ballymena sections which were set out for the board members. Only those for 1890–94 are known; they have been recalculated as annual figures and are compared in the accompanying tables with

Ballyboley Junction, looking west in the 1920s. The line towards Ballymena climbs away in the distance. The Doagh branch is just visible behind the neat signal cabin.

Real Photographs Ltd

CUSHENDALL LINE

RECEIPTS	1880	1890	1891	1892	1893	1894
	£	£	£	£	£	£
Iron ore	11561	4751	3376	2378	2272	2628
Psrs and parcels	–	1099	1184	1169	1192	1349
Goods	553	778	764	678	709	669
Mails	–	40	40	40	40	40
Miscellaneous	19	–	–	–	–	–
Assumed value of b-g wagons	–	1687	1175	842	841	947
Total	12133	6355	6559	5107	5054	5633

WORKING EXPENDITURE						
Maint of way	1385	1187	1055	1039	775	840
Loco power	1220	1323	1264	1286	1341	1073
Carr and wgns	322	753	579	714	884	688
Traffic exps	925	939	879	819	832	919
Rates and insur	128	25	27	28	33	41
Gnl charges	232	–	–	–	–	–
Legal charges	7	–	–	–	–	–
Miscellaneous	14	–	–	–	–	–
Total	4233	4227	3804	3886	3865	3561
Profit	7900	2123	2755	1221	1189	2072
Miles run	43522	56683	54378	47617	46358	50568
Receipts/mile	5s 7d	2s 11d	2s 9d	2s 2d	2s 2d	2s 3d
Expend/mile	1s 11d	1s 6d	1s 5d	1s 8d	1s 8d	1s 5d
Profit/mile	3s 8d	1s 5d	1s 4d	6d	6d	10d

the original owners' returns for the prosperous year of 1880. (See tables above)

On the Cushendall section, the dramatic shrinkage of iron-ore receipts is noteworthy; they fell by over half in the 1880–90 decade and continued their decrease thereafter. Passenger and parcels traffic, once established, brought in only an average of around £3 a day over the years, while the movement of goods contributed only about £2 per day. Once capital had been spent on renewals, expenditure on

permanent way maintenance could be reduced, and this largely accounted for the reduction in working expenditure under the BNCR. But because of the diminishing iron-ore traffic, profitability of the section ever regained its original state; indeed by 1893 the branch was earning only around £3 per day and returning about 1% on capital. By then, it had proved a poor investment for the new owners.

On the Larne section conditions were more stable, since ore traffic generally contributed less than 2% of

BALLYMENA AND LARNE LINE

RECEIPTS	1880	1890	1891	1892	1893	1894
	£	£	£	£	£	£
Passengers	3463	3755	3588	3718	3960	3833
Parcels	67	88	88	81	72	82
Mails	–	20	210	592	592	592
Merchandise	4110	5562	5891	4804	5139	4511
Livestock	327	617	449	430	541	682
Minerals	4934	4832	5478	5417	5837	6023
Iron ore	–	362	291	366	116	272
Rents	–	86	88	90	85	90
Miscellaneous	142	–	–	–	–	–
Total	13043	15322	16083	15498	16342	16085

WORKING EXPENDITURE						
Maint of way	1646	2237	2682	2839	2459	3222
Loco power	2146	2607	3263	3950	4234	3592
Carr and wgns	468	960	1307	1150	1504	1023
Traffic exps	2531	2860	2901	2938	2946	2921
Gnl charges	1038	285	287	286	220	225
Compensation	18	20	22	25	20	31
Rates and taxes	161	90	83	84	101	161
Law charges	–	3	–	–	–	–
Total	8003	9070	10543	11272	11484	11175
Profit	5040	6252	5540	4226	4858	4910
Miles run	101373	126376	132249	145401	144652	145014
Receipts/mile	2s 7d	2s 5d	2s 6d	2s 2d	2s 3d	2s 3d
Expend/mile	1s 7d	1s 5d	1s 7d	1s 7d	1s 7d	1s 7d
Profit/mile	1s 0d	1s 0d	11d	7d	8d	8d

the income. The big earners were coal traffic and general merchandise, which together contributed to about two-thirds of the income, while passengers, livestock and mails made up the rest. Under the BNCR, the train miles run on the B&LR section increased, which is reflected in expenditure on locomotive power, traffic expenses and on carriage and wagon upkeep. But the Larne line was not a highly profitable concern, and though less affected by outside influences than was the Cushendall, its earnings on capital were only 2–3%, while the whole system was earning 5–6% for its ordinary shareholders.

Under English influence

During the second half of 1902 the directors of the BNCR considered a proposal for the purchase of their railway by the Midland Railway of England. That company was preparing to extend its activities across the Irish Sea and were making a branch to Heysham Harbour so that they could enter the Irish Sea steamer traffic. The acquisition of the BNCR would enable them to thrust far into the north-west of the country. The terms were favourable and although the old BNCR had been prosperous, the offer was too tempting to refuse. The Northern Counties' shareholders were getting 5½% at the time. The Midland's terms were:

(1) Each £100 of BNCR 4% debenture stock to be exchanged for £160 of Midland 2½% debenture stock.

(2) Each £100 of BNCR 3% preference stock to be exchanged for £120 of Midland 2½% preference stock.

(3) Each £100 of BNCR 4% preference stock to be exchanged for £160 of Midland 2½% preference stock.

(4) Each £100 of BNCR ordinary stock to be exchanged for £220 of Midland 2½% preference stock.

The 115th half-yearly meeting of the proprietors of the BNCR was held on Friday 13 February 1903 at York Road. After it, a special general meeting was held "for the purpose of considering and, if thought fit, of approving a Bill proposed to be introduced into Parliament in the present Session entitled *A Bill to Provide for the Vesting of the Undertaking of the Belfast and Northern Counties Railway in the Midland Railway Company*".

The chairman, the Rt Hon John Young, DL, spoke at length on the contents of the Bill and formally proposed its approval. Henry McNeill seconded. Strong objection to the motion was then expressed by one shareholder, the Rev John Fawcett, who spoke of the Midland's "twenty-nine millions of bogus capital" and forecast that in ten years' time "they would not get a penny of dividend". He tried to proposed an amendment but the chairman would not receive it. The motion was then passed with this one objector, the chairman remarking that while Mr Fawcett was at liberty as a shareholder to attend the meeting and express his views, he held less than £250 of shares and consequently had no vote.

Ballynure station, looking north, probably in the 1920s. Up to the First World War there had been a goods store where the photographer is standing.

Real Photographs Ltd

Chapter 7

The Midland years

The Northern Counties Committee

The purchase of the Belfast and Northern Counties Railway by the Midland of England was duly authorised by Act of Parliament and the transaction was formalised on 1 July 1903. The take-over was accompanied by the establishment of a committee of management, styled the Northern Counties Committee, which had seven members, both local and cross-channel. The chairman was the Rt Hon John Young of Galgorm Castle, Ballymena, who had been the chairman of the BNCR board of directors for many years. The change in ownership was not accompanied by any noteworthy changes in policy, the Midland being content to have a firm foot in the Irish camp, as the London and North Western had, at Greenore a quarter century before.

The coast again

Soon after the MR(NCC) had assumed management, the vexed question of extending the Cushendall line to the village of that name was again raised. A deputation consisting of Sir Daniel Dixon Bt, and Messrs HM Thompson, C Agnew, R McAllister and A Delargy met the members of the committee on 29 October 1903 and presented a memorial signed by the merchants of Ballymena and the inhabitants of Cushendall and district, urging the Midland to proceed with the extension. Neither memorialists nor members of the deputation seem to have had a clear idea of the historical background to the failure of the BC&RBR to complete the original scheme. Topographical problems were forgotten in the hope that the big English company would conveniently find the wherewithal to carry the line down to the level of the sea from the breezy fastness of Retreat. But the originators of the scheme were to be disappointed for, as the committee minute recorded it, "after the deputation withdrew, the committee had the engineering difficulties explained to them and decided to take no action at present".

The MR(NCC) continued the practice of collaboration with Henry McNeill of Larne in running excursions around the Antrim coast. They also improved the road connection between Retreat and Cushendall during 1905. Berkeley Wise, who had been the BNCR's engineer, and who continued in that office until his retirement in 1906, was instructed to build a shed for a 'road motor'. The building was erected at a cost of £75, and a nominal rent of £1 a year was paid for it. The scheme had only a short life. Four years later, a minute referring to yet a further abortive attempt by the Cushendall people to get a local railway concluded sadly that "efforts to improve the communication between Cushendall and the railway by the use of motor cars have not succeeded, owing to the bad condition of the roads … all that is possible to do at present is to endeavour to provide a good horse service to and from Parkmore station." As late as 1920, the Ballymena Chamber of Commerce tried to promote the construction of a Portglenone–Ballymena–Retreat–Carnlough line, but like others before it, the scheme failed.

Rough runs to the boat

The mail trains made the fastest runs between Ballymena and Larne, and one daily run in each direction connected with the Stranraer steamers. It became the practice for cross-channel travellers from north of Ballymena to change trains there and make for Larne by the narrow gauge, since this shortened the journey and saved time as compared with the broad gauge route via Greenisland. There was undoubtedly more comfort in the broad gauge carriages – perhaps the racing propensities of certain drivers had not been quelled – but there were complaints at a high level of rough running, and this was minuted in February 1904. So serious were the complaints that the chairman asked his officers to consider conveying boat passengers and their luggage via Greenisland. In due course Cowie

S class compound 2-4-2T No 101 at Larne on 22 May 1924. This photograph was taken looking towards the harbour at the point where the narrow gauge lines emerged from under the Circular Road bridge. The locomotive is wearing MR 'invisible green' livery. This engine was one of two built by the MR in 1908-09 as Nos 112 and 113. They were renumbered 102 and 101 in Feb 1920.

Ken Nunn collection, Locomotive Club of Great Britain

S class 2-4-2T No 104 in MR livery on 8-wheel transporter wagon No 3093 at York Road, probably in March 1920, when new.

Ian Stewart collection

and Wise, general manager and engineer, reported that if the scheme were put into effect, alterations would be needed at Larne to hold the additional train; moreover, the expense of 40 additional train miles would be incurred. The conclusion being reached that such a change would not be economically viable. It was formally postponed and the future of the narrow gauge was assured for a time.

Minor improvements

A creamery had been started at Rathkenny and in August 1905 it was decided to make a siding to it. Construction cost the company £254, and the siding was extended to a new store in the autumn of 1920. At the same meeting in 1905, a request was read from a Mr Robert Smith for a siding at Kells, but as it was not authorised "unless he defray the expenses of £150" nothing further was heard of it.

Ballyeaston halt, which had such a short life in B&LR days, was revived during 1911 after a lapse of 29 years. The old stop had become overgrown and £25 was spent on providing a short platform and a shelter. It was an unattended halt, and only a few trains stopped there, on market days.

The Midland fell heir to a pair of well organised narrow gauge lines radiating from Ballymena and, other than continue to run them with their characteristic efficiency, there was not a great deal that had to be done to them. During the first five years of Midland ownership the reports list no capital expenditure on either of the sections, though some consideration was given during 1903 to the purchase of two new engines. In June 1905, the committee declined to make any contribution towards the purchase of bathing boxes at Cushendall, thereby making it evident that they were not to be coerced over fringe benefits.

In 1908, purse strings were loosened and then, in that year and the following one, two compound tank engines were built at Belfast at a cost of £3,400. They were needed to cope with an increase in ore traffic on the Parkmore line, and their construction was followed in 1911 by the expenditure of £2,849 on 50 new wagons. In 1910, £278 went into the building of new workmen's cottages at Ballyboley, and in the succeeding year a new house was built for the Knockanally stationmaster. Three years later the country was at war, and expenditure was thereupon restricted.

'And it grew wondrous cold'

It is unusual to get severe snowfalls in the Antrim hills, and it was never the practice to fit snowploughs to the narrow gauge engines. For many years however there was a narrow gauge snowplough in the Ballymena goods yard, merely a wagon loaded with stone and fitted at one end with angled steel plates. The only severe fall of snow that seems to have been recorded came on the afternoon of 16 January 1905, and the 5.10pm Ballymena–Parkmore and the 5.45pm Ballymena–Larne trains became embedded in drifts and were not released until the following morning.

Government control

Government control of the railways came into effect in Britain on the outbreak of war in August 1914 but similar measures were delayed in Ireland until 1 January 1917. On that date, the MR(NCC) in common with all other Irish railways, came under statutory control administered by the Irish Railways Executive Committee. Control was finally relinquished in August 1921. During this period, the economics of all the railways became peculiarly out of balance for, while wages and the cost of materials both rose steeply, fare increases were delayed by government order until 1 June 1918, when an increase of 50% was allowed.

The government made no direct payment for the conveyance of military personnel and supplies, but the companies were guaranteed the same net earnings as in 1913. In theory, this should have maintained the pre-war status but inflation had altered the picture. By 1921, the 1913 figures were valueless as a basis for compensation; the promised recompense proved to be too difficult to administer and the deficits were eventually wiped off the slate by the Irish Railways (Settlement of Claims) Act of 1921, by which the round sum of £3 million was divided between the various companies and paid in instalments.

Claims and the Troubles

Iron-ore production revived again under war needs and in November 1915 the Antrim Iron Ore Company asked to have the disused Mountcashel branch put into repair. This was done during the summer of 1916. The work involved the extension of the old line to some new mines further along the outcrop, and a large tonnage of fill and ballast was required. This was brought by the railway company in trains of 'blue flats' from the waste tips at Essathohan, beyond Parkmore. Two sets of flats were used, and five or six ballast trains were run every day during the construction work, with corresponding return workings of empties. The mining company reimbursed the railway by paying £6 per ton for the second-hand rails and fishplates that were needed.

From time to time there were minor claims for hay set alight by engine sparks, but something bigger caught alight in July 1918, when a passing train was held responsible for the loss by fire of a small house between Ballygarvey and Ballycloughan containing farm implements belonging to a Mr Robert Dale, at Kenbilly. He claimed £93 5s but, after taking a critical look at the ashes, the company settled for £20.

During the 1914–18 War, internal politics in Ireland had been subjected to increasing strain. The beginning of the end of British rule over Ireland as a whole was marked by the rising in Dublin at Easter 1916. Once the war in Europe ended, events progressed rapidly towards the separation of Ireland into two self-governing portions.

During 1919 and 1920 two governments – Dail Eireann and the British – attempted simultaneously to exercise absolute jurisdiction in Ireland, and a state of active warfare developed. Self-government was established in the six counties of Northern Ireland in June 1921, and at the end of the year a treaty was agreed between London and Dublin establishing the Irish Free State.

County Antrim thus became a part of Northern Ireland from the middle of 1921, but for many months before that date civil disorders placed the county in an uneasy state. Railways became a favourite target for sabotage, though the rail system of County Antrim was much less affected than it was elsewhere, and nothing occurred comparable to the weekly recital of damage suffered by the narrow gauge lines of the north-west of Ireland.

During the night of 19 January 1920, Ballymena station was damaged by fire, and on 26 October a fire in the narrow gauge locomotive shed at Larne was thought to have been of malicious origin, though fortunately the sprinkler system saved the building from destruction.

Then, on 25 March 1921, the crew of the first train

Larne engine shed and shops about 1936. The locomotive visible is 2-4-4T No 110 after rebuilding from a standard 2-4-2T.

L&GRP

74

out of Ballymena ran into Martinstown station – it had been Knockanally until the previous April – to find a detachment of police drawn up on the platform and awaiting transport up the glen. The station buildings at Cross Roads, Cargan, Parkmore and Retreat had all gone up in flames during the small hours. The Retreat goods station was totally destroyed, as were seven wagons standing in it. Martinstown escaped, not through any kind feelings towards it, but because there was a police barracks beside it. According to the local paper, the Sinn Fein Hall at Cargan was burned on the following night in reprisal. Nobody was arrested for the night's work, but it was significant that two permanent-way men decided before long that they had better find alternative employment outside the district.

It was during this time, which everyone called 'The Troubles', that the evening up train was held up on the Cushendall road. They had left Parkmore at 6.30pm, with Johnny McRory driving No 107 and Billy Hanley firing to him. Bob Reilly was the guard. They had come down through Cargan, Cross Roads and Martinstown, and were heading towards Rathkenny.

A mile below Martinstown there was a public level crossing with a gate house, where Sam Swan, the ganger, lived. They passed it, and as they came up to the next overbridge, Hanley saw a red light being waved a short way ahead. "Hold, Johnny", says he, "there must be cattle on the line." On went the brakes, but it was a heavy train and they ran a considerable distance before they came to a stop. They waited in the darkness of the quiet countryside, and after a time up came Bob Reilly to find out what it was that had stopped them. They debated for a while, and when they saw no light coming up from the rear, they decided to go on and ask questions later.

Then up out of the pitch blackness came the gunmen. They knew then that they hadn't imagined the red light. At gun point, the three were herded along the ballast to the van at the rear of the train, where they had to watch the mailbags being slit open and some of the contents taken. That completed, the railwaymen were told to stay where they were, and the gunmen vanished quietly into the night.

Knowing what the consequences might be if they moved, there they stayed until, as was inevitable, the engine began to blow off. It was time to move. McRory and Hanley went along to their engine, only to find that the gauge lamp

had been extinguished during their absence. They put on the injector, moved off and took the train into Rathkenny, where they reported what had happened. They then went on to Ballymena. They had enough of 'The Troubles' for one night, and had experienced the only hold-up on the Ballymena line.

Roddy Millar

One of the two drivers on the Cushendall line during Midland days was Roderick Millar. Physically, he was of small stature and the narrow gauge engines suited him so well that he never migrated to the better pay of the broad gauge. Roddy took immense pride in his engine, which was saddle tank No 101, and although he saw to it that the cleaner in Ballymena yard kept it "like a jeweller's shop", he was not above lending a skilled hand at maintenance.

The boiler of No 101 had a weekly wash out on Saturday nights, and Roddy used to appear at the shed at 3am on Sunday to held complete the preparation. He was not booked on and he drew no pay for the night's work, but he knew that '101' would not have been the same without his loving care, and that was enough reason. The first thing he did was to wash the red buffer beams and the inside of the cab with soap and hot water, while Bill Hanley, who was cleaning then, took bath brick and scouring patch to the lining on the tanks and the side sheets of the cab.

Once the engine was shining in the light of the duck lamps and the boiler was half filled, Roddy would open a bag of raw potatoes he had brought in, cut them up and feed them into the boiler through one of the top plug holes. Now and then, when Roddy's back was turned, Billy Hanley and Johnny Duff, who was cleaning Johnny Frew's engine No 102, would take a few of the spuds to boil and eat them for their breakfast. Not that Roddy would have grudged them their bite, but his engine was all-important, and he knew from experience that his treatment helped to prevent the accumulation of hard scale in No 101's boiler. By the time the cleaning was finished, there was nothing dirty but the bottom of the ashpan, and the engine was ready to go out on another week's work.

Roddy came out again on Monday, not so early, and took out the 7.35am Parkmore train. His daughter, who was teaching in Knockanally school then, went up on the same train and later in the day saw that Roddy got his 'piece' handed to him.

Knockanally had a further connection with the Millars, for near the buffer stops of the siding, between it and the running lines, there was an excellent spring of fresh water. A place to which every engine crew along during the stop to refill their water bottles, it was known to all as 'Roddy's Well' and must have agreed well with its owner for Roddy lived to the ripe old age of 92.

'Merrily did we drop . . .'

The descent from Glenravel to Ballymena could be exciting with a train of loaded ore wagons trying to take charge, and the Cushendall saddle tank engines had only hand brakes until the middle 1890s. Mr Malcolm told the crews more than once that it would have cost over £100 to equip them with steam brakes, so the old engines had to do without. There was the time when Paddy Hannan was taking down a train of ore wagons, with old Sam Crowe in the van. Paddy had been in the Carrick Militia and was better known as 'The Gunner'. On this occasion, one of the vacuum-braked engines was on. 'The Gunner' wasn't too well used to it and had received little or no instruction on the brake. They descended the bank with the wagons alternately buffering up and opening out, the brake van taking the worst of the punishment. It was a rough trip. After they got to Ballymena someone asked Sam what he thought of the new brakes. "Aye," said he, "Bejabers on the way down there, there wasn't a corner of the van that Paddy hadn't me in, and I'd even me arms round the red hot stove pipe, squealing."

There was also the train of eight ore-hoppers that set out from Cargan, and when they came to count the train at Ballymena yard, there were only seven. The guard checked his book, walked the length of the train and counted again, but sure enough, one of the wagons that he'd seen an hour earlier, was not in the train. Yet the train was properly coupled up, though nobody had put on the safety chains. There were no vacuum brakes on them. It was getting late, so they left the mystery to deepen overnight.

The permanent-way gang found the missing hopper wagon during the next morning, lying on its side in a field at the bottom of an embankment, in the dip near Craig's Scutch Mill. The tale was completed when they found wheel marks on the sleepers: some way back the hopper had derailed, bumped merrily along between the front

and the back of the train until both the buffers unlocked. Then with one wild buck, it went over, so quickly and so cleanly that the following hopper missed hitting it. It was on a down grade, front and back parts of the train closed up, the buffers coupled up, and the train went on its way with neither engine crew nor guard any the wiser. For years afterwards the spill was marked in the field by a heap of red ore among the green grass.

The steep bank into Cargan could be troublesome, as Johnny Frew found in 1917 when his passenger train got away on the 1 in 39 as they went past the siding to Evishacrow. He entered Cargan station sounding his whistle as a warning, and found the road was set for the goods shed. It was as well that, by the tine he was in sight of Cargan, Johnny was getting some response from the brakes, for by the time he got his train stopped, the engine was inside the train door and breathing smoke and fire into the rafters. There was a certain amount of damage done, but nobody was hurt, though Johnny, to cool him, received a few days suspension.

When empty wagons had to be taken up to Evishacrow, the mineral train always stopped at Cargan and picked up the stationmaster. His duty on these occasions was to open Pinkerton's 'Patent Box' at the junction with the train staff. Once the siding points were open, the train was propelled towards the bottom of the incline. A short way from the junction, they passed a trap or catch point. Now it happened one day that the permanent-way gang had been up near Parkmore with their bogie, and were on their way down when a mineral train went into the siding and out of sight of the main line. Cathcart was in charge of the gang, and when they came up he found the points set for the siding and the staff sticking in the box. So, to get their bogie past the junction, they reset they road for themselves, which opened the trap points up above. They had a yarn with somebody who was about, forgot to reset the points and went on down the hill towards Cargan. A while later, the mineral train crept down from 'The Drum' – which they called the winding engine of the incline – with the van leading. Sam Crowe was sitting placidly in the van when it went through the trap and fell over on its side. For good measure, four or five wagons followed the van. Old Sam was more surprised than hurt, but he lamented loudly as he picked his way out of the wreckage. He had two fresh eggs in his pocket for breakfast, and he had had no chance to get them boiled before the upset.

Flat out

When a train of the Cushendall tramcar coaches arrived at Parkmore with one of the large brake composites in the rear, it was the practice while remarshalling the train to put a scotch or sprag in between the wheel spoke and hornplate on one of the coaches to prevent it getting on the move by accident.

One morning in June 1920 the 10am from Ballymena came up to Parkmore with Dennis McAdorey driving No 102 and, as usual, they spragged a wheel on a coach. They set off with the 11.15, booked to call at Cargan, Knockanally and Rathkenny. By the time they were getting past the level crossing at Islandtown, it was dawning on the engine crew that they were needing more steam than usual, and instead of running down into Rathkenny, they were having to haul their train downhill. So Billy Hanley, who was firing to Dennis, volunteered to investigate while they were stopped at Rathkenny loading up the creamery traffic. It was a case of great minds thinking alike. Fireman and the guard Davie Thompson met on the same errand, and sure enough, there was the end of the sprag sticking out. That left a fine flat on one set of wheels, after skidding the best part of eight miles.

On another occasion, Johnny Frew, with Aaron Crow firing, was on one of the Cushendall tanks, working some wagons of feeding stuff up to Cargan. About half a mile from Cross Roads, the engine hit and killed a turkey that had strayed on to the line. A few feathers floated away on the breeze as it fell clear and, summing up the situation, the crew went on through Cross Roads in fine style and on up to Cargan. They left the wagons there, ran smartly around, caught the brake van and set off back down the hill. After recovering the turkey and tidying up the scene of the crime, they went on to Martinstown and made a quick line over the way to the inn. There an obliging customer who understood their problem agreed to take charge of it and the turkey for the price of a dozen 3d bottles of stout.

On the Larne road

If Roddy Millar had a counterpart on the old B&LR section, he was James Patrick O'Toole who, in his later days as a Justice of the Peace, was 'JP JP' to his friends. Born in Belfast in 1860, young O'Toole joined the BNCR as a telegraph messenger in 1873. Three years later he was transferred to the locomotive department, and by the time he retired he had completed 54 years with the railway. Much of that long service was spent on the B&LR section and for over 30 years he drove the boat train, where his enthusiasm for a shining and spotless engine had free rein. He had No 105, the younger of the two 2-4-0Ts, for years and everyone between Larne and Ballymena knew that '105' was virtually JP's private property. His cleaner knew what to expect if he had not done his job well: at the end of the day, when the cleaner handed over the docket headed "I hereby certify . . ." for signature, JP would pointedly lay it against the tank as he pencilled it. That done, he turned the form over and looked hard at the back of it. On at least one occasion, the form came off the tank side with its back soiled. When the horrified cleaner got the message, JP slowly rolled the form up and tossed it into the firebox. His footplate was a place of shining brass, as neat as his own kitchen and, as on the kitchen floor, JP had a piece of carpet to stand on. It was not there to keep his feet clean, it was a reminder of good housekeeping.

JP JP's dry humour once dealt with an English visitor at Ballymena who had strolled up to see what was going to haul the train to Larne and then made some derogatory remarks about little '105'. "Oh you know, this isn't the engine, it's the heating apparatus".

The Inver bank

The steep descent of the Inver bank was worse than anything the Cushendall road could offer, for the fall continued all the way to Larne. It was the usual practice with a heavy train to draw up at Millbrook and pin down wagon brakes before coming on to the steepest part of the bank. On several occasions, in spite of precautions, the train crew found their speed increasing and were forced to warn those down at Larne station by a series of prolonged blasts on the whistle.

One memorable whirlwind descent of the bank was in 1918, when a cattle special left Ballymena between twelve and one o'clock every Saturday. There were 30 wagons full of heavy beef cattle behind 'The Bruiser'. Billy McNinch and Billy Hanley had her this day, passed driver and passed fireman, and they were booked to take the cattle train to Larne and return with a football special. They had an uneventful run to Ballyboley and ran merrily along to the head of the bank. Coming up to Millbrook, McNinch

An interesting rear view of a single coach passenger train climbing up the Inver bank. This is taken from the Bridge Street overbridge but looking in the opposite direction to the photo on page 40, taken from the same bridge. The tall chimney is the Bleach Works and St Cedma's Church across the river is hidden in the trees ahead of the train.   Nelson Poots collection

applied the brake and Hanley put on the sander, intending to stop to pin down the wagon brakes. But the train refused to stop, and what was worse, began to pick up speed as the bank steepened. McNinch put 'The Bruiser' into middle gear and away they went round the curves by The Beetles "with the cattle hanging on". It must have been a rough farewell to Ireland for them. Back in the van, the guard knew they were in trouble and had screwed his handbrake on, but to no effect. Nothing they could do seemed to retard the train and Billy McNinch gave the distress signal, a series of lengthy whistle blasts that echoed in the narrowing glen and reached those down at Larne town station. They swung round the last curve, and breathed a sigh of relief when they glimpsed Billy Glass hanging out of the high signal cabin, waving the green flag, though if it had been any other colour there wasn't much they could

have done about it. There was a train at the platform, but the loop was clear, and they wound in and out of it in a way the management never intended. They managed to stop the train on the level stretch towards the Harbour, got down and found the jamb nuts on the pull rods of the brake slacked back out of position. There was no leverage, and they knew then they had come down the length of the Inver bank *without brakes*.

Into the 'twenties

On the Ballymena lines, as on other parts of the Irish railway system, the years that followed the First World War, were grim ones that gave no promise. Five years of diminished maintenance had to be made up, but the traffic was not providing the profits to cover such expenditure. The heavy, double-headed tourist trains that had panted through Cargan towards Parkmore, packed with Lancashire and Yorkshire folk, were rare sights now. The iron-ore trains were finished, and the wartime demand for bauxite had dwindled.

On top of this change of fortune came changes in administration. For three-quarters of a century, Parliament in London had encouraged railway to compete against railway, legalising the duplication of routes in the belief that, with competition, the public would benefit from lowered fares. The war had merely postponed the inevitable reaction to the process, though it had been mooted many years before. In Britain, the numerous separate companies were statutorily grouped into four large concerns, one of which, the London, Midland and Scottish Railway included the former Midland Railway. So the ownership of the Ballymena lines underwent its third change, and from 1 January 1923 they were administered by the LMS(NCC). As before, direction was in the hands of a committee of seven members.

By the mid-twenties, the railways all over Britain no longer possessed a virtual monopoly of long distance transport. The roads which, until the advent of the railways, had been with canals the transport arteries of the country, began to reassert their ascendancy, and to carry an increasing proportion of people, merchandise and minerals. Road motor buses and privately owned cars appeared in increasing numbers, and were joined by motor lorries. The government of the day followed the pattern of earlier years and allowed free competition to develop between rival road transport concerns and between them and the railways. For Ireland, that story has yet to be told in detail, though its broad outlines are well known.*

The public accepted the inevitable lowering of fares and rates, compared them to those of the railways and when they found the latter to be higher, promptly abandoned the railway for the road. Moreover, in many areas motor bus services offered a more convenient and flexible service than the railways could ever do, the frequent stops suiting the roadside dweller better than the necessarily wide separation of railway stations.

On the Irish narrow gauge, only the County Donegal Railways faced up to road competition and, under Henry Forbes' guidance, this comparatively small organisation valiantly offered the public the frequent halts that saved many a long wet walk to a conventionally organised railway station. The Donegal's posters even announced a 'Stop Anywhere' policy. Forbes accomplished this difficult task

with remarkable success because his Stranorlar-based empire was flexible and had the backing of the GNRI shops at Dundalk. Forbes himself assumed almost dictatorial powers and adopted petrol and diesel rail buses contemporaneously with their appearance on the roads. The Donegal's quite remarkable example was followed to a comparable extent on the Irish narrow gauge only on the West Clare section of CIE, and that 30 years too late to save the line from extinction.

On the LMS(NCC), a petrol railcar was run on the Coleraine–Portrush branch in 1924, but the experiment was not extended to other subsidiary lines of the system. On the narrow gauge lines, things continued as they had done for half a century, and no attempt was made to combat the obvious competition of the roads. The managerial ostrich hid its head in the ballast, while the public slowly but surely deserted the railways and betook themselves to the local bus, or bought a car. To move their merchandise, their coal, cattle and sheep they turned towards road haulage, and many a family in Glenwhirry and Glenravel found it far more convenient than anything the railway had ever offered. In these changeful years, the railway administration did try to reclaim some of the traffic which had deserted them by starting road services. But they were not run as feeders to the dying narrow gauge lines, which had to face competition of parallel routes and it was not until 1930 that the LMS(NCC) began a systematic policy of buying out rival bus companies.

Meanwhile, against a background of change in the habits of the travelling public and in the methods of moving merchandise, the traffic on the narrow gauge railways of Antrim dwindled. To quote only one instance: impatient passengers, infuriated by delays associated with the mixed train working, left their seats at Rathkenny and joined the passing bus while the railway staff were busy loading butter. Stops of half an hour were common there, but for local people with shopping to do in Ballymena, a seat in a chilly and stationary railway carriage was gladly forsaken for a seat in a moving bus. In many instances the train never saw them again.

The closures begin

A warning of the tenuous state of the economy of the narrow gauge lines in Antrim had come in March 1924 when the independently-owned Ballycastle Railway ceased

* *However, see Michael Collins'* Road Versus Rail in Ireland 1900-2000 *(Colourpoint 2000)*

After the take over of the Ballycastle Railway, several NCC engines were transferred there. No 106 prepares to leave Ballycastle with the 12.50pm mixed on 11 July 1931. AW Croughton

operations and the company went into liquidation. It sold out to the only possible purchaser, and the LMS(NCC) assumed ownership of the 16 mile line for the sum of £12,500, which was around one-eighth of the Ballycastle's capital expenditure. The ailing Ballycastle line was reorganised and became a convenient repository for surplus carriage and wagon stock from the Ballymena lines.

On the Ballymena narrow gauge lines, the first retrenchment came in 1930 when, as from 1 October, passenger services were withdrawn on the Ballymena–Parkmore and on the Ballyclare–Doagh sections. This effectively ended the use of Parkmore as a rail/road exchange point for tourists, though Glenariff continued to play its part in excursion itineraries. After the burning of Parkmore station in 1921, the railway company had built a remarkably ugly, if utilitarian erection of concrete and glass to shelter the tourists and accommodate the staff (see rear cover). After the passenger service ended, it continued for a time to serve the community as a youth hostel.

Passenger trains continued to run between Ballymena and Larne, with connecting services to Ballyclare from Ballyboley Junction. Beyond Ballyclare, the paper mill continued to provide a comparatively heavy goods traffic in both directions. This abbreviated service continued for just over two years.

The 1933 strike

In the early part of 1933, all the railways in Northern Ireland, with the exception of the Belfast and County Down, were paralysed by a lengthy strike which started on 31 January and ended on 10 April. The trouble arose over a 10% cut in salaries and wages which had been awarded by a majority finding of the Irish Railway Tribunal. During the strike, officials and a few train crews attempted to maintain a skeleton service, and this was supplemented by buses and lorries.

The strike sounded the death knell of the Ballymena narrow gauge lines, for on 28 February the LMS(NCC) gave notice that passenger train services over those sections would terminate as soon as the strike ended. In addition, it was proposed to discontinue the goods service between

The Gardner-Edwards railcar under test at Ballyboley Junction in 1933. It is on its way to Larne and is crossing 2-6-0ST No 109 on a Ballymena-bound coal train.

JH Houston collection

Below: *The railcar on the six-wheel transporter truck at York Road, probably on its way to Ballymena for the test run seen above.*

JH Houston collection

Ballyclare and Doagh. The latter section, the last to be constructed, was therefore the first to be completely closed.

The strike had its lighter side. Before it, Sam McCullough had been firing over the B&LR road, and being one of the few Larne men who elected to remain at work, he took on the duties of driver. Coal traffic from Larne to Ballymena and Ballyclare took precedence, and Sam did what he could to ensure that supplies were kept moving. The Larne boys who were 'out' thought they would call a halt to Sam's activities so they black-soaped the rails at The Beetles, that most difficult part of the Inver bank. Sam had No 109, 'The Bruiser', that day and by dint of giving her a good flakin' out of Larne, he managed to get enough way on his train to carry him over the slippery section. From the slopes above, his performance was watched with professional interest by the strikers. Next day they made a better job of the soaping and brought Sam to grief.

Another day the strikers lifted out part of the Kilwaughter points and threw them in a nearby stream. Sam McCullough had 'Taffy', a little Welshman, firing to him that day. They made their way up to the gap and stopped. Down from the engine climbed 'Taffy', stripped off his trousers, waded into the stream and hauled the points out. Between them they put the bits back into place, got their train on the move,

and continued on their way. So the strike eventually came to an end, and with it all the passenger services over the B&LR section.

First and last

Shortly after the end of the strike, the Larne–Ballymena section had an unusual visitor in the shape of a diesel-engined railcar constructed by the Belfast firm of Gardner-Edwards. This concern had collaborated in railcar design with the County Donegal Railway Joint Committee and had built a railcar for a South American railway. The vehicle was tested over the B&LR section before it was shipped, the first and last of its kind to run on the County Antrim narrow gauge.

'The Bruiser', 2-6-0ST No 109, on a coal train about to enter Ballyclare around 1920. The men are (on the engine) David Warwick (driver) and Sam Girvan (fireman); (L-R in front) WJ Orr (stationmaster), Tom Marshall (porter), Robert Ireland (guard) and John Stewart (driver). The land in the left background is now part of the Leisure Centre.

David Orr collection

The closures continue

For four and a quarter years more, goods working along occupied the remaining 45½ miles of track. It was apparent by now that the upper reaches of the Cushendall section were little used and offered no prospect of a renewal of traffic, so from 10 April 1937 services ended over the Rathkenny–Retreat section and, but for the Rathkenny creamery traffic, the entire Cushendall road would have closed. As it was, the railways of Ireland ceased to have a 'summit' of over 1,000 feet above sea level.

Two years more, and the country was again at war. For nearly a year the *status quo* of the narrow gauge was maintained until, on 2 June 1940, two-thirds of the remaining 35½ miles was closed. Ballymena station lost both its narrow gauge lines, as the amputated stump of the Cushendall line was turned over to road lorries. The

Ballymena–Ballyboley portion of the old B&LR road was also closed, the lines being lifted soon afterwards and shipped to Europe for use with the British Expeditionary Force.

With this fourth stage of closure, the remaining mileage had shrunk to just over 12, and was maintained by the traffic between Larne Harbour and the paper mill at Ballyclare. Ballyboley ceased to be a junction, and became merely a grass-grown platform and a water-tank, devoid alike of traffic and station premises.

The impact of the Second World War on the Larne–Ballyclare line was perhaps less than on other railways in Northern Ireland, where they were temporarily rejuvenated by the diversion on to them of much road traffic. The Larne narrow gauge line continued to stare closure serenely in the face, owing its existence to one local industry, and knowing that there was no other future for it.

As well as transfers of NCC locomotives to the Ballycastle section, the two large BR 4-4-2Ts saw service on the Ballymena to Larne section after being renumbered 113 and 114. This view of No 113 at Larne Harbour in 1936, emphasises the impressive bulk of these machines. L&GRP

The final changes in ownership came after the war. On 1 October 1948, the LMS became a part of British Railways and for six months the descendents of the MR(NCC) were ruled by the Railway Executive (NCC). That came to an end when British Railways shed their unprofitable Irish possessions and sold the NCC to the Northern Ireland government for the sum of £2,668,000. From the first day of April 1949 – surely an inauspicious date – an Ulster Transport Authority took over, the sixth organisation to control the narrow gauge line out of Larne in a period of just over 70 years.

Quietly into oblivion

Then, in 1950, the paper mill ceased operations at Ballyclare, the combined result of cross-channel competition and high local transport charges. The slender thread on which the Larne narrow gauge had depended, frayed and snapped. The UTA, charged with making their lines pay, were not slow to act and gave notice in the early part of May 1950 of their intention to discontinue services on certain sections of the NCC lines. The Larne–Ballyclare line was among them. No formal objections were made to the proposal and, from Monday 3 July 1950, the line was closed to traffic. The Ballycastle section was closed on the same day, leaving County Antrim without narrow gauge railways. The Larne line had indeed already slipped quietly into oblivion. There was nothing for it to do and, on 20 May, No 42 had hauled the last train and withdrawn herself into the darkness of the Larne shed. There was no public protest, there were no train loads of fervent enthusiasts, no volleys of exploding detonators, no souvenir hunters. There was not even a hint of a preservation society. It was all a little sad, but it was inevitable, and the writing had been of the wall for 17 years.

Chapter 8

The locomotives

The Glenariff engines

Only two engines were owned by the Glenariff Iron Ore and Harbour Company. They were built by Messrs Robert Stephenson and Co and were the first three foot gauge engines in Ireland. Their design was based on 3ft 6in gauge engines supplied to Japan in 1872. Both were 2-4-0 side tanks, with inside frames, Bissel trucks and 15in outside cylinders. Their delivery date is not known, but was probably in the summer of 1873. It seems likely that they were shipped to their owners in Carrivemurphy townland or else to the existing harbour at Red Bay.

The use, performance and livery of these engines in Glenariff have not been recorded, but it is known that their active life there only covered three years. Thereafter, they lay in the stone-built shed near the shore until, in October 1880,

one was steamed again and used to haul a train of promoters of the Glenariff Railway and Pier Company. That project languished and the engines continued to lie at the foot of the glen until the spring 1885. Their purchase by Messrs McCrea and McFarland, and their later removal by sea from Red Bay pier to Derry has already been related in Chapter 2.

They were put to work on the Buncrana section of the Londonderry and Lough Swilly Railway, becoming Nos 5 and 6 in that company's stock. When one considers the praise which Basil McCrea lavished on them at the time of their purchase, their short life of 14 years on the Swilly is surprising and suggests that they were, in fact, in poor order when auctioned, a legacy perhaps of neglect when they lay idle from 1876 to 1885.

Their leading dimensions were:

Cylinders	15" x 20"	Tubes	136 x 1¹³⁄₁₆"
Leading wheels	2' 6"	Tank capacity	600 gallons
Driving wheels	3' 9"	Grate area	10½ sq ft
Wheelbase	5' 6" + 6' 6"	Heating surface	54 + 642½ sq ft
Boiler	3' 9" x 10'0"	Total weight	26½ tons

The Cushendall engines

To work mineral and goods trains between Ballymena and Retreat, the Ballymena, Cushendall and Red Bay Railway Company ordered three identical engines from Messrs Black, Hawthorn and Co of Gateshead-on-Tyne in

September 1873. The agreed delivery dates were January, March and May 1874, but deliveries were not in fact made until April 1874 (No 1) and April 1875 (Nos 2 and 3). All three were the maker's standard 0-4-2 saddle tank type (Maker's numbers 301-3).

Their leading dimensions were:

Cylinders	12" x 19"	Bunker capacity	8 cwt
Driving wheels	3' 1"	Firebox length	4' 0"
Trailing wheels	2' 7"	Firebox inner	3' 6" x 1' 10½"
Wheelbase	6' 4" + 5' 6"	Heating surface	47 + 410 sq ft
Boiler	3' 0¼" x 9'0"	Weight	22½ tons
Boiler tubes	104 x 1⅝"	Working pressure	140 psi
Tank capacity	500 gallons	Cost, each	£1470

Cushendall 0-4-2ST No 1 running as BNCR No 60 around 1895, before rebuilding. Note the dome and spring balance safety valves above the firebox.

Author's collection

The same locomotive as BNCR No 101 after reboilering in 1897. It now has the dome in a more conventional position and is fitted with an exhaust steam ejector.

Real photographs Ltd

No builder's or owning company's description of the livery of these engines is known to survive but their colour has been stated to be dark green. As built, the dome was on the firebox, but later reboilering sited the dome on the middle of the barrel.

On being taken over by the Belfast and Northern Counties Railway in 1884 they were renumbered, Nos 1, 2 and 3 becoming Nos 60, 61 and 62. At this time broad gauge engine numbers ran up to No 49 and the next nine numbers were left vacant to allow for increases in the broad gauge stock. Events showed that the blank spaces were insufficient to accommodate the growing broad gauge stock and in January 1897 the ex-Cushendall narrow gauge engines were again renumbered, becoming Nos 101–103. In early Midland days, they were placed in Class '0'.

No 1/60/101 was reboiled in 1897, probably with fewer tubes. It entered reserve stock as No 101A in February 1920 and was withdrawn in 1923.

No 2/61/102 was rebuilt in July 1893, when the saddle tanks were extended to be flush with the front of the smoke box. After 15 years thus, the tanks were shortened to their original dimensions. The engine became No 102A in February 1920 and was withdrawn in 1923.

No 3/62/103 was given an extended saddle tank in March 1893, and retained this feature until it was withdrawn in February 1911 after 36 years service.

She was then sold to one of the mining companies in Glenravel and overhauled some years later at Ballymena running shed, but the date of her scrapping is not known.

In February 1920, Mr WH McAdoo, traffic manager of the Cavan and Leitrim Railway, asked the Irish Railways Executive Committee for the loan of three engines on the construction and working of the Arigna valley extension. As a result, Nos 101A and 102A were commandeered by Government order and taken to work on the C&L. Here they spent 19 months, principally working coal trains from Arigna but finding their way to every part of the C&L lines at one time or another. According to Dr P Flanagan in his book *The Cavan and Leitrim Railway*, 'the wee northerners' were very highly thought of on the C&L. A weak brake was their only fault and the men were sorry to lose them when they returned to the NCC at the end of control. They were taken north in November 1921 and were never used again, lying idle for over two years until they were scrapped.

An interested aspect of the activities of the Cushendall's locomotive superintendent has been noted by Mr RN Clements. In *The Engineer* of 17 March 1882 there appeared the following advertisement: "Small 3ft gauge tank locomotive for sale, nearly new, by Fox Walker & Co of Bristol. Can be seen by applying to Mr James Donaghey, Loco. Supt. BCRBR, Ballymena, Ireland."

The use of a Fox Walker engine is well established. This engine was built in 1878 and was a 0-40 saddle tank with 9 x 14in cylinders and 2ft 6in wheels. It was brought by the Harbour Commissioners in 1882 and must have come from the Ballymena sale. Since the minute books of the BC&RBR do not refer to any such sale, it seems likely that the engine was purchased new by one of the mining companies in the area, perhaps not paid for owing to the depression in the iron-ore trade, and the put up for sale by the builders. The Cushendall company appear to have been merely selling agents, and there is no indication that they ever made use of the engine themselves.

The Ballymena and Larne engines

Brief and tantalising reference is made in this company's minute book to early contacts with RF Fairlie and with the Baldwin Locomotive Company. Thus, in the record of the board meeting of 17 March 1876 a letter is mentioned, written on 8 March by the secretary, CH Brett, to Fairlie and a reply of 10 March. Copies of both letters were ordered to be sent for the scrutiny of Mr Robert McCalmont of Eaton Square, London, a large shareholder and a member of the board of directors. It is probable that the exchange of correspondence was nothing more than an enquiry as to what Fairlie had to offer and nothing further can be traced regarding the matter. Had something materialised, double-boiler Fairlies might have run on the line and wakened the echoes on the Inver bank.

On 28 August 1876 the board instructed their engineer,

William Lewis, to write to the Baldwin Locomotive Company of Philadelphia, USA "in conformity with Mr McCalmont's letter". The only other references to the Baldwin enquiry were on 20 October, when Lewis was told to send the correspondence to McCalmont "for his opinion" and finally, on 18 December, when the plans and papers of the Baldwin engines were passed on to Lewis. What was offered is not disclosed by the brief minutes which Brett wrote.

While approaches were made to the Baldwin company, the first definite move was taken toward acquisition of engine power. During October 1876 there was contact with Messrs Beyer, Peacock and Co of Gorton, and at the board meeting that month James Chaine moved and OB Graham seconded, "That an engine, a duplicate of *The Sutherland*, Isle of Man engine, be ordered at once from Beyer, Peacock & Company, provided they can deliver within three months". The Isle of Man Company were finding their Beyer-built 2-4-0 engines admirable suited to their line, their design having been based on a 3ft 6in 2-4-0T made in 1866 for Norway.

But although the Ballymena and Larne directors referred specifically to *Sutherland*, by the time their order came to be placed with Beyer, Peacock, the 10MR had a stud of no less than six 2-4-0 tanks, three of which had been built in 1873, including No 1 *Sutherland*, two had come in 1874 and their latest, No 6 named *Peveril*, had been delivered in 1875. Beyer, Peacock's shop order for the B&LR engine is dated 31 October 1876 and states that it is for a locomotive "to be the same as one Tank Engine No 3310 of February 18th 1875', which was the 10MR *Peveril*. The shop order further states that the engine was to be delivered by the end of January 1877.

Thus the B&LR was supplied with a copy of *Peveril*, which differed from *Sutherland* in having larger side tanks. 2ft 6in high and holding 385 gallons, in place of the earlier two foot ones which held only 320 gallons. The spectacle glasses on *Sutherland* were circular, those on *Peveril* and the B&LR engine were rectangular. The Irish engine had its buffers placed 1ft 10½in above the rail, while the Manx engines had theirs set 4½in higher. On all the 10MR engines the height of the roof of what Beyer's drawings delightfully term the 'house' was 6ft 6in above the footplate; on the B&LR, the more restricted loading gauge required the cab roof to be lowered by three inches.

Having thus embarked on the purchase of a Beyer, Peacock engine, the B&LR went on eventually to own six Gorton engines of three different designs, built for them at various dates between 1877 and 1883:

Type	B&LR No	Built	Maker's Stock No	Maker's Progressive No
2-4-0T	1	1877	3525	1687
	4	1878	3714	1828
0-6-0T	2	1877	3560	1700
	3	1877	3560	1701
	6	1883	6291	2304
2-6-0ST	5	1880	3897	1947

The first of the 2-4-0T engine was tried in steam at Gorton works on 19 January 1877, but before it was dispatched, another shop order was issued on 12 March covering alterations to suit the fitting of Smith's vacuum brake. The Isle of Man engines had merely hand and steam brakes, with wooden blocks, on the driving wheels. As a result of this further modification, B&LR No 1 did not leave the works until 26 March 1877. It had 11 x 18in outside cylinders, inclined at 1 in 9, and the side valves had Allan straight link motion. Smokebox and valve chests were integral, and the smokebox door was tilted backwards. The boiler was 2ft 10¾in actual outside diameter (not over the cladding), and the length between tubeplates was 7ft 8¼in. The bell-mouth dome housed the Salter safety valves.

The driving cab, the 'house' of the maker's drawing, was made from a wrap-around plate which formed the front, roof and back. The side sheets were short when the engine was delivered, but the crew were later given additional protection by extending the side sheets backwards. The bunker was enclosed by the cab roof and held a ton of coal. The engine cost £1,432 15s 6d, which was paid to Beyers on 20 April 1877.

Ballymena and Larne Railway 2-4-0T No 4 of 1878. This locomotive differed slightly from No 1 (Page 36), but was based on the successful Isle of Man design. Note the higher side tanks and the different position of the injector. The cab was also longer. These engines had the old-fashioned spring balance safety valves fitted on the dome.
Beyer Peacock

The B&LR minutes state on 24 April 1878 that a Mr Jack had arranged with Beyer, Peacock for the supply of "a duplicate of No 1 engine". This arrangement must have been quite informal and much in advance of any definite instructions, for Beyer's shop order of No 3714 was not issued until 9 August 1878. It was a development of B&LR No 1 and, since the Isle of Man Railway had not extended their engine stock beyond their No 6, the improvements incorporated in the new Larne engine were the result of 16 months operating experience on the B&LR road.

Apart from the statement that the locomotive was to be numbered '4' in B&LR stock and was to have Smith's vacuum brake, the shop order contains little information and gives no details of either the livery or the proposed delivery date. However, the progressive number book reveals that the engine was tried in steam on 28 September 1878 and delivered on 11 October 1878. It differed from B&LR No 1 in having deeper side tanks holding 450 gallons of water, and a larger fuel bunker of 32 cubic feet capacity. In place of No 1's awkward fitment for sanding inside the front corners of the cab, the sand boxes on No 4 were sited in front of the side tanks. The weight of the engine empty was 18½cwt more, and loaded, 31³⁄₅ cwt more than No 1.

Both Nos 1 and 4 had the graceful, long, tapering chimney with copper cap which survived on some of the Isle of Man engines long after the Irish examples had gone. While the 10MR engines carried their numbers in brass on

each side of the chimney and in the middle off the back sheet of the cab, the B&LR chose to place their numbers in the middle of the side tanks, a large serified numeral, set in an oval plate and surmounted with "B&LR Ry Co". On No 1, the maker's plate was carried on the first ring of the boiler barrel, on No 4 it was placed on the side of the bunker.

In 1889, Nos 1 and 4 passed into BNCR stock and were then renumbered '63' and '64'. They got their second renumbering to '104' and '105' in January 1897, and about 1904 were classified 'P'. They retained these numbers into MR(NCC) times, and in the case of No 105 into the LMS(NCC) era.

The first engine, No 1/63/104, was rebuilt in 1893 with 12½ x 18in cylinders, and reboiled at the same time. The new boiler had 88 tubes. This engine was withdrawn in February 1920.

No 4/64/105 was given 12½in cylinders in 1889. It spent a short time on the Ballycastle section of the LMS(NCC) during 1926. During 1928, it was withdrawn and sold to the Castlederg and Victoria Bridge Tramway Company, a small concern operating a roadside line in County Derry. On that line it was fitted with a skirt over the motion and wheels on the right side, which was next to the public road, and it worked for around five years until it was scrapped in 1933. To the end, it retained its bell-mouth dome.

The story of the 0-6-0 tank engines began in October 1876, more or less contemporaneously with the decision to order the first of the 2-4-0 engines. Nothing however, is mentioned of this in the B&LR minute book. On 19 October 1876 Beyer, Peacock prepared for B&LR a weight diagram for a 0-6-0 locomotive with side tanks and 13½ x 18in outside cylinders. It

A later view of 2-4-0T No 4, as NCC No 105, inside Larne shed on 22 May 1924. The sandbox has been moved from the side of the boiler to the bunker. After a trial on the Ballycastle section in 1926, this engine was sold to the Castlederg and Victoria Bridge Tramway in 1928.

Real Photographs Ltd

Top: *Ballymena and Larne Railway 0-6-0T No 3 as built by Beyer Peacock in 1877. The original cab was open at the rear and the engine had spring-balance safety valves on the dome. Note the prominent Beyer builder's plate.*

Beyer Peacock

Ballymena and Larne Railway 0-6-0T No 3 as LMS(NCC) No 107 at Larne about 1930. Note the cast 'BNCR' lettering above the number. Ross pop safety valves are now carried on the dome.

CP Friel collection

was not until 6 November 1876 that a full drawing was prepared for the proposed locomotive and it was from this drawing, with minor changes, that two engines were built for the B&LR. Since their line was not yet finished, the company were in no particular haste to order, so it was not yet finished, the company were in no particular haste to order, so it was not until 2 February 1877 that, according to the minute books, James Chaine was empowered to buy "two engines with breaks" from Beyer, Peacock. Even then, the order was not placed for another three months. Beyer, Peacock issued their shop order on 18 May 1877, and a

note giving details of the proposed delivery date "no later than 20th August next and as much earlier as possible" was added to the shop order on 30 May. The engines were to be fitted with Smith's vacuum break.

These two 0-6-0 tank engines, Nos 2 and 3 of the B&LR, were tried in steam at Gorton works on 27 and 28 July respectively, and both left the works on 17 August 1877. At Gorton, an official photograph was taken of No 3, but not of No 2. Gravity sanders were fitted, the front sand box being placed on the running plate in front of the leading driving wheel, while the rear sand box was in the

Ballymena and Larne Railway 0-6-0T No 2 as MR(NCC) No 106 on transporter truck No 3045 at York Road about 1920.

CP Friel collection

Beyer, Peacock's proposed 0-6-0T for B & LR, July 1878

Cylinders 15in x 20in	Width 7ft 9in over tanks
D.W. 3ft 3in	Boiler 3ft 9¼ x 8ft 11in
Wheelbase 5ft 0in + 5ft 6in	Tanks 650 gallons
Length 21ft 6in	

which is dated 26 July. Then, on 21 October 1878, another drawing was made, this time for a 14½ x 20in outside cylinder, again on 3ft 3in wheels. A full proposal drawing for the 14½in engine was prepared on 23 October 1878, but nothing came of the scheme.

The first shop order covering the third of the 0-6-0 tank engines was issued by Beyer, Peacock on 6 September 1882 and was followed by a more detailed order dated 11 October 1882. The orders state that the engine was "to be delivered by December next" and was to be fitted with the vacuum brake. "The engine to be numbered 6 and to be the same as two engines 3560 May 18th 1877" with minor exceptions, including the fitting of Rowan's patent pistons, alterations to the coal bunker, coupling rods, platforms, framing, brake shift carriers and levers. The firebox back was deepened, causing

driving cab. At first, the cab was open at the back.

Although five years were to elapse before another 0-6-0 tank engine was built for the Ballymena and Larne, Beyers were not idle on their behalf and interest was being taken in a more powerful version of the two already supplied. On 25 July 1878 just under a year after the delivery of Nos 2 and 3, a weight diagram was prepared for a proposed 0-6-0 side tank with 15 x 20in outside cylinders and 3ft 3in driving wheels, and this was followed by a detailed drawing the alteration of the ashpan and firebars, the front buffer beam was bolted and not riveted. Alterations were made in the vacuum brake arrangements, the ejectors being of cast iron and of a different pattern to those previously used. The leading wheels had brake blocks fitted and this caused the frames, piston rods and slidebars to be lengthened. Minor changes were made in the sand boxes, toolboxes and brake screw casing. The cab was improved by the provision of a "back cab weather plate" which had "fixed windows and a sliding door in the middle above the handrail", while the top of the side sheet was curved in the way which was to characterise Beyer engines for many years afterwards. The depth of the cab, front to back, was increased by 8½in to a fraction under 5ft. The engine was tried in steam on 19 January 1883 and delivered on 16 February.

Under the BNCR, Nos 2, 3 and 6 became Nos 65, 66 and 67, the second renumbering in 1897 making them

Nos 106, 107 and 108. They were placed in Class 'Q'. On all the engines, the original spring balance safety valves were later replaced by Ross pop valves set in tandem on the dome casing.

These three engines survived until the 1930s. No 107 went first in December 1931. No 108 was withdrawn in December 1932, and No 106 remained the survivor of the class until June 1933. They retained their numbers from 1897. They were eventually used on both the Larne and the Parkmore sections and were also transferred to the Ballycastle section after it came under LMS ownership in 1924. No 107 was probably in use at Ballycastle in 1927–8, whilst the other two, once taken to Ballycastle in 1924, seem to have spent most of their remaining lives there. No 106 had the distinction of running over one million miles before it was withdrawn; it also had the highest annual and the highest average annual mileages for its class:

Mileage under BNCR and NCC	No 106	No 107	No 108
Total	1,041,899	922,725	857,955
Maximum annual	48,300 (1905)	41,470 (1897)	37,137 (1908)
Average annual	23,200	20,459	19,400

Ballymena and Larne Railway 0-6-0T No 6 as built in 1883. This locomotive had an enclosed cab from the start.

Beyer Peacock

Odd man out on the Ballymena and Larne was 2-6-0ST No 5, a unique type for the Irish narrow gauge. Essentially, this engine was a tank version of the outside cylinder 2-6-0 tender design which Beyer, Peacock supplied to the South Australia Railway in 1877–82 (the W class). Beyer, Peacock prepared a proposal drawing, dated 26 June 1879, for an engine with 14 x 18in outside cylinders, 2ft leading

wheels and 3ft 3in driving wheels The weight diagram for this locomotive was not prepared until 14 February 1880. The relevant shop orders were dated 3 February and 6 March 1880, and the engine was "to be delivered by the end of April". A note dated 21 July 1880 was subsequently added to the shop order and referred to the "alteration in the feedcock arrangements" and since this note was

B&LR 0-6-0T No 6 is seen as NCC No 108 at Ballycastle in 1931. Compared to the previous photo, the jacks have been moved to the tank tops and replaced by toolboxes and Ross 'pop' safety valves have been fitted.

L&GRP

B&LR 2-6-0ST No 5 as built by Beyer, Peacock in 1880. This engine carried Ramsbottom safety valves rather than the Spring Balance type fitted to the other B&LR engines.

Beyer, Peacock

added some two months after it had been delivered to the B&LR, it would appear that there were some shortcomings as built and that these were later made good by Beyers. The locomotive was tried in steam on 29 April 1880 and delivered on 26 May 1880. Its cost was £1,700.

On No 5, the inclined outside cylinders with the footplating raised above them, the front truck with outside bearings, and the sloping smokebox door all mirrored the design of the 2-4-0 tank engines, while the six-coupled driving wheels and 14in cylinders were the outcome of the need for more traction and adhesion. The saddle tank held 500 gallons and gave better access to the motion than the side tanks of the other engines. The loaded weight of

just over 25½tons was around 4½tons more than any of its stable-mates, but the axle loading was slightly less. On incorporation into the BNCR stock it became No 68, and then No 109 in 1897. Around 1904 it was made the sole representative of Class 'R'. It was reboiled in 1899 and withdrawn in May 1934. It soon established a reputation as the most powerful engine on the line, and the enginemen nicknamed it 'The Bruiser'. It was not popular with the firemen, because the cramped short cab made it difficult to get a good swing with the shovel. As one senior driver said of his days as a fireman, "It was just torture cleaning the fire on a warm day – you had to use a rake and a short shovel and by the time you'd finished, there wasn't a dry stitch on you". But its performance with the heavy goods and coal trains out of Larne was legendary. Its BNCR/NCC mileage totalled 892,874, a yearly average of 19,400. The greatest annual mileage was 36,228 in 1891. As far as is known, No 5 worked entirely on the Ballymena–Larne section, mainly on the Doagh branch where it did good work on the Doagh–Larne trains. It was regularly shedded at Doagh, and descended to spend a night at Larne only on the occasions of its boiler washout.

Details of the livery of the Ballymena and Larne engines is most elusive, and nothing is mentioned about this aspect of the engines in the minute books. It has been stated in the literature, though without any reference to the source, as "light green". The first mention in Beyer, Peacock's records is contained in the shop orders for Nos 2 and 3, where the colour was to be "Quaker green similar to engine No 3525", that is similar to B&LR No 1. Identical colour was prescribed for 'The Bruiser' and for the third of the 0-6-

0 tanks. From an examination of the maker's photographs, it seems likely that the smokebox and funnel were black. Lining details are not known, and all that can be deduced from the maker's photographs is that a broad band with radiused corners, perhaps 1½in wide and probably in red, was applied as a panel on the boiler bands, the tanks and the cab side sheet. The side of the bunker on No 4 was similarly lined. On each side of this colour band narrow lines of a light colour, perhaps yellow, were run, while about 1½in inside this combination there was another colour line, narrow and difficult to distinguish in the photographs from the background green, so that it may well have been orange. The chimney cap was of polished copper. The bell-mouth domes on Nos 1 and 4 were of polished brass. On No 2, 3 and 6 there was no bell-mouth, only a hole for the safety valve, and the domes appear to have been painted. No 5 had a closed-top dome which was painted.

The leading dimensions of the engines were:

B&LR No	1/4	2 and 3	6	5
Type	2-4-0T	0-6-0T	0-6-0T	2-6-0T
Cylinders	11" x 18"	13½" x 18"	13½" x 18"	14" x 18"
L/wheel dia	2' 0"	–	–	2' 0"
D/wheel dia	3' 9"	3' 3"	3' 3"	3' 3"
Wheelbase	8' 0" + 6' 3"	5' 0" + 5' 6"	5' 0" + 5' 6"	5' 6" + 3' 6" + 3' 6"
Boiler:				
length	7' 8¼"	8' 0"	8' 4½"	9' 2"
diameter	2' 10"	3' 3"	3' 3"	3' 5¾"
tubes (1⅝ in)	103	132	132	160
hgt of centreline	4' 10"	4' 10½"	4' 10½"	5' 0½"
working pressure (psi)	120/140	140	140	140
Total heating surface (sq ft)	43 + 349	43 + 464	44 + 485	54 + 641
Grate area (sq ft)	6.95	9.1	9.1	10.5
Tractive Effort (lbs)	4,937 (5,759)	10,009	10,009	10,765
Weight loaded (tcq)	17.12.0*	21.2.0	22.9.2	25.13.2
Weight empty (tcq)	14.12.0*	17.7.2	18.9.3	21.2.0
Tank capacity (galls)	385/450	450	450	500
Coal capacity (tons)	1/1.3	1	1.1	1.2
Lgth over headstocks	20' 1¾"	20' 3¾"	20' 3¾"	21' 10⅝"

* The increased weight of No 4 is referred to in the text.

B&LR 2-6-0ST No 5 was popularly known as 'The Bruiser'. It is seen here in late MR days at Harryville, Ballymena, as No 109. The only obvious change from new is the vacuum reservoir positioned below the cab.

Real Photographs Ltd

Below: *No 109 at the Cushendall Yard, Ballymena in the early 1930s. Coal was now stored over the top of the firebox, a practice that probably did little for the efficiency of the safety valves!*

Real Photographs Ltd

The Northern Counties engines

Having fallen heir to a variety of narrow gauge engines whose design was largely that of their builders, and of which he cannot have entirely approved since the nine engines were of four different types, Bowman Malcolm set about the design of a new class of locomotive. He was a pioneer in compound working and in 1890 had taken delivery of the first 5ft 3in gauge passenger compounds. Goods compounds followed in May 1892 and the stage was seemingly set for compounding on the narrow gauge.

Malcolm wrote the Beyer, Peacock and Co on 27 March

1891 regarding new narrow gauge locomotives, and outlined eight requirements:

(i)   to be suitable for both goods and passenger working

(ii)   to have four-coupled 3 ft 9 in driving wheels

(iii)   to have a pony truck in front, or radial axleboxes front and back

(iv)   to have cylinders 15 x 18 in or 14 x 20 in

(v)   to be "as powerful as any we have"

(vi)   tanks to hold 500 gallons (saddle tanks preferred)

(vii)   load on any pair of wheels not to exceed ten tons

(viii)   "would there be any difficulty in compounding these engines?"

Design work by S Rendall began at Beyer's works on 31 March 1891. By mid-April the basis of the new design had evolved and a provisional sketch had been drafted. Despite Bowman Malcolm's expressed preference for saddle tanks – which he probably inherited from his knowledge of 'The Bruiser' – side tanks holding 600 gallons were shown. When detailed weight calculations were made, it was found difficult to get a distribution of weight within the required ten ton limit and the design was abandoned. The following note was appended to the calculations, "the weight all comes off the hind end, and none off the front, which will make the distribution of weight very unequal when the tanks are nearly empty."

Concurrently, Bowman Malcolm was giving thought to standardisation and to some aspects of the design, and he wrote again to Beyer, Peacock suggesting that:

(i)   the leading and trailing wheels be the same size (2 ft) as those of the existing B&LR engines, so as to use the same tyres

(ii)   the boiler to be similar to that on No 68 ('The Bruiser'), if of sufficient capacity

(iii)   as many parts as possible to be duplicates of the B&LR engines, or of other engines recently made for]the BNCR

(iv)   the coupling rods to have solid ends of standard type

(v)   injectors and double sand blast of Graham and Craven's make, similar to those on standard-gauge compounds

(vi)   if compounded, a sight feed lubricator, Vacuum Oil Co's pattern, to be supplied

(vii)   both steam and automatic vacuum brakes to be fitted.

Further work on the drawing board followed and a design was submitted to the BNCR on 15 April 1891. This differed from the earlier proposal in having a saddle tank holding 570 gallons, while leading and trailing wheels were both 2ft in diameter. Either simple or compound working was envisaged, the boiler pressure being calculated at 150psi for simple and 170psi for compounding working. Later, both pressures were increased by 10psi.

A gap exists in the preserved Beyer, Peacock correspondence over the following four months, and the next link in the story was forged on 7 August 1891 when an un-numbered drawing was prepared. This no longer survives, but according to records it was an enlarged copy of the saddle tank drawing of April 1891. Since it only gives details covering compound working, it would seem that the idea of simple working had been dropped. Then, on 10 August 1891, drawing No 48084 was made: again, this was based on the April saddle

Beyer, Peacock's proposed 2-4-2 ST for B & NCR, April 1891

Cylinders 14in x 20in (simple) or 15in/21¾in x 20in (compound)	Weight 28¾ tons (simple) 29½ tons (compound)
L.W. & T.W. 2ft 0in diam.	Boiler 3ft 6in x 9ft 5in
D.W. 3ft 9in diam.	Tank 570 gallons
Wheelbase 6ft 3in + 6ft 0in + 8ft 0in	

Left: *Compound 2-4-2T No 110 (originally 69) at Larne in the 1920s, before rebuilding as a 2-4-4T in 1931. Note the Walschaerts valve gear.*

Real Photographs Ltd

Below: *A broadside view of 2-4-2T No 111 (originally 70) at Ballymena in 1931, after fitting with Ross 'pop' safety valves.*

JAGH Coltas

tank sketch but shows side tanks and Walschaert's valve gear. There are no records of detailed calculations being made at this stage for a locomotive with side tanks, but the change in design was probably due to the vexed matter of axle loading.

During October and November 1891 Beyers made further calculations for the side tank design. On 27 October it was suggested that the high pressure cylinder should be altered from 15 x 20in to the dimension ultimately adopted, 14¾ x 20in. It was further suggested that the boiler be reduced from 180psi to the original 170psi. Then there is a last reference to the possibility of simple working, a mere note in brackets that for such a design the boiler pressure would be better at 150 than 160psi.

Further consideration of the design extended into December 1891. A final proposal drawing was made on 29 December 1891 and was basically a weight sketch of the engine as built, with the low-pressure cylinder shown of 21in diameter.

On 12 January 1892 a shop order for two narrow gauge compound side tank engines was issued at Gorton. The engines were given stock number 7511 and progressive numbers 2463 and 3464, and were to carry BNCR numbers 69 and 70. The boilers were to have 170psi working pressure and were to be tested hydraulically to 220psi. Delivery was to be "next March". Painting was to be "similar to engine 7504" which was an order for two compound, inside-cylinder, 5ft 3in gauge goods engines, with Beyer, Peacock progressive numbers 2457/8. The shop order for these two engines yields the following information: "The engines to receive not less than one coat of red lead, two coats of lead colour, then rubbed down and finished with two coats of dark green lined out and varnished with three coats of best engine copal varnish. The buffer plank, number plates and inside of cab to be painted vermilion. No oil of any kind to be used in paints. Surface of figures and edge of plates [in number plates] to be bright." The number plates were to be made of brass. The letters 'BCNR' were to be placed on the side tanks, but a later note amends this and 'backplate' is substituted. The transfers were to be supplied by the railway company.

During the building of the locomotives, two notes were added to the shop orders. Thus on 12 January 1892, "Balance weights solid forged", and on 3 April 1892, "Blow off cock not wanted, 1¾-in mud cock to be put in place".

No 3463 (BNCR No 69) was tried in steam on 5 April 1892 and left Gorton works en route for Belfast on 13 May. No 2464 (BNCR No 70) was tried in steam on 6 April 1892 and left the works on 21 May.

These two engines, the first members of a class that was eventually to comprise six engines, carried Nos 69 and 70 for only five years, and then became Nos 110 and 111 in the 1897 renumbering. They subsequently formed Class 'S'. As built and as first running on the B&LR section, these locomotives appear to have been rather troublesome and a visit was paid to the line by a Mr Worthington, a technical representative of the builders, in December 1894. Defects were admitted by Beyers and Worthington's report notes:

(a) Balance beams between the bogie (*sic*) and coupled axles to be introduced if possible to prevent excessive slipping of the coupled wheels

(b) Side play of the bogies (*sic*) has been increased ¼in each way for each bogie. This has been allowed for when the locos were built, when 1½in side play was given, although 1¾in was allowed for

(c) The diameter of the valve spindles to be increased

(d) Air relief valves on cylinders to be made of our best mixture and to be redesigned in order to prevent fracture of the hollow spindle and damage to the stop

(e) The front sand-traps to be kept further away from the valve spindle glands in order to prevent moisture from them being drawn into the sand pipes

(f) The spindles of injector steam cocks to be strengthened

(g) The coupling rods to have a solid bush at the driving crank pin, if a satisfactory job can be made of the outside crank arm

(h) The bushes in large end of eccentric rod to be made of mild steel, case-hardened to prevent excessive wear

(i) Crossheads to be fitted with cast-iron slides instead of white metal

(j) Provision to be made for carrying the weight of the low-pressure piston to prevent the rapid wear of cylinders

(k) Motion pins in reversing lever to have more surface and if possible the arm on reversing shaft to be lengthened in order to reduce the strain on lever and crank bolt

(l) Injector feed pipes to be so arranged that they can empty the tanks when running either forward or backward over their heaviest grades; this may be done by arranging for one injector to feed from the front end of the tank and the other injector from the hind end.

These items were merely recommendations to the builders, to be taken into account if and when further orders were placed.

Up to 1931, No 110 ran 931,086 miles, an average of 24,000 miles per year. During that period, a new boiler was fitted in February 1910 and there were general overhauls in December 1919, October 1921, December 1925 and December 1928.

In 1931, it was decided to rebuild her extensively, the major part of the operation being the replacement of the trailing radial truck by a bogie, giving the engine the unusual wheel arrangement of 2-4-4T, which was unique in Ireland. Its class symbol became 'S2'. The overall length was increased by a fraction under four feet, and a rear bunker was added which held one and a half tons of coal. At the same time, a larger boiler was fitted, a modified G6S as used on the broad gauge (but without a superheater), 7ft longer and 6¾in greater in diameter than the original, and with the working pressure raised from 160 to 200psi. This extensive piece of surgery increased the weight by 10¼tons but only put 1ton 8cwt more on each driving axle.

The modification was done at Belfast, and was not a success, for after it No 110 derailed repeatedly, was too rigid on the curves and slipped so badly that John Gamble remarked after a day driving 110, "Lough Neagh wouldn't have kept her going in sand." After becoming a 2-4-4T engine, her highest annual mileage was 15,124 in 1932;

thereafter she was avoided by everyone if at all possible and only 3,000 miles were run during 1934. Though the tractive effort had been raised from 13,159lb to 16,435lb, the added power could not be fully utilised. After the outbreak of World War II, No 110 was briefly pressed into service but, though she covered 2,000 miles in 1941, her mileage was nil in 1940, and nil from 1942 until 1946. The S2 rebuild was a failure, and No 110 was officially withdrawn in February 1946. She remained in Larne shed for some months before being scrapped.

More successful in every way was No 70/111 which ran over a million miles in a working life of 58 years. This engine was never rebuilt but was again renumbered in December 1948, becoming No 44. Reboilering was carried out in 1911 and in 1926. For many of her latter years she worked the Ballycastle section.

No further developments seem to have taken place until October 1903, when Beyer, Peacock made calculations and a proposal drawing for a 4-6-0T for the MR(NCC)'s narrow gauge lines. Regrettably little information has survived concerning this abortive scheme. The design was based directly on the 2-4-2T engines and, as can be seen from the drawing, the projected locomotive would have had many points of similarity with them. Compounding

and Walschaert's valve gear were determined on from the start and, apart from the wheel arrangement, the most noticeable difference was the increase in water capacity to 650 gallons. Although a perusal of the builder's files has not uncovered the reasons behind the new design, it was probably to determine whether better adhesion could be achieved by the use of an extra driving axle. The project was scarcely novel on the Irish narrow gauge, for it came ten years after a class of six 4-6-0Ts had been built by Neilson of Glasgow for the Donegal Railway, and one year after Barclay of Kilmarnock had turned out four similar engines for the Londonderry and Lough Swilly. Whatever the reason, the project was not pursued further either by the MR(NCC) or by Beyer, Peacock.

After the purchase of the two compound locomotives in 1892, 16 years elapsed before the class was augmented. During that period the company and its successor, the MR(NCC), had 11 narrow gauge engines at work into Ballymena. The next new narrow gauge engine was built, not at Gorton but at York Road, Belfast, and emerged in October 1908 as No 112.

In February 1920 No 112 was renumbered '102'. Then, in November 1939, it became '42' and remained thus until it was scrapped in 1954. In 1930, it was altered to increase its coal capacity, the length of the rear radial truck, wheelbase and overall length were all increased by two feet and a bunker was placed behind the cab. The weight was increased by 1ton 3cwt. It was reclassified to 'S1'. On the modified engine, although the coal capacity was nominally unaltered at one ton, the bunker enabled the footplate to be kept free of coal and thus improved conditions in the rather restricted cabs. As No 102, this engine worked for a time between Ballymoney and

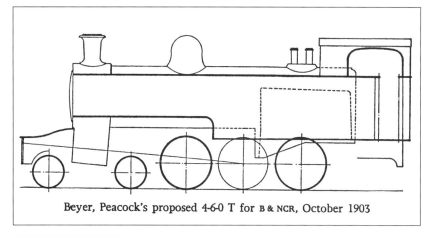

Beyer, Peacock's proposed 4-6-0 T for B & NCR, October 1903

Cylinders	14¾/21" x 20"	Boiler	3' 5" x 9' 4"
Leading wheels	2' 0"	Boiler tubes	150 x 1⅝"
Driving wheels	3' 3"	Heating surface	615 + 65 sq ft
Wheelbase	5' 4" + 3' 7" + 3' 9" + 3' 9"	Working pressure	180 psi
Weight	(2 x 4t 5c) + (3 x 9t 0c) = 35½ tons		
Tank capacity	650 gallons		

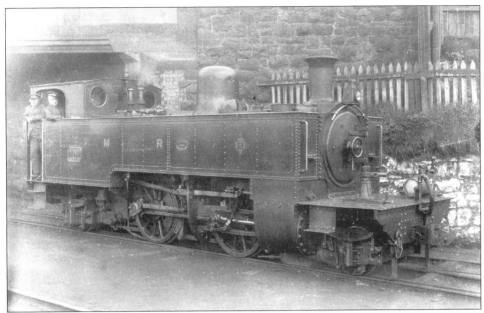

The second brace of 2-4-2Ts were Nos 112 and 113, built in 1908 and 1909. In February 1920 they were renumbered 102 and 101 respectively. No 101 (ex-113) is seen with its crew near the Circular Road overbridge at Larne on 22 May 1924, still in MR livery.

Real Photographs Ltd

Ballycastle, and was there in 1936 when a sister engine, No 41, was away for heavy overhaul. Its last years were spent working from Larne to the Ballyclare paper mill.

From the Belfast shops in March 1909 No 113 went into service. Like its sister engine, it was renumbered in February 1920 and became '101'. Eight years later it was rebuilt with the rear bunker to Class S1. A second renumbering in June 1939 made it '41'. Most of its later career was spent on the Ballycastle road where, though worked hard, it was efficient and popular with the crews.

The last pair of compound tanks to be built were Nos 103 and 104, also constructed at York Road. They went into service in September 1919 and March 1920. Both of these engines retained their original Class S characteristics through their working life.

Of the six compounds, No 103 was the shortest lived member, and at the end of 1938 she was scrapped after lying out of use for two years while awaiting a general overhaul. For her short span of 19 years, redundancy alone was to blame.

No 104 was shedded at Ballymena for many years, and became '43' in October 1942. Four years later, following a heavy repair she was sent to the Ballycastle line. Rejuvenated, she put up at tremendous mileage, her 42,407 miles in 1948 being the highest annual mileage of any of the compounds. No 43 worked on the Ballycastle section until it was closed in 1950, remained in stock until early 1954 and was then scrapped.

The mileages covered by the six compounds are given in the following table:

Mileage	69/110	110 (as S2)	70/111/44	112/102/42	113/101/41	103	104/43
Total	931,006	52,088	1,156,774	614,217	469,761	309,583	444,080
Max annual	not known	15,124 (1931)	39,808 (1894)	37,918 (1944)	35,136 (1943)	26,338 (1930)	42,407 (1948)
Average annual	23,900	3,500	19,700	14,900	11,200	18,200	14,900

Bowman Malcolm's compound tanks were outstanding little engines which, between them, shouldered the bulk of the narrow gauge work in north-east Ireland. They were scrapped when there were no facilities for preservation and it is unfortunate that one of the dainty little Class S engines was unable to find a home in Belfast's Transport Museum.

The final pair of 2-4-2Ts were No 103 and 104, built at York Road in 1919 and 1920 respectively. The first of the pair, No 103, was photographed at Ballymena yard in 1936.   Real Photographs Ltd

Two of the class, Nos 101 and 102, were rebuilt in 1928 and 1930 respectively with the rear radial truck lengthened and a coal bunker added, thus becoming Class S1. No 102 is seen on a passenger train at Larne Harbour shortly after rebuilding.

CP Friel collection

The leading dimensions of Classes S, S1 and S2 were as follows:

Class	S	S1	S2
Type	2-4-2T	2-4-2T	2-4-4T
No in class	6	2	1
Maker	BP and NCC	NCC	NCC
Wheelbase	6' 9" + 6' 3" + 7' 3"	6' 9" + 6' 3" + 9' 3"	6' 9" + 6' 3" + 8' 3" + 4' 6"
Wheel diameter			
Leading	2' 0"	2' 0"	2' 0"
Coupled	3' 9"	3' 9"	3' 9"
Trailing	2' 0"	2' 0"	2' 0"
Cylinders (2 outside)	14¾/21 x 20"		14¾/21 x 20"
Boiler*			
Length	9' 4"		9' 11"
Diameter (outside)	3' 5¼"		4' 0"
Tubes	150 x 1⅝" diam		164 x 1¾" diam
Pressure (psi)	160		200
Centreline above rail	5' 5"		6' 1"
Heating surface (sq ft)			
Firebox	58.2		83
Tubes	614.8		742
Total	673.0		825
Grate area	11.3		12
Weight in working order (tons/cwt/qr)	31.17.2	33.0.0	42.1.0§
Weight distribution (tc)			
Leading wheels	5.8	5.1	6.0
Driving wheels (both)	10.0	10.0	11.8
Trailing wheels	6.9	7.1	6.2/7.3
Tank capacity (galls)	570	570	570
Coal capacity (tons)	1	1	1½
Length over headstocks	25' 6½"	27' 6½"	29' 6"
Length over buffers	27' 9⅞"	27' 9⅞"	31' 9½"
Height from rail	9' 8"	9' 8"	10' 1¼"
Tractive effort at 85% boiler pressure (lbs)	13,150	13,150	16,438

*   Boiler dimensions of Class S are taken from Beyer, Peacock drawings, which give 170 lbs as the working pressure. Heating surface areas are from original Beyer, Peacock records.

§   In *The Locomotive*, page 382, 15 Nov 1932, the total weight is given as 44 tons 4 cwt, with correspondingly heavier axle loadings, those of the driving axles being shown as 12 tons.

In 1931 S class 2-4-2T No 110 was extensively rebuilt with a G6S boiler as fitted to the main line A1 class 4-4-0s. At the same time a bogie replaced the rear radial truck and a large coal bunker was added. Although an impressive looking and powerful machine, she had poor adhesion and was not deemed a success. She is seen in action at Larne shortly after rebuilding.

RG Jarvis

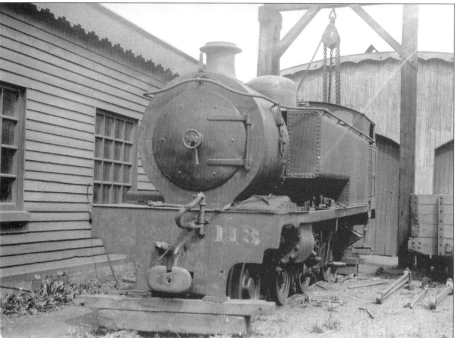

Left: *Ex-Ballycastle Railway 4-4-2T No 3, as NCC T class No 113, outside Larne Works on 14 July 1937.*

AW Croughton

Opposite: *The rarely photographed T class No 114, outside Larne shed, its 'NCC' lettering barely visible.*

Real Photographs Ltd

The ex-Ballycastle engines

While a variety of B&LR, BNCR and Midland engines gravitated to the Ballycastle section and ended their working days there, a reverse tendency was exhibited by two engines which Kitson and Co built in 1908 for the Ballycastle Railway Co. For the previous 28 years that company had worked its 16 miles of railway with fair success using three six-coupled saddle tanks. They needed new engine stock and the locomotive superintendent, George Bradshaw, designed a class or two 4-4-2T engines, for which the order was placed in November 1907. The directors' minutes of the Ballycastle Railway Company mention that the design was approved by Bowman Malcolm. The fact that Malcolm was asked to cast an eye over the new design is not remarkable, for the NCC held a large block of Ballycastle share capital, but what is surprising was the unsatisfactory nature of the product. One is tempted to think that Malcolm may not have had much say in the design, though his successful Class S engines may have inspired it. With a leading bogie to match the Ballycastle curves, there was simple propulsion rather than compound, but the engine was four-coupled and the fixed wheelbase of 6ft 6in compared with the 6ft 3in of Class S, while the driving wheels were 2in smaller to give added traction.

Lack of adhesion was the downfall of the Kitson engines for, of the total weight of almost 40 tons, only just over 21 tons was carried on the driving wheels and they became notorious for slipping. On the Ballycastle line, the long, hard climb to Capecastle proved their undoing time and time again, with the steam sanders useless once the sandboxes were emptied. Apart from that serious defect, the engines were reliable enough and served the Ballycastle company without any heavy repairs from 1908, until that unfortunate company went into liquidation in 1924.

In 1924 the Ballycastle Railway was taken over by the LMS(NCC) and the two Kitson engines, Nos 3 and 4 went into Northern Counties stock at Nos 113 and 114. Judging by Ballycastle reports, No 3 was then in reasonably good condition, but the firebox of No 4 needed urgent replacement. So they both went to the York Road shops, and their place at Ballycastle was taken by the Class Q 0-6-0Ts. So that the Kitsons could run on the Larne road, where bridge clearances were less than at Ballycastle, the cabs and boiler mountains were reduced in height. New boilers were fitted, to No 113 in December 1926 and to No 114 in November 1927. With the lowering of the cab roofs, the round porthole in the side sheets was obliterated, and the round front spectacle glasses were replaced by radiused rectangular ones. They formed Class T.

Nos 113 and 114 worked on the B&LR section for the rest of their lives, apart from a brief transfer of No 113 to the Ballycastle section in 1942. Under NCC ownership, the mileage worked by these locomotives was as follows:

	No 113	No 114
Mileage		
Total	152,120 (1926–46)	100,805 (1927–41)
Max annual	27,850 (1927)	14,164 (1938)
Average annual	7,500	7,700

These averages, calculated on complete years only, are markedly less than those of the compounds and the three engines of Class Q. No 113 was withdrawn from stock on 30 September 1940 and lay out of use during the whole of 1941. Then, in February 1942, No 114 was withdrawn, being in bad repair, while No 113, which was still fit for work, received a wartime reprieve and was put back into stock. During 1942 she covered 13,379 miles, and 3,283, 8,403 and 8,940 miles in 1943/4/5. During 1946. No 114, withdrawn and sold in 1942, was used for a time by the contractor who bought her as a stationary engine for steam pile-driving at Larne Harbour. The leading dimensions of the Class engines, after rebuilding were:

Numbers on NCC	113 and 114
Maker's numbers	4565 and 4566
Cylinders (2 outside)	14½ x 21"
Wheel diameters	
Leading	2' 6"
Driving	3' 7"
Trailing	2' 6"
Wheelbase	5' 0" + 5' 8" + 6' 6" + 6" 6"
Boiler	
Outside diameter	4' 0"
Barrel length	9' 6"
Tubes	170 x 1¾in
Pressure (psi)	160
Centre line above rail	6ft 6in
Heating surface (sq ft)	
Firebox	83
Tubes	769
Total	852
Grate area	12
Weight in working order	39tons 11cwt

Weight distribution (t c q)	
Leading wheels	5.6.2
	5.6.2
Driving wheels	10.13.0
	10.15.0
Trailing wheels	7.10.0
Tank capacity (gall)	800
Coal capacity (tons)	1¾
Length over buffers	31' 1½"
Height above rail	10' 2½"
Tractive effort @ 85%	
of boiler pressure	13,964 lb

Livery

Under the BNCR, the colour of the engines is believed to have been a dark laurel green lined out in crimson/light blue/chrome yellow, the latter being outermost.

When the MR(NCC) took control, the engines were painted 'invisible green', a dark colour which approached black. lining appears to have been the same as in BNCR days. The initials 'MR' in shaded, sans-seriff gold capitals were on the side tanks flanking the number plate. Buffer beams were vermilion red, and the smoke box was black.

The LMS(NCC) colour copied the old Midland of England, and was crimson lake or maroon, with black smokebox and red buffer beams. The LMS(NCC) crest was on the cab side-sheets. The initials 'NCC' were on the side tanks, either as small block letters, or as small or large Roman letters. On the three Class Q engines, the numberplate was in the middle of the tank, and 'NCC' was placed behind the plate. The number plate background colour was maroon at first, but later red. On the compounds, the number plate was on the tanks, in line with the front of the cab. Lining consisted of a broad band of black with a line of yellow ochre along the inside edge.

During much of World War II the narrow gauge engines were painted unlined black, and only the red buffer beams and number plate backgrounds relieved the sombre effect. Under the UTA, black continued to be used but was lined with yellow and vermilion. The UTA roundel, 14in in diameter and with 'Ulster Transport' in orange block capitals lined in red, encircled a white shield bearing a red hand. The roundel had a mid-green background and was placed in the middle of the side tanks of the locomotives which remained.

The style of the number plates remained a BNCR characteristic throughout succeeding ownerships. They were brass, in a horizontal rectangular format with radiused corners. The size was about 18 x 10in and a raised edge surrounded the plate. The plates of the first BNCR number series (Nos 60–70) contained boldly serified numbers alone. The 1897 renumbering introduced a series of plates which had 'BNCR' in small block capitals above the digits. This BNCR series was used into MR(NCC) and LMS(NCC) times, and probably the last survival was on 'The Bruiser', No 109. When No 110 was rebuilt to Class S2, someone ordered that the 'BNCR' letter be milled off the plates, and in consequence the numbers became offset towards the bottom of the plate. The MR(NCC) renumberings of 112/102 and 113/101, and the numbering of 103 and 104 when built, gave these plates digits only, otherwise their appearance followed earlier practice. The principle was maintained in the last renumbering to Nos 41–44.

Originally No 104, but renumbered in October 1942, S class 2-4-2T No 43 is seen at Ballycastle shed in 1948. She was transferred to Ballycastle in 1946 and, after the closure of the line in 1950, remained at Ballycastle until it was cut up in 1954.

L&GRP

Chapter 9

Carriages and wagons

Ballymena and Larne Railway stock

The chairman was authorised on 2 February 1877 . . .

. . . to order rolling stock at his discretion on the following basis:

	Bristol	Midland	Price each
Composite carriages	3	–	£600
Lime or tip wagons	–	10	£41
Open wagons or coal wagons	10	–	£49
Open wagons or coal wagons	–	40	£42
Platform wagons 14 in side	–	10	£37
Platform wagons 24 in side	–	10	£40
Covered goods vans	10	–	£66
Cattle wagons	7	–	£55
Breakvans with vac. break	3	–	£80

The passenger carriages and breakvans to be fitted with vacuum breaks as recommended by Mr McDonnell. *

In spite of the reference to the Midland Wagon Co, the entire B&LR rolling stock came from the Bristol Wagon Works. The first order, somewhat modified, was discussed in a letter from Chaine dated 9 February 1877:

> Ballymena and Larne Railway.
> Messrs Bristol Wagon Works Co, Ltd,
> Gentlemen,
> On behalf of the above Railway Company, I beg to place in your hands the following order for 3ft-gauge rolling stock.
> *Two composite* Bogie carriages at £577–10 each as fully described in your Specification dated Dec. 12/76 but subject to the following additions and/or alterations viz:
> 1st the wheels to be of the kind known as Mansells.
> 2nd the Smith Vacuum Brake to be fitted complete to each carriage in addition to hand brake.
> 3rd the springs used to be made either by Krupps or Turton and Co and the tyres and axles by Bolton Co, Krupp or Bessemer.
> 4th the cushioning both in 3rd and 1st only to reach shoulder height and in the 1st to be of real Morocco leather of approved colour.
> 5th the glass in lantern to be engraved to an approved pattern.
> 6th the carriages to be 2ft longer in body than specified, such additional length being added to the guards compartment, which is to be provided with side look-out for guard and two plain seats hinged so as to fall down.
> 7th two continuous steps the lowest 14in on under side from rail.
> 8th cord to pass along inside of lantern with brass snap hooks at either end, & passing through I.R. washers so arranged as to show in which compartment it has been pulled.
> 9th the partition in 3rd to go to the roof.
> *Twenty open* goods or coal wagons as per specification dated 12 Dec. except that the axles are to be of Bessemer steel made by Krupp, Bessemer or Bolton Co, the buffers fitted with Stapleford's safety hooks, and the ends of the bodies are to be arched 5in and each wagon fitted with plain single brake. Price £45.

* Of the Great Southern and Western Railway, which was then using Smith's type of vacuum brake.

Ten covered good wagons similar to brake vans, specified steel axles, Stapleford's hook, plain hand brake and as above. Priced £52.

Seven cattle wagons as specified with steel axles, Stapleford's hook, plain brakes etc. Price £53.

Three goods brake vans fitted with Smith's vacuum break (sic), complete in addition to hand break, steel axles, Stapleford's hook and other detail as per specification. Price £75.

. . . the wagons to be delivered half in March, half in April and the carriages within 3 months from this date.

Truly yours,

JAMES CHAINE, Chairman.

On 30 May 1877 it was decided to order a first class saloon carriage costing £700 from Bristol "to be delivered on or before 23 July at Belfast or Larne", and also "ten coal or open trucks at £45 and ten timber trucks or platform wagons at £47 10s". All preceding orders were listed in an account furnished by the Bristol Company in October 1877, which shows that some reductions in the price had been agreed to in the interim:

10 covered goods wagons	@	£62	
7 cattle wagons	@	£53	
60 open goods wagons	@	£45	
10 platform wagons	@	£47	10s
3 goods brake vans	@	£75	
2 composite bogie carriages	@	£577	10s
1 saloon carriage	@	£700	
Total		£6,246	

Although 'bogie' vehicles are referred to in these 1877 transactions, the composite carriages were six-wheelers of the Cleminson type.

Not until four days after the line had been opened to Ballymena were any steps taken to increase the small coaching stock, which must have been quite insufficient. On 28 August 1878 two composites were ordered, the minute merely noting "details as recommended by manager". They differed from the existing pair of composites in having bogies, and were delivered in 1879. In March of that year, five new bogie carriages were placed on order, bringing the total up to ten vehicles. Some disagreement arose over the bridge carriages and on 28 May 1879 a complaint was raised that Bristol had charged £16 16s for 42 blinds and £25 as part freight "on the last carriages delivered at the

harbour", whereas "contract was for free delivery, and the blinds should not have been charged."

Last additions to the coaching stock were five small third class carriages in 1881–2. In the minute book, no mention is made of their being ordered from an outside supplier and, since the returns of rolling stock for 1881 and 1882 show their acquisition with a corresponding drop in the number of covered wagons, it seems that they were home-made conversions. They were four-wheelers and, with one compartment seating 16, must have been bleak vehicles.

The coaching stock of the B&LR is summarised in the table on page 108, with the BNCR numbers allocated to them after transfer and retained by them until final withdrawal. Only in three cases are the original B&LR numbers known: B&LR No 5 is believed to have become BNCR No 315, and Nos 7 and 8 became Nos 321 and 322 respectively.

One of the 1878 bogie composites is illustrated in RM Livesey's 1912 pamphlet describing Irish narrow gauge rolling stock. The compartments are arranged 133133. Bogie wheels are of 2ft 1¾in diameter, set at 4ft 9in centres, and the bogie centres are 24ft 7in apart.

An early photograph of a B&LR train leaving Larne Harbour (page 39) shows locomotive No 4 hauling four carriages. In the lead is No 5, a six-wheeled brake composite, with a pair of passenger compartments both fore and aft of the central guard's compartment with its side ducket. Following it are two bogie brake composites; their numbers cannot be determined, but they appear to have three passenger compartments on each side of the guard's compartment. The total of six compartments for passengers suggests that one of them is the 41ft 3in vehicle which became BNCR No 305. They seem to be identical, which does not fit in with the detail of the NCC list in the above table, where the three bogie brake composites differ from each other. It may be conjectured that one of the vehicles in the photograph was later converted to BNCR composite No 318. The last vehicle in the train is the first class saloon, clerestory-roofed, which later became BNCR No 304.

It was BNCR No 304 which did duty in a royal train when, in July 1903, King Edward VII and Queen Alexandra visited Ireland. Landing at Buncrana in County Donegal, they were conveyed by the Londonderry and Lough Swilly Railway to the city of Londonderry. The LLSR had no saloon carriages, and while the conveyance

Top left: *Ex-B&LR First Class saloon coach No 304, photographed at Pennyburn Yard, Londonderry, when it was loaned to the LLSR for use by King Edward VII on their Royal Train in July 1903.*

LLSR

Opposite: *A Larne-bound train makes a spirited departure from Ballymena in the early 1900s, hauled by P class 2-4-0T No 104. The train comprises bogie Parcel Post Van No 324, an unidentified Brake/Composite and Composite No 318.*

L&GRP

Lower left: *'The Bruiser' (No 109) at Ballyboley with the Doagh branch train on 9 August 1930. The two vehicle train comprises a 4-wheel goods brake van and bogie Brake/Composite No 321.*

HC Casserley

Delivery date	Type	Wheels	Length	Width	Compts (Seats) 1st	3rd	BNCR No
1877	Brake/Composite	6	29' 6"	6' 6"	1 (6)	3 (24)	301
1877	Brake/Composite	6	29' 6"	6' 6"	1 (6)	3 (24)	315
1877	1st Saloon	Bogie	33' 0"	7' 0"	1 (20)	–	304
1879	Composite	Bogie	34' 9"	6' 6"	2 (12)	4 (32)	302
1879	Composite	Bogie	34' 9"	6' 8"	1 (6)	5 (40)	322
1879	Brake/Composite	Bogie	34' 9"	6' 8"	1 (6)	4 (32)	321
1879	Composite	Bogie	35' 6"	6' 8"	2 (12)	4 (32)	303
1879	Brake/Composite	Bogie	35' 6"	6' 8"	2 (12)	2 (16)	314
1879	Composite	Bogie	41' 3"	6' 8"	3 (18)	4 (32)	318
1879	Brake/Composite	Bogie	41' 3"	6' 8"	2 (12)	4 (32)	305
1881/2	Third	4	14' 1"	6' 7"	1 (16)	–	308
1881/2	Third	4	14' 1"	6' 7"	1 (16)	–	309
1881/2	Third	4	14' 1"	6' 7"	1 (16)	–	310
1881/2	Third	4	14' 1"	6' 7"	1 (16)	–	311
1881/2	Third	4	14' 1"	6' 7"	1 (16)	–	313

of royalty in one of their compartment vehicles might have been an apt introduction to Ireland and to its railways, it was not regarded as appropriate to the occasion. The Swilly had neither financial resources nor workshops to tackle a conversion job. For some reason, the Donegal Railway were not asked to help, though they had a six-wheeled saloon which might have done. John McFarland, the Swilly's chairman, was an old Northern Counties man and there they turned for the loan. The 26 year old, ex-B&LR saloon was chosen for the task. The BNCR, within weeks of being taken over by the Midland, rose nobly to refurbishing the elderly carriage. It went through the shops and was completely refurnished in drawing-room style by a Belfast warehouse, the total cost being around £300. After its duty was done, it was returned to the MR(NCC). At their meeting on 19 August 1903, the committee gave some thought to the carriage "specially upholstered and renovated at the request of the LLSR". Dismantling of its grandeur was being postponed until it was decided whether or not to retain it as it stood. If it was to be retained, it was felt that the Swilly should pay part of the cost. By the following month its retention as decided upon, and the Swilly were asked to pay half the cost. Had it survived, it would have been made a star exhibit in the Belfast Transport Museum, but the only glimpse we can now have of its magnificence is a photograph taken beside the water tank at Pennyburn yard in Derry, with two worthies grasping the white-painted veranda rails and gazing anxiously towards Buncrana.

A pamphlet on *Narrow gauge Railways, Ireland* by William Lewis in 1882 depicts both a six-wheel composite and a bogie brake composite of the B&LR, but neither figure is completely consistent with later NCC information. The six-wheeler is given a length of 33ft, whereas 29ft 6in is correct. It has four third-class compartments, whereas three were listed by the NCC. The bogie brake composite is shown with lateral semi-elliptic springs to each axle, while a detail sketch of the bogie has the proper transverse springs. Guard's compartments and ducket are at one end, and the five passenger compartments are arranged 33133. Wheel centres are spaced at 5ft, and while no overall length is marked, this may be calculated as about 32½ft. Evidence suggests that it may be the shortest of the three bogie brake composites (BNCR No 321) more or less in its original state.

All B&LR coaching was flat sided. Originally the roofs

of six-wheel and bogie vehicles were of the clerestory type, but later photographs show them replaced by elliptical roofs. No detailed information is known about their livery, but it seems from photographs to have been dark brown, without elaborate lining. Waist-level mouldings border the full legend 'FIRST CLASS' etc on compartment doors and a roundel appears twice on each side, below the waist line.

The apparently random numbering adopted by the BNCR resulted from the vehicles being numbered serially as they went through the carriage and wagon shops for repair and repainting. The numbers were unrelated to building dates.

Withdrawals of the six-wheeled and bogie vehicles took place over a seven year period, as dictated by the end of passenger workings:

1927:	Nos 301 and 305
1928:	No 318
1929:	No 302
1930:	No 322
1931:	none
1932:	Nos 303 and 315
1933:	none
1934:	Nos 304, 314 and 321

Most of the little four-wheel thirds were withdrawn earlier than their larger brethren, and all were converted back to covered wagons:

1919: Nos 310 and 311. The wagons were renumbered 5310 and 5311 in December 1934, and were withdrawn in 1954.

1926: No 308. This wagon was renumbered 5308 in December 1934 and was withdrawn in 1954.

1929: Nos 309 and 313. The wagons were renumbered 5309 and 5313 in December 1934 and were withdrawn in 1954.

Most numerous among the B&LR goods stock were open wagons, their total became 190 by the end of 1878, and thereafter remained constant. They handled the heavy coal traffic out of Larne. 'Mineral wagons' were not listed separately until after the line was linked with that of the Cushendall in 1880, at the end of that year 50 are listed in the half-yearly return and these include 20 iron hopper wagons mentioned in the minute of 6 July as "well in hand", and on 17 September as "received from the Bristol Wagon Co but wheels had not been turned up and brakes do not fit". The remainder were 30 end-tip wagons ordered in October from Bristol at £41 each. Fifty more end-tip wagons were ordered in September 1882, bringing the mineral wagon total to 100 vehicles. Some conversion of hoppers to end-tippers was discussed at the board meeting on 12 October 1887, the object being to make more wagons available for traffic.

The covered wagon stock of 20 at the end of 1878

A posed shot of a Cushendall line train at Ballymena in the 1890s with 0-4-2ST No 60. This shows the original curved roof profile of the carriages. Note the signal cabin, later replaced.

Ian Stewart collection

remained static for only two years, then, as mentioned, five were converted to third class carriages and one to a brake van, so reducing the total to 14. During 1883, the total became 13 when another brake van was built. Small increases in the 1882–7 total of 100 mineral wagons came in 1888 and in 1889, the stock becoming 101 and 102,

though without mention in the minute book of the facts behind the change.

The varying totals of coaching and goods stock are given in the accompanying table, abstracted from the company's half-yearly reports:

Date	Coaching Stock			Goods Stock						
	Saloon	3rd	Composite	Covered Wagon	Open Wagon	Timber Trucks	Cattle Trucks	B/Vans	Ballast Wagons	Mineral Wagons
12/77	1	–	2	10	60	10	7	3	–	
12/78	1	–	2	20	190	10	17	3	–	
6/79	1	–	4	20	190	10	17	3	–	
12/79	1	–	9	20	190	10	17	3	–	
6/80	1	–	9	20	190	10	17	3	12	
12/80	1	–	9	20	190	10	17	3	12	50
12/81	1	3	9	17	190	10	17	3	12	50
12/82	1	5	9	14	190	10	17	4	12	100
6/83	1	5	9	14	190	10	17	4	12	100
12/83	1	5	9	13	190	10	17	5	12	100
12/87	1	5	9	13	190	10	17	5	12	100
6/88	1	5	9	13	190	10	17	5	12	100
6/89	1	5	9	13	190	10	17	5	12	100

Cushendall stock

The first Board of Trade return of the Cushendall's rolling stock is for 1875 and comprised 145 "Wagons of all kinds used for the conveyance of Live Stock, Minerals, or General Merchandise", together with two of "Any other Carriages or Waggons used on the Railway not included in

the preceding columns". Inevitably, these statistics present a picture which lacks detail, for not only were open and covered cattle wagons not separated, but both narrow and broad gauge vehicles were included in the statutory totals.

The Board of Trade returns for rolling stock may be summarised:

	1875	1876	1877	1878-9	1880–4
Locomotives	3	3	3	3	3
Carriages used for the conveyance of passengers only	–	–	1	1	1
Other vehicles attached to passenger trains	–	–	–	–	–
Wagons of all kinds, etc	145	175	210	209	241
Any other carriages or wagons &c not included in the preceding columns	2	2	2	2	2

In the minute books of the company the first reference to rolling stock occurs on 22 September 1873, when the directors decided to obtain sample narrow gauge wagons, "iron-ore trucks holding four tons" from the Midland Wagon Co and from the Railway Carriage Co of Oldbury. A sample arrived from Oldbury before the board meeting

on 31 December 1873 and was offered at £54 each for 60, or at ten guineas a year over seven years. Although the Midland sample had not arrived by the end of the year, it must have come soon afterwards, for on 11 March 1874 the minutes refer to an agreement having been sealed with the Midland Wagon Co for "hire and purchase of 20 narrow gauge tip wagons and ten broad gauge platform wagons'. No further dealings with Oldbury are mentioned.

Twenty more eight-ton broad gauge wagons with steel wheels were ordered from the Midland Company in April 1875, and at the same time 20 sets of steel wheels and axles for narrow gauge trucks were obtained, "these being necessary to replace the cast-iron wheels on the first trucks delivered, which were found unfit for the work." In August, the Midland Wagon Co offered £4 per ton, delivered in Birmingham for the cast iron wheels, but the company were not satisfied with that offer and the secretary was told to sell them in Belfast and so avoid shipping costs.

Further purchases from the Midland Wagon Company were negotiated in March and June 1877. The first was for ten eight-ton broad gauge wagons at £66, and of narrow gauge stock 17 'hoppered' wagons at £45, three covered wagons 13ft 6in long and 9ft high at £60, and two open goods wagons at £40 – delivery to be in mid-May. The June order was for ten broad gauge wagons and 22 narrow gauge wagons, the latter comprising three covered, 17 hopper and two open.

According to the minutes, the final wagon order was placed with the Railway Carriage in Co in January 1880, and was for 32 'hopper trucks' at £48 10s, presumably narrow gauge.

From the minute books, there is thus evidence of the purchase of 50 broad gauge wagons, all of which would have been open and used for the movement of ore between Ballymena and Belfast. Of narrow gauge stock, 98 are mentioned. The combined total of 148 falls short of the final Board of Trade total by no less than 93 vehicles, though 60 may be accounted for if the Oldbury offer of December 1873 was taken up. The two 'other' vehicles which appear in the Board of Trade totals were brake vans, one of which became No 323 of BCNR stock.

Apart from wagons, the government returns include from 1877 one "Carriage used for the conveyance of passengers only", evidence that the company allowed itself the unjustified luxury of a directors' saloon. This was a bogie vehicle, peculiar in being only 22ft 6in long. It was 6ft 3in wide, and in BNCR days had one compartment for 22 passengers. For a time, the BNCR numbered their Cushendall carriages in a separate series, and assigned No 1 to the saloon, though it later became No 312 and was demoted to third class. It survived until 1934. The history of

its purchase began in May 1874, when at the board meeting a letter was read from the Railway Carriage Company with a sketch for a first class carriage but consideration was left for a rolling-stock committee. However the order was given to the Midland Wagon Co, for at the board meeting on 19 May 1876 it was minuted that "the first class carriage sent from Midland Wagon Co is considered satisfactory". The only subsequent mention was on 28 November 1876 when a complaint was made of the wheels "as not being fit for it".

Northern Counties stock

Because of heavy damage to the station and offices at York Road, Belfast, in the air raids of 1941, no complete record survives of the totals and rebuilding dates of the carriage and wagon stock.

The acquisition of the Cushendall line by the BNCR was followed by the production at Belfast of carriages suited to the dominantly tourist traffic of the line. Unlike the compartment coaching stock of the Ballymena and Larne and Ballycastle Railways, the new Cushendall stock had veranda ends. Two were made for the 1886 opening and eight more added over the next 13 years as tourist traffic developed. For a few years they were numbered in a separate Cushendall series, in which pride of place was given to No 1, the ex-BC&RBR directors' saloon. Then about 1889–90, as they came to the shops for repainting, the BNCR incorporated them into a general narrow gauge series whose numbers eventually ran from 301 to 333.

The Cushendall coaches were originally all eight-wheeled, with a rather peculiar semi-rigid suspension recently described by Mr DG Coakham:

> Its most peculiar feature lay in the suspension as the two four-wheeled trucks were not conventional bogies, having neither bolsters nor pivots . . . The axleboxes did not have any side-play in the trucks, which were merely two plates 8 x ½in connected laterally by one 5 by ½in member, and the only flexibility achieved was through a system of links between the leaf springs and brackets rigidly fixed to the main frames of the coach. Hornplates, set wide apart to allow for axlebox movement must have been very restricted and a lot would have depended on the elasticity of the truck frame.

The general arrangement of these was of a flat-sided saloon, partitioned into two unequal parts and with a communicating door. Longitudinal seats were of slatted wood. There were ten windows along each side, three belonging to the smaller compartment. Early photographs show steeply curved roofs but rebuilding (believed to be in 1909 for Nos 306 and 307) reduced the roof curvature and replaced panelled sides with vertical matchboarding. One early photograph (page 61) shows two carriages in a train with clerestory roofs and 16 side windows, but it is not known which of the ten vehicles these were.

The ten vehicles, officially termed 'tramcars', were:

Built	BNCR No	Compts		Seats		Length	Width	Remarks	Withdrawn
		1st	3rd	1st	3rd				
1886	306	–	2	–	40	36' 9"	6' 3"	No 2 Cushendall	1954
1886	307	–	2	–	40	36' 9"	6' 3"	No 3 Cushendall	1932
1889	319	–	2	–	40	36' 9"	6' 3"	No 4 Cushendall	1932
1889	320	–	2	–	40	36' 9"	6' 3"	No 5 Cushendall	1929
1891	316	–	2	–	40	36' 9"	6' 3"		1934
1891	317	–	2	–	40	36' 9"	6' 3"		1930
1898	329	1	1	12	32	40' 0"	6' 3"		1932
1898	330	1	1	12	32	40' 0"	6' 3"		1932
1898	331	–	2	–	44	40' 0"	6' 3"		1929
1898	332	–	2	–	44	40' 0"	6' 3"		1929

Cushendal coach No 5, photographed before renumbering into BNCR stock as No 320.   Author's collection

Steel channel solebars, 6 x 2¾in, ran the length of the saloon body to form the main frame, while the end platforms were supported on cantilever frames. In the case of the 1886 tramcars, the wheelbase of the trucks was 3ft 9in, and the wheel diameter 2ft. The total wheelbase was 27ft 9½in. The saloon body measured 31ft 10½in. Similar dimensions are believed to have applied to the 1889 and 1891 vehicles, but those built in 1898 were about 3ft longer.

Veranda ends were covered by the roof, the ends of which were supported on ¾in diameter pillars which carried metal lattice panels forming end and side gates. Pivoted fall plates allowed a passage between the vehicles. Lighting was by oil gas, stored in a cylinder below the frame. To judge by early photographs which show short stove pipes projecting through the roof, heating was by solid fuel.

A brake van, No 333 with a length of 33ft, was built in 1898, and had veranda ends to match the other tramcars.

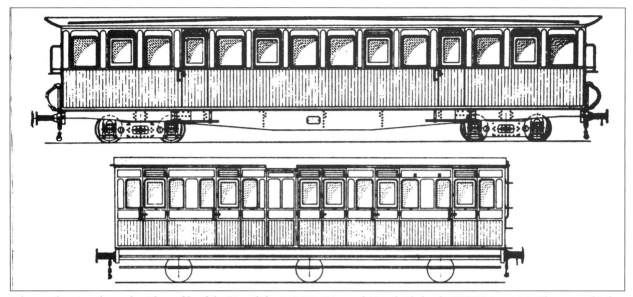

The top drawing shows the side profile of the 'Doagh bogies', Nos 327 and 328, built by the BNCR in 1895. They were third class vehicles seating 40 in two compartments. In 1937 they were withdrawn and converted to caravan coaches. The lower illustration shows ex-B&LR six-wheel brake composite No 315.   DG Coakham

Its flat panelled sides carried two pairs of windows and were without side duckets.

In addition to these tramcars, two bogie tramcars were built in 1895, with pressed steel underframes. These were known as the 'Doagh Bogies' and were converted to caravan coaches Nos 16 and 21 in 1937 and 1938:

BNCR No	Compts 3rd	Seats	Length	Width	W'drawn	Converted
327	2	42	40' 0"	6' 2"	1937	CC 16
328	2	42	40' 0"	6' 2"	1937	CC 21

To handle cross-channel mails to Larne Harbour, the BNCR built a brake parcel post van in 1892. This was No 324, a bogie vehicle 27ft 6in x 6ft 8in, with a conspicuous central ducket (photo page 109). It was withdrawn in 1929 and later used as a hut at Ballymoney.

No more coaching stock was produced until 1928. In that year the LMS(NCC) built five new narrow gauge bogie carriages, four of them of new construction while the fifth was based on the underframe of ex-B&LR Composite No 318. In its new form the rebuild held 52 third class passengers. It was used on the Ballycastle until that was closed in 1950, and in 1952 was sold to the County Donegal Railways Joint Committee, where it became No 58 and was used until that line closed at the end of 1959.

The four new coaches built in 1928 were primarily for the Ballymena–Larne boat trains, and were numbered 350–353. They departed from tradition in being 8ft in width and in having corridor connections and lavatory accommodation. In comfort, they were far in advance of anything that had run on an Irish narrow gauge railway but they were built at a time when passenger usage of the B&LR section was declining. Since the 1933 strike ended passenger workings over the section, the new coaches had only five years service on the Larne boat trains. They were then transferred to the Ballycastle section of the LMS(NCC), to replace some old BNCR tramcars that were there. Details of the 1928 corridor stock are as follows:

No	Type	Length	Compts 1st	3rd	Seats 1st	3rd
350	Compo	50' 0"	2	2	12	31
351	Compo	50' 0"	2	2	12	31
352	Bk/3rd	50' 0"	–	2	–	24
353	Bk/Compo	50' 0"	2	2	12	31

Nos 350 and 351 were identical, with end vestibules off which were lavatories. Smoking and non-smoking compartments were available in each class, and a central corridor ran the length of the vehicle.

No 352 was built as a brake/third, but was altered in

Details of the dimensions of the compartments are given on pages 110–113 of The Ballycastle Railway, Second Edition *published in 2006.*

Above: A posed photo in the Cushendal yard, Ballymena, showing ex-BR 4-4-2T No 113 with the new 'Boat Train' set in 1928. From the front, the carriages are Nos 350, 352 and 353.

Real Photographs Ltd

Left: At Larne Harbour on 11 July 1937, the crew of 2-4-2T No 102 keep a wary eye on the photographer. As passenger services to Ballymena had ceased in 1933, coach 353 must have been on a special.

Real Photographs Ltd

1936 to a third. No 353 was a unique vehicle and, owing to the size of the guard's compartment, the single end vestibule was very small.

Goods stock taken over from the Cushendall and B&LR companies comprised almost 600 vehicles, of which at least 50 were the Cushendall's broad gauge ore wagons. They were listed and their values estimated by the BNCR as follows:

Ex-BC&RBR

	Est value
3 covered wagons	£236 19s 0d
239 open wagons	£9,155 9s 4d
2 brake vans	£105 0s 0d

Ex-B&LR

30 covered and cattle wagons	£1,080 0s 0d
293 open wagons	£7,909 8s 7d
10 timber trucks	£270 0s 0d
5 brake vans	£180 0s 0d
12 ballast wagons	£304 0s 0d

For some unexplained reason, the total of B&LR open wagons comes to three more than the combined totals of open and mineral wagons which were given in the Board of Trade returns.

An unidentified four-wheel brake at Larne in 1931.

Real Photographs Ltd

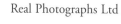

Class 13 hopper wagon No 4009 at Larne in 1936.

L&GRP

Open wagon No 4299, six ton van No 4110 and brake van No 4255 at Larne in 1936.

L&GRP

Six-ton end-tipping open wagon No 4293 at Larne in 1931.

L&GRP

High-sided open wagon No 4488 at Ballymoney on 21 November 1950.

DG Coakham

Piped goods van No 5310, in red oxide livery, at Ballymoney on 21 November 1950.

DG Coakham

Under the NCC these wagons, and new acquisitions built since take-over, were placed for engineering purposes into 25 classes. These were:

End-tip wagons (various)	Classes 1–9
8-ton open wagons	Class 10
Timber truck	Class 11
4-ton hopper	Class 12
8-ton hopper	Class 13
6-ton ballast wagon	Class 14

8-ton ballast wagon	Class 15
Covered wagons (6 ton)	Classes 16–18
Cattle wagon (short)	Class 19
Cattle wagon (6 ton)	Classes 20 & 21
Brake van (ex-B&LR)	Class 22
Brake vans	Classes 23 & 24
Covered wagons	Class 25

The main dimensions of these were as follows:

Class	Length over headstocks	Overall height	Overall width	Wheelbase	Average tare weight	Capacity cubic
1	12' 6"	3' 9¼"	6' 6"	7' 0"	2.8	100
2	12' 6"	4' 5¼"	6' 6'	7' 0"	2.10	137
3	11' 4"	5' 3¼"	5' 10½"	5' 4"	2.8	143
4	11' 4"	5' 3¼"	5' 10½"	5' 4"	2.8	143
5	11' 4"	5' 3¼"	6' 6"	5' 4"	2.8	158
6	12' 6"	5' 1¼"	6' 10"	7' 0"	2.12	168
7	12' 6"	5' 1¼"	6' 10"	7' 0"	2.13	187
8	c12' 5"	5' 8¼"	6' 10"	7' 0"	3.2	231
9	14' 0"	6' 2"	7' 0"	8' 0"	3.7	280
10	14' 0"	5' 11¾"	7' 0"	8' 0"	3.7	280
11	12' 6"	3' 9¼"	6' 6"	7' 0"	2.11	–
12	9' 0"	5' 9"	5' 9"	5' 3½"	2.7½	76
13	9' 8"	6' 8¾"	5' 9"	6' 2"	2.19	143
14	12' 6"	3' 11¼"	6' 6"	7' 0"	2.7	99
15	14' 0"	5' 1¾"	7' 0"	8' 0"	3.7	205
16	14' 0"	9' 0¼"	6' 6"	8' 0"	3.14	466
17	14' 5"	8' 8½"	6' 8"	8' 0"	3.11	484
18	14' 5"	9' 0¼"	6' 8"	8' 0"	3.16	522
19	12' 6"	8' 4¼"	6' 6"	7' 0"	3.11	245
20	14' 0"	8' 4¼"	6' 6"	8' 0"	3.13	298
21	14' 0"	9' 6¾"	7' 0"	8' 0"	3.15	535
22	16' 6"	9' 5"	6' 7¾"	7' 0"	–	322
23	16' 6"	9' 3¾"	8' 4"	9' 0"	5.4	539
24	14' 6"	8' 9"	6' 7½"	8' 0"	5.3	483

Differences between the nine classes of end-tip wagons reflected minor original variations in the specifications, but details of their origin appear to have been lost.

At the closure of the Larne–Ballyclare section, the surviving rolling-stock consisted of 62 open wagons of various types and one brake van. The latter was No 4251 of Class 24.

The wagons were numbered as follows:

End-tip (6 ton) (Total 32)   Nos 4210/60/68/83/93, 4304/14/25/30/31/33/35/66/78/80/97, 4408/12/20/25/28/ 43/50/56/57/71/96, 4515/25/42/43/51

End-tip (8 ton) (Total 2)   Nos 4211 & 4390

Centre-door (6 ton) (Total 8)   Nos 4285, 4319/34/68/82, 4483, 4553/55

Centre-door (8 ton) (Total 19)   Nos 4204/05/26/40/41/56/ 62/63/95, 4358/88/99, 4402/09/72/89, 4501/33/38

Ballast wagon (8 ton) (Total 1)   No 4200 (Class 15)

Under the MR(NCC), wagons were painted grey with the initials of the owning company on the centre door; 'MR' above in large plain block or shaded block capitals, and 'NCC' below in smaller capitals. Under the London, Midland and Scottish (NCC) the legend was either 'LMS' in large plain block capitals, or 'LMS NCC' with the second half in smaller letters. In later days, 'LMS NCC' was sometimes relegated to the lower left corner of the wagon side, in smaller letters, or even omitted altogether. In MR days, all the wagons were given heavy rectangular cast-iron number plates of horizontal format with a raised edge and radiused corners. Their size was about 12 x 6in, and on them the raised letters 'MR.NCC' were above the number, both letters and digits being boldly serified. These number plates were usually situated in the lower left corner of each side.

No information is known to exist of the complete MR(NCC) stock, nor of the individual scrapping dates.

Trans-shipment trucks

To move locomotives and carriages to and from the Belfast workshops, three trans-shipment vehicles were built to run on the broad gauge. The first was made to convey Cushendall carriages and although its nominal load was only 12 tons, photographs show it to have been used to carry locomotives. The LMS(NCC) built two more: a six-wheeler with a wheelbase of 11ft + 11ft, used solely for locomotives, and a long vehicle with two bogies set at 44ft centres, used for carriages (opposite).

Built	No	Reno	Type	Load	Tare	Length	Haulage
1889	3093	921	8-wheel	12 tons	7t 13c		General haulage
1926	3045	–	6-wheel	35 tons	6t 15c	35' 6"	Locomotive haulage
1930	3095	–	Bogie	20 tons		54' 4"	Carriage haulage

Ex-BR 4-4-2T No 113 climbing the Inver bank at Larne with a coal train for Ballymena. The train comprises a mixture of three and four plank open wagons.

Photomatic

Mobile hand crane No 4124 at Ballymoney on 21 November 1950.
DG Coakham

Cattle truck No 5507 at Ballymoney on 21 November 1950.
DG Coakham

Four-wheel grey brake van No 4251 with a coal train for Ballyclare on the Inver bank in 1946. The locomotive, No 113, had gone forward to Kilwaughter siding to drop off some wagons. Leaning from the window is well-known local enthusiast, the late Reg Ludgate.

DG Coakham

Bogie transporter wagon No 3095 at Ballymena when new, on 9 August 1930. It was built for moving bogie carriages. This view shows Ballymena shed in the background and the special track for loading/unloading narrow gauge stock.

HC Casserley

Chapter 10

Train services and operating methods

The Ballymena and Larne line

The B&LR started their services on 24 August 1878 with three mixed trains in each direction on the main line on weekdays. These left Larne Harbour at 8.10am, 1.45pm and 6pm, and Ballymena Harryville at 7.45am, 1.20pm and 5.30pm. The runs either way were timed at 75 minutes, with stops at Kells, Ballyclare Junction and Larne. No other stations were open yet. At the Junction, connections ran to and from Ballyclare. On Sundays, passenger trains left Larne Harbour at 8.30am and 5.30pm, each timed at 70 minutes to Harryville, while return trips were made at 10am and 7pm. On weekdays, additional trains ran between Larne Harbour and Larne, and between Larne and Millbrook Bank siding and the Junction when required.

Ten years later, four mixed trains ran each way on the main line on weekdays, crossing at Ballyboley Junction, where the Doagh branch connection came out to connect, at 8.25am, 10.50am, 2.30pm and 6.40pm. The journey times varied from 75 minutes to as much as 120 minutes, depending on the amount of shunting. On Saturdays, there was a passenger train which left Ballymena at 3.50pm, went only as far as Kells, and was back in Ballymena by 4.17pm. The Sunday service was much the same as in the opening year, with minor differences in times.

By 1890, the service had reached maturity. First on the move was the 6.15am Larne–Doagh, which took 65 minutes with stops at Kilwaughter, the Junction, Ballynure, Ballyclare and the paper mill siding. The engine then took out the 7.25am Doagh–Ballyboley train, which was met at the junction by the 7.20am Larne–

Ballymena, along with the 6.40am Ballymena–Larne. The two main-line trains went on their way, while the Doagh connection returned to its terminus at 8.25am. The two

FROM	To Ballymena.		To Larne.		To Ballyclare.	
	1st cl.	3rd cl.	1st cl.	3rd cl.	1st cl.	3rd cl.
Larne Harbour	3s 0d	1s 9d	–	—	1s 8d	0s 11d
Larne	2s 10d	1s 8d	—	—	1s 6d	0s 10d
† Kilwaughter	2s 8d	1s 6d	0s 9d	0s 5d	1s 2d	0s 8d
Headwood ..	2s 3d	1s 4d	1s 0d	0s 7d	1s 0d	0s 7d
Ballyclare Jun.	2s 1d	1s 3d	1s 0d	0s 7d	—	—
Ballynure ..	2s 6d	1s 5d	1s 2d	0s 8d	—	—
Ballyclare ..	2s 8d	1s 6d	1s 6d	0s 10d	—	—
Ballynashee ..	1s 9d	1s 0d	1s 6d	0s 10d	0s 10d	0s 6d
† Collin ..	1s 6d	0s 10d	1s 10d	1s 1d	1s 6d	0s 10d
Moorfields ..	—	—	2s 1d	1s 3d	1s 9d	1s 0d
Kells ..	—	—	2s 8d	1s 6d	2s 1d	1s 3d
Ballymena ..	—	—	2s 10d	1s 8d	2s 8d	1s 6d

MARKET TICKETS DAILY BY ALL ORDINARY TRAINS, AT REDUCED FARES, AVAILABLE FOR RETURN SAME DAY.

† For issue from Kilwaughter and Collin, see Advertisement, "Extra Stops on Market Days" on other side.

Charges for market tickets, from the B&LR 1883 pocket timetable.

DOWN. WEEK-DAYS. SUNDAYS

Miles from Larne Harbour		STATIONS. All Trains 1st and 3rd Class.	1	2 Boat Express	3 Mixed	4 mxd		Saturdays only.	Sundays 1	Sundays 2	Sundays 3
			a.m	noon	p.m.	p.m.		p.m.	a.m.	p.m.	p.m.
		Larne Harbour ... dep.	8 0	12 0	1 45	6 0	..	8 15	...	5 30	7 30
1		Larne... ... ... ,,	8 5	12 5	1 50	6 5	..	8 20	8 15	5 35	7 35
6¼		Headwood(Flag station) ,,	8 18	..	..	6 18	..	8 33	8 28	5 48	..
7¾		Ballyclare Junc. ,,	8 28	12 25	2 30	6 30	..	8 40	8 35	5 55	7 55
9½	BRANCH.	Ballynu·e ... ... arr.	8 33	12 30	2 40	6 35	..	8 45	8 40	6 0	8 0
11¼	BRANCH.	Ballyclare ... ... ,,	8 40	12 35	2 50	6 45	..	8 50	8 47	6 7	8 7
—	BRANCH.	Ballyclare .. .. dep.	8 10	12 10	2 15	6 15	..	..	8 20	5 4	7 40
—	BRANCH.	Ballynure ... ... ,,	8 15	12 15	2 20	6 20	..	..	8 25	5 45	7 45
12		Ballynashee.. .. ,,	8 40	12 37	2 45	6 45	..	..	8 47	6 7	8 10
17½		Moorfields ... ... ,,	8 53	12 48	3 0	7 0	..	..	9 0	6 20	8 25
20½		Kells ... . ,,	9 3	12 55	3 15	7 10	..	..	9 10	6 30	8 33
24¾		Ballymena ... ... arr.	9 15	1 5	3 30	7 25	..	..	9 22	6 42	8 45
..	BNCR	Ballymena .. .. dep	9 27	..	5 19	...	..	..	..	8 15	..
..	BNCR	Belfast ... ... arr.	10 25	..	6 45	...	..	..	..	9 45	..
..	BNCR	Ballymena .. ... dep.	11 15	1 21	4 55	...	..	..	..	...	..
..	BNCR	Derry .. .. arr.	1 45	3 55	7 30	..	..	..	..	...	..

UP. WEEK-DAYS. SUNDAYS

Miles from Ballymena.		STATIONS	1	2 Mixed	3	4 Mixed	D mixed	Sundays 1	Sundays 2	Sundays 3
			a.m.	a.m.	p m.	p.m.	a m.	a.m.	p.m.	p.m.
..	BNCR	Derry... ... .. dep.	7 0	10 30	Boat Express	2 45	See foot note.	..	..	2 30
..	BNCR	Ballymena ... ... arr.	9 22	1 0		5 12		..	..	5 14
..	BNCR	Belfast .. ... dep.	6 10	12 0		3 30		6 10	..	5 0
..	BNCR	Ballymena .. ... arr.	7 25	1 16		4 50		7 30	..	6 33
				p m.						
...		Ballymena ... ... dep.	9 40	1 30	3 35	5 35	7 0	9 45	2 45	7 5
4½		Kells ... ... ,,	9 52	1 45	3 45	5 50	7 15	9 57	2 57	7 17
7½		Moorfields ... ... ,,	10 0	...	3 53	6 0	7 23	10 5	3 5	7 25
12¾		B.llynashee .. .. ,,	10 15	2 15	4 7	6 15	8 0	10 20	3 20	7 40
18¾	BRANCH.	Ballynure ... ... arr.	10 35	2 40	4 25	6 35	8 30	10 37	3 37	8 0
20¾	BRANCH.	Ballyclare ... ... ,,	10 45	2 50	4 35	6 45	8 40	10 45	3 45	8 7
	BRANCH.	Ballyclare .. .. dep	10 10	2 15	4 5	6 15	8 10	10 20	3 20	7 40
	BRANCH.	Ballynure ... .. ,,	10 15	2 20	4 10	6 20	8 15	10 25	3 25	7 45
17		Ballyclare Junc.	10 30	2 35	4 20	6 40	8 27	10 32	3 32	7 55
18½		Headwood (Flag station)..	10 33	2 38	..	6 43	8 30	10 35	..	7 58
23¾		Larne...	10 50	3 0	4 40	7 10	9 0	10 55	3 55	8 15
24¾		Larne Harbour ... arr	10 55	3 5	4 45	7 15	9 5	11 0	4 0	..

D 7.0 a.m. runs on Wednesdays, Second Thursday each month, & Larne Half-yearly Fairs only

B&LR public timetable for the summer of 1883.

Left: Class Q 0-6-0T No 106 would appear to be arriving at Ballymena from Parkmore in this picture. However, the locomotive and stock suggest it is more lokely to be a Ballymena train moving up to the platform to pick up its passengers.

L&GRP

Right: An interesting view of Ballymena shed in 1936. Narrow gauge engines used the two roads on the left side of the shed and the broad gauge the other two. The Cushendall line runs to the left of the shed, with a mixed gauge yard on the left.

L&GRP

main-line trains returned from Larne Harbour at 10am and from Ballymena at 9.35am, crossing again around 10.40am at Ballyboley where the 10am ex-Doagh had been sitting since 10.25am.

These morning workings of 1890 were separated from afternoon runs by a break, during which a path was available for what the time-table termed 'a special goods'. This ran express from Doagh at 11.30am, was in Larne at 12.30pm and returned to Doagh at 12.50pm. The afternoon peace of Ballyboley was again disturbed around half past two by the arrival of the 2pm from Doagh, the 2pm from Larne and the 1.25pm from Ballymena. By 2.37, all three had gone their ways rejoicing. A special goods working to Doagh, Thursday excepted, slipped out of Larne at 4.45pm and was in Doagh an hour later.

Meanwhile, Ballymena saw the departure of a 5.35pm mixed, which crossed with the 6pm mixed ex-Larne at the junction, where the branch train had been simmering since 6.30pm. The main-line workings were into Larne at 7.10pm, and into Ballymena at 7.40pm. The connecting 6.40pm to Doagh arrived there at 7.05pm, after which that station closed for the day. On Thursdays only, Larne dispatched a goods train up the main line at 8.10pm, calling only at the junction on its way to Harryville where it stopped at 9.45pm. In the reverse direction on Thursdays was the 8pm passenger train, which crossed with the Thursday evening goods at Ballyboley and was into Larne at 9.10pm, a working which, though listed as an express,

Advertisement from the B&LR 1883 pocket timetable.

would obligingly stop anywhere to set down. The Saturday afternoon Ballymena–Kells and return was still shown. Shunting at the paper mill siding and at Ballyclare yard was done by the branch engine.

Sunday workings lacked the recurring frenzy at Ballyboley junction. In the 1890s under the BNCR, the 7.35am ex-Larne got unimpeded to Ballymena by 8.50am and after ten minutes returned to Larne. Meanwhile, the 8.30am Larne–Doagh train had ended its run at 9.08am, had turned, and was back at the junction to connect with the 9am ex-Ballymena. The branch train then worked back to Doagh, whereupon the engine did a smart run around and was timed to be away at 10.15am. It reached Ballyboley at 10.35am, where the engine again ran around and took its train to Ballymena, reaching that town at 11.28am. Peace then reigned for three and a half hours.

Next on the move was the 3pm from Ballymena, into Larne at 4.30pm. After a pause there, it returned to the junction and ended its run at Doagh at 5.53pm. The last main-line workings of the Sunday were the 6.30pm from the Harbour, which reached Ballymena at 7.50pm, leaving again at 8.15pm to be back into Larne by 9.30pm. Last

movements were a train from Ballyboley at 9.10pm to Doagh and its return working at 9.30pm to Larne town, thus ending a remarkably heavy day's working in spite of the protests of Sabbatarians.

With small changes, this general pattern continued into the twentieth century and into MR(NCC) days, summer and winter services being little different. In 1912, the 6.30am mixed from Ballymena led off the day, meeting the 6.50am from Larne at Ballyboley at 7.15am. The latter train was on its leisurely way from Moorfields to Kells when Larne Harbour sent off the Mail on its tail at 7.55am, with passengers off the Scottish boat. The mail train slipped its mail van at the town station and went on post-haste up the Inver bank, to pause only at Kells before getting to Ballymena at 8.55am.

On Saturdays, the Mail was followed by the 8am Doagh–Ballyboley–Ballymena passenger train, while on other weekdays this train ran mixed to Larne town, where it crossed with a Doagh-bound goods coming up from the Harbour station. Two main-line trains in mid-morning were the 10.10am passenger from Ballymena and the 10.20am mixed from Larne. They crossed at Ballyboley around 11am. On its way to Larne goods, the 10.10am train passed at Kells the

Week-Day Excursions
TO
GLENARM & CARNLOUGH

Via Larne and Coast Road,

By 9-40 a.m. Train, due at Larne at 10-50, thence per Mr. Henry M'Neill's Coast Conveyance; returning from Carnlough and Glenarm in connection with 6-0 p.m. Train.

FROM

BALLYMENA, KELLS, & MOORFIELDS

	1st Class	3rd Class
To GLENARM AND BACK,	3/3	2/6
To CARNLOUGH AND BACK	3/9	3/-

Tickets for the Coast Conveyance are sold at the B. & L. R. Co.'s Booking Office. Harryville Terminus, Kells and Moorfields Stations.

The above Fares include Rail and Conveyance.

Advertisement from the B&LR 1883 pocket timetable.

9.15am Harryville–Larne goods, which had been shunted. The goods then left Kells as soon as the section was clear, and at Ballynashee crossed with the 10.20am from Larne.

Before the next mixed trains ran along the main line, a special goods left Doagh on some days at 11.30am for Larne Harbour. It crossed another special Doagh goods at Larne town, which had left the Harbour at 12.15pm and was due in Doagh at 1.55pm. There then set out from Larne Harbour, at 1.30pm, a pick-up goods, which tarried from 2.30 until 3.30pm at Ballyboley and eventually reached Harryville at 4.50pm. At the junction, this slow goods met the 2.15pm mixed from Ballymena and allowed to 2.40pm passenger from the Harbour to Ballymena to pass, while, to make a fourth as it were, the branch connection came out from Doagh. While the 1.30pm goods was spending its time at Ballyboley on Saturdays, a cattle train came over the hill from Ballymena, crossed with the goods and went on down to Larne and Larne Harbour, where the beasts were shipped.

A path was arranged for two special goods workings in mid-afternoon: these were the 4pm from Doagh, into the Harbour at 5.35pm, and the 4pm from the Harbour, due in Doagh at 5.40pm.

To connect with the departure of the evening steamer to Stranraer, the 5.50pm mail train from Ballymena thundered along on its 60 minute run to the Harbour, checking speed only to exchange staff or tablet. The 6.15pm mixed followed it, stopping everywhere and due in Larne at 7.50pm. At Ballyboley, it crossed with the last

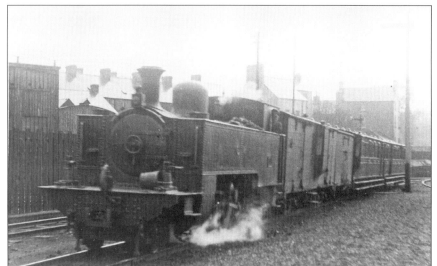

Left: The 5.45pm Ballymena to Larne Harbour boat train arrives at the Harbour behind 2-4-2T No 101 on 22 May 1924. The leading vehicle is the parcel post van.

Ken Nunn collection, LCGB

Opposite: An unidentified 2-4-2T, on a Larne Harbour to Ballymena mixed train, takes water at Ballyboley Junction in the late 1920s or early 1930s.

CP Friel collection

working out of Larne town, the 6.55pm, which reached Ballymena at 8.25pm. Banking assistance was provided, if needed, for the 12.15pm and 1.30pm trains.

Such was the service provided throughout the year before the First World War. There were no Sunday trains in winter, but summer Sundays saw quite an intensive service. Larne sent out a Ballymena train at 7.35am; it met a Doagh connection at Ballyboley, and went on to terminate at Ballymena at 8.47am. The engine ran around and took its train back towards the coast at 9.15am, taking 83 minutes for the journey. A return trip from Larne at 10.55am was into Ballymena at 12.15pm. Sunday lunches then dictated a break in the service, after which the 2.30pm departure from Ballymena took many a family down for a breath of sea air. The return train from Larne Harbour to Ballymena left at 6.30pm, a load of Doagh folk having been taken home an hour earlier. A return to Larne from Doagh was made at 6.35pm. Last train on the main line was the 8.30pm from Ballymena which, at Ballyboley Junction, met a late evening train to Doagh, which had left the Harbour station at 9pm.

Summer trains on Sundays dropped out during the First World War, and the timetable of summer 1918 looks decidedly bleak. On weekdays then, there were only two trains in each direction over from Ballymena in the morning, and the 5.40pm mixed from the Harbour and the 5.15pm passenger from Ballymena – the pairs crossing at Ballyboley and meeting the Doagh connection there. There were no express workings. Apart from these, there was an early Doagh–Larne run at 6.30am and a Larne Harbour–Doagh mixed at 2.40pm, which crossed with the 2.45pm Doagh–Larne Harbour working.

After the war, an express boat train was reinstated from Larne Harbour. In the winter of 1921–2, Ballymena trains left Larne at 7.35am and the Harbour at 9am, 2.40pm and 5.50pm, while workings to Larne left Ballymena at 7.10am, 10.25am, 2.15pm and 5.40pm, all with the usual branch-line connections. The day of the busy Sunday services was virtually over, however, and in that particular timetable no trains ran on Sundays.

The summer of 1929 saw much the same pattern of movements, with a late run from the Harbour to Ballymena on Wednesdays and Saturdays only. The Sunday service, a mere ghost of what it had been, left Doagh for Larne at 2.30pm and returned to Doagh from Larne at 8.30pm. The buses had won the day.

The services tottered into the early 1930s with nearly empty trains, three in each direction on weekdays, plus a

A delightful scene at Doagh on 9 August 1930, showing Class R 2-6-0ST No 109 blowing off as it waits to depart with the 7.10pm branch train to Ballyboley. With no passengers in sight, the porter chats to the driver and guard, who are relaxing on the bench seat. The goods shed is visible to the right. Passenger services to Doagh ended on 1 October 1930, two months later.

HC Casserley

single Doagh goods that left Larne Harbour at 12.30pm, and returned there, leaving Doagh at 2.40pm. There were paths available for three special goods trains between the Harbour and the paper mill siding. It was in these twilight years that the LMS(NCC) made their brave attempt to resuscitate the line and distinguish it as the only narrow gauge railway in the British Isles to operate a boat express of modern *corridor* coaches. The steamer was due into Larne at 8.55am and the narrow gauge was scheduled to leave at 9am, but it could be held up to 70 minutes if the boat was delayed.

The run to Ballymena took 60 minutes, with a call at Kells at 9.49am. Derry passengers had 26 minutes in which to make their broad gauge connection at Ballymena and, if they were off a late boat, could well be further delayed at Ballymena awaiting a later train, though they had the compensation of a good refreshment room.

The return boat train pulled out of Ballymena at 5.47pm and, with stops at Ballyboley and Larne Town, plus another at Ballynashee on a Saturday, was allowed 64 minutes to reach the Harbour station.

The Cushendall line

For the first 20 years of working the Cushendall branch, the BNCR provided two trains in each direction during the winter. The first of these left Ballymena at 7.35am, connecting with the 6.30am Belfast–Derry Mail and arrived in Parkmore at about 8.20am. After its departure there was a long period of apparent quiescence, to judge from the working timetable, for the evening train leaving Ballymena at 5.15pm was the next scheduled passenger train, reaching Parkmore at 6pm and returning down the hill at 6.20pm. However, between the morning and evening runs, the line was anything but quiet, for it then reverted to its original purpose of bringing ore down from the mining sidings into Ballymena, much of it for trans-shipment into broad gauge trucks there, though some ran through to Larne. But passengers were not forgotten during the working day, and the working timetables of the 1890s supplied the encouraging information that "Passengers desirous of travelling from Ballymena, between the hours

CUSHENDALL BRANCH.

BALLYMENA TO PARKMORE.

DOWN	1	A 2	G.&P. 3	4	Suns. 1
	a m	a m	p m	p m	a.m.
Ballymena .. dep.	7 35	10 0	1 40	5 5	10 10
*Ballygarvey	7 42	10 7	1 47	5 12	10 17
Ballycloughan	7 47	10 12	1 52	5 17	10 22
Rathkenny	7 52	10 17	1 57	5 22	10 27
Clough Road	7 56	..	B	5 26	10 31
Knockanally	8 1	10 27	2 8	5 33	10 37
Cross Roads	8 7	10 35	2 16	5 42	10 45
Cargan	8 14	10 41	2 23	5 49	10 51
Parkmore .. arr.	8 22	10 50	2 30	5 57	11 0

PARKMORE TO BALLYMENA.

UP	1	Gds 2	3	4	5	Suns. 1
	a m	a m	p.m.	p.m.	p.m	p.m.
Parkmore .. dep.	8 30	1115	3 30	5 45	6 10	7 0
Cargan ..	8 35	..	..	5 50	6 15	7 5
Cross Roads ..	8 40	..	..	..	6 20	7 10
Knockanally ..	8 47	..	3 50	..	6 28	7 18
Clough Road ..	8 53	..	..	..	6 35	7 25
Rathkenny ..	8 57	..	C	..	6 40	7 30
Ballycloughan ..	9 2	..	C	..	6 45	7 35
*Ballygarvey ..	9 6	..	..	..	6 51	7 41
Ballymena .. arr.	9 13	1230	4 15	6 30	7 0	7 50

(Column 4, up direction: Runs Fridays only)

Trains timed at Ballygarvey stop only by signal or on notice being given to Guard

A On Mondays, Wednesdays and Saturdays, 10-0 a.m. waits until 10-20 a.m., and connects with 9-15 a.m. from Belfast.

B Stops at Clough Road on Saturdays to set down Passengers.

C Stops on Notice to Guard or Station Master.

Passengers desirous of travelling between Stations on the Cushendall Branch, between the hours fixed for the morning and evening passenger trains, can do so by the following Mineral train, which may be stopped at any intermediate station required except Clough Road :—

Parkmore to Ballymena about 11-15 a.m.

Mineral Trains run on this Branch as the traffic demands, under the direction of Mr. Harris, Station Master at Ballymena.

Timetable for the Cushendall line from the MR(NCC) working timetable, July–September 1912.

fixed for the Morning and Evening Trains, can do so by any Mineral Train that may happen to be running . . . Mineral Trains run on this branch as Traffic demands under the direction of Mr Rigby, station Master at B'mena".

The public timetables were more specific and informed the travellers that they could move about "by the following Mineral Train: Cross Roads to Ballymena, about 11.0 am, stopping at any intermediate Station, except Clough Road, Ballymena to Parkmore, about 1.0 pm".

In summertime, the service was more generous and there were three trains a day in each direction during the 1890s. The movements began as before with the 7.35am ex-Ballymena, which was back there from Parkmore at 9.08am. Then there was the 10.30am out of Ballymena, with passengers joining it off the 9.05am Belfast–Derry train, full of anticipation of a lunch in Glenariff. The return

working from Parkmore was not until 4.35pm, a fast train that stopped only at Knockanally and Rathkenny, and met the 3pm Derry–Belfast Mail. The third working out of Ballymena left at 5.25pm, taking the glen folk after their day's shopping or work. At Parkmore, it collected late-moving tourists, left at 6.20pm and was into Ballymena just after 7pm, in time to catch the evening train to Belfast. Quite often, the 5.25pm out of Ballymena would be heavily loaded, with seven or eight carriages behind two engines. If the traffic demanded it, the train would go all the way to Parkmore, but more often they would only take four carriages beyond Cargan with one of the engines.

There were no trains on Sundays until about 1910. Then, from the first week in June, a train left Ballymena at 10.10am. City people who fancied a day in the hills could leave Belfast at 9.05am and, after the inevitable Greenisland

Class O 0-4-2ST No 102 waiting to depart from Parkmore with a mixed train for Ballymena some time around 1900.

L&GRP

stop, be in Ballymena at 10.02am. Their narrow gauge train had them in Parkmore around 11am, but there was no return working to take them back to civilisation until 7pm. Once on to the evening train, they were in Ballymena at 7.50pm and caught the 7pm ex-Portrush, which deposited them at Belfast at 9pm. There was no connection towards Derry.

By autumn 1911, the working timetable showed four trains in each direction. In addition to the well-established early morning and evening passenger trains, there were others at 10am and 1.40pm out of Ballymena, the first one going only as far as Cargan, except on Mondays and Saturdays when it continued to Parkmore. In the up direction, Cargan sent off a goods at 11.15am and Parkmore one at 3.15pm. All the goods or mineral trains carried persons "desirous of travelling".

In the spring of 1912 a coal strike caused some curtailment of services over the whole of the NCC's system, but its only effect on the Cushendall line was to stop the morning goods ex-Cargan, and an early mineral working

that left Ballymena at 6am and which was not listed in the working book.

Sunday trains came to an end during the First World War and were never resumed, but the war seems to have had no effect on the services on summer weekdays, as the June 1918 timetable showed the 7.35am, 10am, 1.45pm and 5.10pm ex-Ballymena, and the 8.35am, 11.15am, 3.35pm and 6.15pm ex-Parkmore.

Although Retreat never handled passenger traffic, the MR(NCC) showed it in their public timetables, though with the apologetic footnote that only goods traffic was handled there. It was not the practice to mention Retreat in the working timetables at all until they were published in a larger page format after October 1912.

Then, for some odd reason, Retreat was only listed in the town direction, with the statement that, "The 1.40 pm train from Ballymena to Parkmore works Goods through to Retreat on Mondays, Wednesdays and Fridays". Quite often, however, there was sufficient traffic to warrant a Parkmore–Retreat working on other days, but it was always sandwiched between the arrival of the 1.40pm ex-Ballymena and the return working from Parkmore. The Retreat workings were small ones, and although no loads were set down in the working timetable for the section, the train crews treated the run with respect and limited their loads to four or five wagons. They took their train up to the summit at Essathohan and there stopped to pin down wagon brakes before making the descent down the 1 in 39 to the outpost of the NCC and its dead-end. The same stationmaster was at Retreat for many years and could count on having a warm house after the thrice-weekly visits, as the enginemen made sure some coal was spilled out of their bunker. And if a dozen or more fresh eggs went back to Ballymena on the return journey, it merely maintained 'the balance of payments'.

The mine sidings needed equally careful working, with steep grades down towards the valley bottom, a steep curve into the main line and always a heavy train behind the engine. There was a bad runaway on the Mountcashel siding in 1916. Paddy Hannan had worked a train of empties to the mine with one of the Cushendall saddle tanks. He hooked off, ran around and picked up his train. Before he could get coupled up to his brake van, his heavy train got the better of him and they set off down the hill out of control, leaving old Sam Crowe sitting in the guard's van up at the mine. In spite of Paddy's efforts, the train picked up speed but stayed on the road until they went under the first arch at Martinstown. Then the first wagon broke loose, went over on its side and dumped its load in the field, and the other wagons followed its example. Paddy stayed on his engine, which kept the rails, but after the coupling was torn out, a pipe to the steam brake cylinder snapped and filled the cab with steam. Poor Paddy was very badly scalded and had to spend many weeks in hospital. There was no heavy crane on the narrow gauge, so the breakdown crew had to do their best with a light hand crane and jacks, and getting the derailed wagons back on to the line kept them occupied for the greater part of a week.

Under the BNCR, advertised excursions played a large part in maintaining the income of the branch. They were arranged from early June to late September. During the 1890s "the most varied and charming ONE DAY CIRCULAR TRIP in the North of Ireland" was billed "to the Vale of Glenariff, Cushendall and the Antrim coast", and it could be taken clockwise or anti-clockwise, while

two times of departure were allowed. Early birds could leave Belfast at 6.30am on the broad gauge mail train and be in Ballymena at 7.30am. There they changed to the Cushendall train, left at 7.35am and were in Parkmore at 8.22am. They then clambered on to 'McNeill's Car', went down Glenariff as the morning sun was flooding the slopes, reached the store at Waterfoot and continued into Cushendall, where they arrived at 9.20am with nearly five hours before them. Another of McNeill's cars was meanwhile making its ponderous way along the coast from Larne, carrying tourists who had taken the reverse route. The car was in Cushendall at mid-day, horses were changed and at 2.10pm it left to return to Larne. All being well, the traverse of the coast road took until 5.45pm; the travellers were then put on the 6.05pm at Larne town station and were back in Belfast by 7.05pm.

In the reverse direction, only 1 hr 40 min was given at Cushendall, and the 3.45pm train from Parkmore was caught, while the Belfast arrival was timed for 5.45pm. In both directions the excursion could be taken later in the day, leaving for Parkmore at 8.30am, or for Larne at 9.30am, with arrivals back in Belfast at 9.35pm or 9pm respectively. The fare "including Rail and Coach" first class was 9s, second class was 7s 6d and third class 6s 6d. Those willing to pay for their comforts were warned "there is only one kind of carriage on the Cushendall Branch, but a compartment is specially set aside for holders of First class Tickets".

Another such tour in the 1890s was "Glenariff, Cushendall and Ballycastle in One Day". Cushendall was reached via Parkmore and McNeill's Car. After two and a half hours there, Delargy's Car went over the mountain road past the Vanishing Lake of Loughareema and was in Ballycastle at 2.15pm. The return could be made either by the 3pm or the 6.15pm train. It was not a little heroic for some on the mountain road for, apart from an occasional ass cart, the only conveyance they were likely to meet would be the other Delargy Car, coming with tourists who were doing the round trip in the other direction.

A few specials, usually five to six coaches of organised excursions, worked through from Larne to Parkmore where a fleet of sidecars were waiting to take them to Glenariff and, after suitable refreshments, down to the coast road and back to Larne.

The Cushendall service in the last summer of passenger

trains followed much the same pattern of 20 years earlier. The 7.35am still set out from Ballymena, and returned at 8.30am from Parkmore. The evening passenger workings were the 5.15pm from Ballymena and the 6.10pm from Parkmore. Between these pairs of workings the others were mixed "and cannot observe stated times", as the public timetable warned. Of them, there was the 10.35am from Ballymena, and the 11.40am from Parkmore. On Mondays, wednesdays and Fridays only, ballymena sent off a mixed train at 1.40pm, which returned from Parkmore at 3.30pm. Finally, there was a 2pm mixed from Ballymena on Saturdays only. The Retreat goods workings had ended and the timetable stated that "Goods Traffic to and from Cushendall district is dealt with at Parkmore Station."

Operating the B&LR line

Goods traffic seems to have begun between Larne and the Ballyclare paper mill as early as September 1877 but,

as the line was still not properly signalled, the niceties of train staff working would not have been considered. After Colonel Rich's inspection, the following undertaking was given on 19 August 1878:

SYSTEM FOR WORKING TRAINS PENDING
ERECTION OF TELEGRAPH

To Col Rich RE, Inspecting Officer, Board of Trade

Sir,

The Ballymena and Larne Rly Co undertake to adopt the Block Telegraph in addition to the Train Staff and Ticket Regulations immediately on completion of the Telegraphy Line now being erected by the Government Engineer, and pending the adoption of Block Telegraph they undertake that only one Engine in Steam or two or more Engines coupled together shall be allowed to be upon one of the following sections of single line at one and the same time:

Sections: Larne Harbour and Larne
Larne and Ballyclare Junction

Between Larne Harbour and Larne town stations, the broad and narrow gauge tracks ran in parallel. This view, on 22 June 1937, is looking back towards the harbour as 4-4-2T No 113 wends its way west with a ballast or coal train. The tide is out on Larne Lough, but nowadays the railway is on a new alignment to the right, its original route being under the modern police station. The houses on the left are in Hope Street, also now under the police station.

HC Casserley

Ballyclare Junction and Ballyclare
Ballyclare Junction and Ballymena

This will be carried out by using the Train Staff only and no Tickets till the Block Telegraph is completed.

The official opening of the line came very shortly afterwards, on Saturday 24 August, when both goods and passenger workings began from Larne Harbour and Harryville, and from Ballyclare to the Junction. The main line was divided into five sections, four of which were operated by train staff and ticket:

Section	Colour of staff and ticket	Form of staff
Larne Harbour and Larne	red	round
Larne and Junction	yellow	square
Junction and Ballyclare	green	round
Junction and Kells	red	3-sided
Kells and Ballymena	blue	round

Between Larne and the harbour station, train tickets were not issued and the train staff only was used in that section. The first working timetable dated 24 August 1878 contained detailed instructions as to how the staff and ticket system was to be worked. The procedure adopted when the trains were to be assisted is of particular interest, for its shows that on the Inver bank both piloting and banking were in vogue:

> When trains are assisted by a second Engine in the front, the leading Engine must carry the Staff or Ticket; but when the Assistant Engine is behind pushing the Train, the Train Engine must carry a Ticket, and the Assistant Engine the Staff, except in cases where the Train and Assistant Engines are travelling over the entire length of Section, and have to be followed by another Train or Engine, when the Train and Assistant Engine must each have a Ticket. When the Assistant Engine is intended to return to the station from which it started, without running through the entire Section, it must always carry the Staff.

Propelling was done between Larne and the Harbour, and under 'Instructions' we read:

> *Pushing Trains from Larne to Harbour* – Guards of all Trains pushing wagons from Larne to Harbour after dark, must ride in the front Wagon and show a 'White Light' towards the Harbour.

The handling of special trains was also considered:

> *Special Trains* – A 'Red Board' or 'Flag' by Day, or an 'Extra Red Light' by Night behind any Train or Engine denotes that a Special Train is to follow: and such Special Train signal must, if possible, be shown on the Train immediately preceding the Special Train; but it may happen that Special Trains may be dispatched without any previous notice having been given: *it is therefore necessary to be at all times prepared for unexpected Trains.*

When Ballynashee was opened in 1879, it broke the long section between the Junction and Kells into two parts. The red, three-sided staff from Junction to Kells thereafter covered the Junction–Ballynashee section only, and a new square section green staff was introduced between the Ballynashee and Kells.

With the opening of the Harryville–Ballymena passenger section in September 1880, a sixth section was added, handled by a square green staff with green tickets similar to the Ballynashee–Kells staff.

The Ballyclare–Doagh section was completed in 1884, goods trains beginning of 8 February and passenger trains from 1 May. A further train staff was put into use, red and square in section.

Once established, the division of the line was continued into BNCR days and it was not until the 1890s that a change took place with the introduction of the train tablet system. Tablet working had been started on the broad gauge single line between Carrick Junction (later Greenisland) and Carrickfergus in November 1889, and it was gradually extended until the entire line to Larne Harbour was covered, as well as most of the single-line parts of the main line. The broad gauge tablet from Larne to the harbour had a three-sided hole in it, while that for the same narrow gauge section, once it was introduced, had a round hole.

Between October and November 1901 the Kells and Ballymena section went over to tablet working, the tablets having a square hole. Then, some time between 1901 and 1908, tablets replaced staffs on the Harryville–Ballymena passenger and Larne–Ballyboley sections. By 1908, the operational sections were handled as follows:

Section	
Larne Harbour and Larne	Tablet (round hole)
Larne and Ballyboley Jnct	Tablet (diamond hole)
Ballyboley Junction and Ballyclare	Staff and Ticket (round/green)

Above: *On Friday 18 August 1939, as war clouds were gathering on the European horizon, the photographer has captured S2 class 2-4-4T No 110 shunting a train of hopper wagons at Larne Harbour, with the Stranraer ferry visible in the background.*

SS Cunningham, courtesy CP Friel

Right: *S1 class 2-4-2T No 42 passes Ballyboley with a paper mill train in the late 1940s.*

CP Friel collection

Ballyclare and Doagh	Staff and Ticket (square/red)
Ballyboley and Ballynashee	Staff and Ticket (3-sided/red)
Ballynashee and Kells	Staff and Ticket (square/green)
Kells and Harryville	Tablet (square hole)
Harryville and Ballymena Passenger	Tablet (triangular hole)

In February 1920, the board minutes make one of their rare references to the tablet and staff working:

> On the intermediate sections Kells–Ballynashee, Ballynashee–Ballyboley, blocking is done by the Station Masters by means of the speaking telegraph instruments. The introduction of the 8-hour day raises the question of relief ad as it would be very expensive to have qualified telegraphists to relieve at Kells, Ballynashee and Ballyboley, it is proposed to install the Electric Train Tablet at these intermediate stations,

With Larne Aluminium Works in the background, U2 class 4-4-0 No 73 passes a healthy collection of narrow gauge wagons as it arrives at Larne Harbour.
Courtesy S Magee, photographer unknown

in which case a member of the platform staff can be trained to work the tablet apparatus and thus provide relief. The estimated cost of erecting the line would be £501, plus 4 instruments £465.

So far as it known the change was never made and the state of affairs at 1908 persisted up to 1933, when the strike brought passenger services to an end. Thereafter, goods trains were run "as occasion demands" and drastic simplification became possible. Tablets were retained for the two sections between the Harbour and Ballyboley, but from there to Ballymena one very long section of 17½ miles was worked, controlled by the old Kells–Harryville tablet instruments. The entire Doagh branch became one section controlled by a round brass staff under the principle of "one engine in steam, or two or more engines coupled together". Then, in 1940, The Ballyboley–Ballymena section was closed and lifted, leaving only the fragment from Larne Harbour to the paper mill in existence.

Operating the Cushendall line

The early story of this line under the BC&RBR is shrouded in mystery. The company records which now exist contain no reference to the purchase of signals, telegraph instruments or to any system of block working. It was not until 6 February 1876 that the board formally resolved, "That the Rules and Regulations of the Belfast and Northern Counties Railway Company be, and hereby are, adopted for the conduct of the Traffic and the guidance and instruction of the Officers and Men of the Ballymena, Cushendall and Red Bay Railway Company." The BC&RBR then re-issued the leather-bound 1875 rule-book of the BNCR, a volume of 144 pages, having inserted a slip inside the front cover stating that they had adopted it. Now the BNCR, being as passenger carrying line, were working their single lines on the train staff and ticket system and pages 34–39 of the rule-book laid down the usual details. But there is no evidence that the Cushendall company did, in fact, adopt that section of the rule book and it is unlikely that they did so.

By 1881, dwindling income forced the Cushendall to look into the question of carrying passengers, and Silas Evans' approach to Colonel Rich of the Board of Trade makes it clear that the line was not signalled. All three engines must have been in use simultaneously and it seems more than likely that a crude time interval system was used intelligently so that no accidents of any moment took place.

Under the BNCR, the development of passenger traffic demanded that the working of the Cushendall line be regularised. Colonel Rich gave permission in March 1886 to work the Ballymena–Knockanally section using a staff, with one engine in steam. By the time the entire section was open to Parkmore for passengers, three block sections were in use, operated by Wise's patent train staffs (designed by Berkeley D Wise of the BNCR, at the time when he was with the Belfast and Co Down Railway):

Section	Colour of staff and ticket	Form of staff
Ballymena & Knockanally	red	round
Knockanally and Cargan	brass staff & blue lettered permits	fluted
Cargan and Parkmore	black	square

The Wise's staffs enabled the usual train ticket boxes and printed train tickets to be dispensed with. At each end of the patent staff there were two compartments or pockets, containing metal tablets called 'train permits'. These were engraved with the name of the station to which they authorised the train to proceed, performing the same function as train tickets. Permits for down trains were kept at one end of the staff, and those for up trains at the other. The permits were released from the staff, one at a time, by means of a key in the possession of the station-master at each end of the section, the keys being only capable of opening the appropriate pockets. By this means, three trains could be sent in succession in the same direction, but no more, the first and second trains carrying the permits and the third train the staff. On arrival at the end of the section, the driver gave up the permit to the station-master, who kept them safely until the staff was brought along by the following train, whereupon he pushed the permit into its pocket, which locked automatically. Before a train started from a staff station, all the permits for trains coming from the other end of the section in advance were to be locked in the pocket, and were to be seen by the driver.

Between Parkmore and Retreat, a staff without tickets or permits was used, so that it was, in effect worked by one engine in steam.

Some time between 1901 and 1908 the Wise's patent staffs were replaced by the staff and ticket system, and the form of the Knockanally–Cargan staff changed to a three-sided yellow one. Between 1908 and 1911 this section was divided at Cross Roads, the three-sided yellow staff being used between there and Knockanally, while a new round brass staff with green tickets were introduced between Cross Roads and Cargan. From about 1905 the Parkmore–Retreat section began to be worked by staff and ticket, using a round staff of a red colour.

The Annett's key on the staffs and tablets controlled the various sidings, and in the 1908–11 period these sidings were located as follows:

Sidings controlled by train staff:

Ballyclare siding, at Ballyclare station

Paper Mill siding, between Ballyclare and Doagh

Kirk's or Tannybrack siding, between Moorfields and Kells

Ballycloughan siding

Rathkenny siding

Rathkenny creamery siding, between Rathkenny and Knockanally

Evishacrow siding, between Cargan and Parkmore

Sidings controlled by train tablet:

Kilwaughter siding, between Larne and Ballyboley

Ballyrickard siding, between Kilwaughter and Larne

McQuiston's siding, between Kells and Ballymena

Gasworks siding, at Harryville

On the withdrawal of the passenger trains to Parkmore in 1930, the Cushendall section was worked by a single brass staff.

Accidents

Perusal of the minute books of the Cushendall and B&LR companies would suggest that the former company enjoyed comparative freedom from accidents, while the latter encountered their fair share. The true facts are inaccessible now, but one feels that the BC&RBR, working their mineral railway reasonably far from public gaze, felt that both trouble and paper would be saved if the Board of Trade did not become too closely concerned with minor accidents, so long as no one got badly hurt. Only three accidents are listed in the company's books. The first happened on 22 April 1875 to "James Johnston, engine driver of this Company", but it "was considered trivial" and "need not be reported to the Board of Trade". The fashion had been set. The second accident was a tragic one; it occurred during the summer of 1881 and resulted in the death of Mrs O'Boyle, the wife of the Cross Roads station-master, No details are given in the minute book, but it is likely that it involved the crossing gates. What was recorded was the acceptance of a bill for £4 4s for attendance by the local doctor.

On 27 February 1882 the first accident in a bad year resulted in the death of porter Pat Henry of the BC&RBR. He was injured while pushing a wagon into a siding in the Cushendall yard at Ballymena. While doing so, he was struck by a B&LR train which was being propelled into the yard on the same line. The jury found both companies negligent.

At later dates during 1882 the B&LR suffered three accidents. The first was a spectacular breakaway. The 9.40am up passenger train was on its way towards Larne on 18 April when "two carriages containing about 12 third class passengers broke away at Moorfields and ran to Kells viaduct (two miles) where they were overtaken by the engine and resumed their journey without damage." The occurrence highlights the dangers of the non-automatic vacuum brake.

A second breakaway took place two days later. Some Cushendall wagons were damaged "by the coupling hook getting detached between Collin and Moorfields on the night of 20th April". The secretary was asked to draw the attention of Mr Cotton – general manager of the BNCR and also managing the affairs of the Cushendall line – to the "want of shackles" on BC&RBR stock.

Larne station on 18 August 1882 saw a collision when the 3.45pm ex-Ballymena came into the station and hit an empty wagon that had been left on the line. The fate of the wagon was not recorded but the collision cannot have been violent for the minute book records with gratitude that no passengers were injured and that the train proceeded on its way to the harbour after a delay of ten minutes.

There were two accidents during 1885. The first was another breakaway and took place on the morning of 3 February when the 7am mixed train parted on the Ballygowan bank, due to a faulty coupling on a side tip wagon. The minute book does not detail what vehicles ran back, but they covered three miles before they came to a standstill.

On 11 July 1885 two carriages of the Doagh branch train were turned on to the wrong line at the junction. An empty carriage left the rails and a second carriage containing passengers was stopped before any damage could be done. Driver McClure was fined 20s for running past a signal at danger. The signalman was fined 5s "for neglecting to look out before he altered the points".

A short way from the junction, the Ballyboley iron ore siding was the scene of a buffer collision on 23 February 1886. It must have been a good one as the repairs cost the company £50. The explanation given was that "the guard failed to catch his brake as it passed him at the points and the rails being wet he could not overtake the train."

A level crossing accident was almost inevitable. On 4 July 1887 a ballast train collided with a horse and cart on McAuley's crossing. The company admitted some liability and attended to the repairs to the damaged cart. Whether the horse was also damaged is not stated; it may have escaped with a warning, but at the time the company were heavily mortgaged and in no mood to be generous.

Under the BNCR and the Midland, improvements in track maintenance and operating methods together reduced the accident rate. Some of the occurrences have been mentioned in the text but two derailments may be recorded. The first caused much damage to the main line of the B&LR section when, on 15 October 1904, a wagon of iron ore came off the rails at Kilwaughter "due to excessive oscillation", a cause that could cover a multitude of sins. On the bank, the speed would have been fairly high and the guard would have had difficulty in drawing the attention of the enginemen to the fact that something was wrong. That was, if he noticed it. The wagon was dragged a distance of 1,140 yards before it was halted.

The Mountcashel iron ore siding was the scene of a derailment on 2 August 1908. Sixteen side-tip wagons derailed on the 1 in 30 gradient, and 11 of them were badly damaged.

A tragic accident involving the death of a driver occurred on 1 September 1920. Bob Mitchell was a passed driver firing on the Larne broad gauge road. He was relieving a Larne narrow gauge driver and was bringing the 5.30pm boat train from Ballymena. After Moorfields, he heard knocking on the fireman's side and mentioned to John

Graham, who was firing to him, that he hoped it would get no worse if they were to keep to time. On the approach to Collin halt, Mitchell crossed over to Graham's side of the engine and put his head well outside to hear the knock in the motion better. A moment later his head struck against a wooden hut that formed the support for an old water tank; he was severely injured and fell to the ground. Graham stopped the train, the guard ran up, and with the assistance of passengers they lifted Mitchell into the guard's van. Fireman and guard took the train on towards Larne, while some passengers remained with poor Mitchell in the van. They did what they could for him, but he died on the way to Larne.

The Larne slip workings

Passing reference has been made earlier in this chapter to the practice of slipping a mail van at Larne from the down mail train. This interesting manoeuvre was unique on the Irish narrow gauge and took place for a number of years prior to World War I. During 1908 and 1909, the Mail left Larne Harbour at 7.51am and a note in the working timetable states, "A carriage is slipped from the 7.51 a.m. Express at Larne".

During the coalminer's strike in March 1912 the services over the B&LR section were drastically curtailed and express workings ceased for a short time. After the strike, the mail train was retimed and left at 8.05am. The slip carriage was replaced by what the working timetable called a 'mail van'. Slip working was continued up to the start of the war, but terminated with the end of the express workings during the war and was never reinstated.

To operate the slip workings with the mail van, a spare brake van was placed at the stop block in the Harbour station and, on the arrival of the steamer, was loaded with mail bags and parcels for Larne town. The coupling hook on this van was attached at the Ballymena end, as were the hooks on the other train vehicles but, unlike them, the hook on the van was fitted with a heavy metal ring near its front end. A chain with a split link was attached to the ring and reached into the van through the window. The van was manned by a competent porter and was not vacuum braked. Having accelerated out of the Harbour station, the driver shut off steam about a quarter of a mile from Larne, and then gave his train a touch of the vacuum. This took the strain off the hook, whereupon the porter pulled it up clear and thus uncoupled the van. The train then drew ahead and made at its best speed for the Inver bank, while the van coasted in under the control of the handbrake and was brought to a stop at the platform exit.

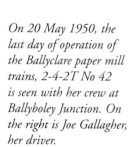

On 20 May 1950, the last day of operation of the Ballyclare paper mill trains, 2-4-2T No 42 is seen with her crew at Ballyboley Junction. On the right is Joe Gallagher, her driver.

Brian Gallagher
collection

Chapter 11

Conclusion

Iron ore the stimulus

Unlike the Ballycastle Railway in the north of County Antrim, the Ballymena lines owned their genesis to the promise of heavy mineral traffic. Their precursor was a mineral line in Glenariff, that loveliest of Antrim glens, which had an active life of only three years. Though it failed because of faulty prospecting, it set the fashion for a gauge of three feet, a fashion which was to spread over much of Ireland as separate disconnected companies.

As an independent company, the Ballymena, Cushendall and Red Bay Railway had a brief career and operated for only nine years. No passengers were carried, the company preferring to put all its eggs into one basket and to funnel a tremendous tonnage of iron ore down to Ballymena for subsequent shipment. The line was characterised by lengthy

mine sidings, owned by the mining companies but worked mainly by the three saddle-tank engines of the Cushendall company. By the middle 1880s requirements were falling off for the grade of ore that Antrim could produce and the company were glad to dispose of their assets to the Belfast and Northern Counties Railway.

On the Ballymena and Larne Railway, traffic was less one-sided than on the Cushendall and, although mineral traffic made a valuable contribution to the revenue, it was more than balanced by passenger and general merchandise and by the inland haulage of coal from the port of Larne. But the company had never been prosperous and such success as they had achieved came only as a result of cheese-paring tactics. After 11 difficult years, the BNCR made a tempting offer which the B&LR could not refuse. The late James Chaine's vision of a narrow gauge railway from Larne

A Permanent Way gang at Moorfields in 1925. Left to right: W Hill, WJ Wilson, R McCullough, H Armstrong, W Service, S Clarke, H McKerry and S McKee.

J Jamieson collection

137

Driver JP O'Toole, JP, at Ballyclare, about 1925.

H Herron collection

to Londonderry must have seemed very far away then.

Under the BNCR, the prosperous trunk system carried the two narrow gauge lines on its broad gauge back. The narrow gauge took its place as a feeder to the main lines in a regime that could survive only so long as wages and fuel costs were low. During this epoch the local management succumbed to the blandishments of the cross-channel Midland Railway and sold out. From 1903, management was through a subordinate directorate styled the Northern Counties Committee.

Anglicisation brought the novelty of slip working on the Larne line, a unique practice on the Irish narrow gauge. It also perpetuated the *status quo* for 11 years, until war brought an abnormal environment and government control was imposed. Financial inflation followed, and all the railways of the country emerged from it weakened and ill-prepared to withstand the impact of the loss of their monopoly of transport to the roads.

The Long Run Down

By the end of the 1920s the Cushendall line was virtually finished. The once fashionable tourist excursions to Glenariff had lost their charm, the mineral traffic was but a ghost of its former self and only the freight to and from a creamery kept the line open. On the Larne line, things were a little better but showed no visible signs of improvement,

The labour troubles of early 1933, culminating in strike action, gave the committee excuse for a stage-by-stage closure, which, logically, should have already begun. By the end of seven years only a quarter of the original narrow gauge mileage was still being operated and this was tied to the needs of a local paper mill. That fragment of the former Ballymena lines remained a fascinating relic which it took two years under the Ulster Transport Authority and the closure of the paper mill to efface. The last train ran, unheralded and unsung, a few weeks before the date of official closure, which coincided with that of the Ballycastle section. With their extinction, County Antrim lost the last of its narrow gauge lines, the first of which had been laid 77 years before.

Chapter 12

The Narrow Gauge Routes in 2007

Although it is almost 60 years since the last section of the mid-Antrim narrow gauge lines closed, a surprising amount still remains today. Essential tools for following the route descriptions below are Ordnance Survey 1:50,000 scale maps Nos 9 (Larne) and 15 (Belfast), the detailed April Sky 1:10,000 scale street maps of Ballymena and Larne and Alan Godfrey's historic map of Larne in 1903. At Ballymena station recent changes to the Permanent Way Yard have obliterated most traces of the narrow gauge, including the engine shed, which was there until 2005.

Ballymena to Retreat

Ballymena town

Our starting point for exploring the route of the Ballymena, Cushendall and Red Bay Railway is the new 'Park and Ride' facility at Ballymena station. Access to this is from Upper Princes Street (from either the Galgorm

Road or the Cullybackey Road). The road in takes you past the NIR permanent way yard and brings you to what was an island platform in narrow gauge days. The parking bays adjoining the platform occupy the track that served the narrow gauge (see cover painting).

In the area to the right, behind all the fences, was an extensive yard serving both gauges, including the four-track engine shed, carriage sidings, interchange facilities and, just where you turned in from Upper Princes Street, the 'Cushendall yard', which was the goods facility for the narrow gauge. The route of the line to Parkmore and Retreat was roughly on the west side of the road into the station carpark.

Because of the extensive housing development on the west side of Ballymena, much of the route of the line has been completely obliterated in recent years. To see what remains drive back out of the carpark to Upper Princes Street, turning left and then left again at the Cullybackey Road. The line passed under the road just round the corner and the bridge is still there, though filled in. Trackbed is visible on the north side, the line passing to the east of Carndale Meadows on a gradual right hand curve. At the time of writing (March 2007), the trackbed can still be seen on a building site at Carndale Meadows (off Carniney Road, just beyond the bridge).

From here the line climbed north to cross the Ballymoney Road opposite Ardena Grange. It was from near here that I believe the photo at the bottom of page 61 was taken. It then passed along the south side of Loughan School turning gradually eastwards. It crossed the

Car park in the former narrow gauge yard in Ballymena station.

N Johnston

Surviving stretch of narrow gauge embankment to the west of Ballymena, visible from the Ballygarvey Road.   N Johnston

Ballygarvey station house today.   N Johnston

and emerge in open countryside.

To get to this point more quickly from the Cullybackey Road bridge, go up the Carniney Road, turn right after three quarters of a mile into Carnburn Road and straight across the roundabout into Grove Road which, after a mile, brings you to the Cushendall Road (A43) at a roundabout. Take the second exit to pass under the M2.

Ballymena–Rathkenny

Just after passing under the M2, turn right onto the Ballygarvey Road. A short distance up this road (opposite Nos 36/38) the line can be seen on the right climbing up out of Ballymena on a curving embankment. Two hundred yards beyond this it passed under the road on a skew. Four hundred yards beyond this again the line crossed the lane from No 60, and a partly removed embankment can be seen to the left. After another half mile turn left onto Parade Road. **Ballygarvey station** is on the left after half a mile. The station house is much rebuilt and modernised. Across the field on the right is a hedge and the stone wall in part of it marks where the line originally crossed the field as it swung north.

Continue to the end of Parade Road and turn right at the Cushendall Road. After 50 yards turn right into Pillarbrae Road. About a mile down this road the railway crossed under the road, from the right, on a skew bridge which still survives. Take next left (Quarrytown Road). **Ballycloughan station** (No 29) is a short distance up here on the right. The sun parlour is a modern edition.

Continue to the end of the road and turn right onto the Cushendall Road again. After a mile and a half, look out on the right for a small bridge which carried the Carncoagh

Old Ballymoney Road between the school and Parkside Rise, passed the end of Circular Park and crossed Doury Road and Sandown Park, just north of the Independent Methodist Church.

It then swung north between Kew Link and Waveney Brow to avoid the Cemetery (today the route is partly within the expanded cemetery) and swung north-east again to cross the Cushendall Road at Herbison Park. The trackbed is now under the Dunfane Estate, but it emerged through Dunfane School to pass under the M2 Motorway

Road over the railway. It is just after a farm house, amidst trees. From here on, the line follows a course close to the road, on the right hand side as far as Cargan and then on the left. The site of **Rathkenny station**, which once served a large creamery, is now under the Wilson car sales complex on the right. From Rathkenny a short branch went off up the hill to the right, to Rathkenny iron ore mine.

Rathkenny–Retreat

Continue along the A43 for three quarters of a mile to where the B94 (Clough Road) creates a crossroads at McGregor's Corner. Turtle's Peugeot garage marks the site of what was **Clough Road station**. About a mile beyond this on the right is a former gatehouse, where the line crossed Islandtown Road.

We now come to the considerable settlement of Martinstown, once called Knockanally. In railway days, this was a tiny settlement; today it is virtually a small town. **Martinstown station** was behind the Glensway Tavern and from here a two mile branch to the mines at Mount

Cashel went off to the right, diverging gradually from the main line. The station is now gone, though a stone wall still stands on the Rathkenny side of the tavern. Pull into the Tavern carpark, just short of the bridge, and you can see the piers of the railway bridge over the Glenravel Water river (compare page 23).

No trace now remains of the next stopping place, **Crossroads station**, which was located where the Glens Brae Road crosses the A43, about a mile and a half beyond Martinstown. A new house occupies the site of the station house. The station was a few yards up the road to the right, the line crossing it on the level, and had both up and down platforms, a passing loop and a signal cabin.

In railway days Cargan had four houses and a pub. Now it is growing rapidly. If the large settlements here and at Martinstown had existed in the 1920s, the line might have survived much longer. A short distance before Cargan the railway diverged a bit from the road to follow lower ground and then crossed under the road in a deep cutting just where Costcutters is now. **Cargan station** occupied the

Top: *Cargan looking north – only the station house survives (behind the hedge).*

Centre left: *Well preserved embankment north of Cargan.*

Centre right: *Bridge and embankment between Cargan and Parkmore.*

All N Johnston

Bottom left: *Parkmore station as it was in June 1963. It is still largely intact but the near end wall has now collapsed.*

Bottom right: *Parkmore station in June 1963 viewed from the north and showing the (smaller) gents toilet block.*

Both R Whitford

site of the small housing estate on the left side of the road but only the station house survives. However, there are clear traces to be seen of two mineral branches diverging south across the road again to Dungonnell mines and north up the hill to Crommelin, where the stone supports for the winding gear can be seen.

For the next two miles the line is below the level of the road and follows the Cargan Water river valley on the left.

Top left: *The interior of the station at Parkmore looking north. The platform was on the left side.*

Top right: *The well preserved water tower at the north end of Parkmore station. Rumour has it that the tank still has water!*

Left: *The stone bridge that once carried the railway over the Essathohan Burn some distance north of Parkmore. The adjacent road bridge is to the left.*

Bottom left: *The station house at Retreat. It is currently being refurbished.*

Bottom right: *The end of the line at Retreat showing the loading bank.*

All N Johnston

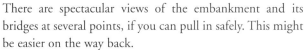

There are spectacular views of the embankment and its bridges at several points, if you can pull in safely. This might be easier on the way back.

The highlight of this line is undoubtedly **Parkmore station** which is at the divergence of the A43 to Glenariff and the B14 to Cushendall. Old photographs from the 1890s give an impression of the station being in a barren moorland (page 128), but today the area is heavily forested. The station is just behind the high laurel bushes (Hint: If you can't find an NCC station, look out for laurel bushes or a yew tree! The NCC commonly planted these to provide shelter). The original 1888 station was of timber but the present building is a concrete replacement following the destruction of the original by arson in 1921. The station building survives and with the near end gone, entry is not difficult! Note the station name cast in concrete, the gents urinals at the far end and the water tower, allegedly still full of water!

From Parkmore, we move up the line to the final destination, Retreat. The line continues on the left for a short distance as we plunge into Parkmore Forest, but passes under the road just past a white cottage on the left, slightly under a mile from Parkmore. A short distance on, immediately after an 'S' bend, look out for a surviving railway bridge on the right, crossing the Essathohan Burn alongside the road bridge, the former railway bridge now being used by a path. It was half a mile beyond this that the Trostan Mineral Railway diverged (page 165).

Retreat station is about two miles beyond this point, the line diverging slightly to climb up a hill to the right. A lane leads up to the station house which at the time of writing is being renovated. Note the loading ramp beyond the house. This was never a passenger station, the facilities being a station house, a goods store, a run round loop and a headshunt. Retreat Castle lies in ruins below the house.

We now return to Ballymena to follow the Ballymena and Larne Railway.

Ballymena to Larne

Ballymena Town

Before the link to the present Ballymena station was created in 1880, the Ballymena and Larne Railway had a terminus at Harryville, which we shall come to shortly. First we must trace the route from the main line station to Harryville. The Larne line made an end on connection with the Cushendall line at the island platform we visited at the 'Park and Ride' earlier and ran parallel to the broad gauge as far as Railway Street. The Galgorm Road, the River Braid and Railway Street were crossed on parallel bridges but traces of the Galgorm Road bridge were erased in 1957 when the bridge was reconstructed. However, the abutments of the River Braid viaduct can still be seen from the adjacent fire station, off Waveney Road (Remember, this is a one way street!). After crossing Railway Street on a bridge shared with the broad gauge (Railway Street accessed the original 1847 station before the move to Galgorm Road.), the line diverged sharply to the left to cross Queen Street.

Harryville station is at Paradise Avenue and can be entered from Queen Street, directly opposite the stone-built railway goods store on the right. If approaching from the Belfast direction, leave the A26 dual carriageway at Ballee Roundabout, following the signposts for *Ballymena, Harryville*. Proceed into town for about a mile and turn right into Paradise Avenue, opposite the stone warehouse referred to above.

Today Paradise Avenue merges with Douglas Terrace but in narrow gauge days these were two dead-end streets separated by an extensive railway yard which occupied the land on both sides of the present street. The main yard was on the north side, its eastern boundary being marked by a brick wall. On the opposite side, the odd angle of the gable on No 28 Douglas Avenue, indicates where the line crossed the road. Nothing survives at Harryville, other than the site, most of it being now John Crane's yard.

Leaving Harryville, the line followed a course midway between the Antrim and Larne roads, which took it behind the King George's playing field, across Wakehurst Road and the John Simpson Memorial playing fields at Harryville. It then ran close to Lettercreeve and Kincora in the Ballee estate, across a stream by the Penny Bridge, on the route of the present public footpath before following the west bank of the stream to pass under a private road at O'Hare's Bridge and curve southwards to cross the route of the present Ballee Road East dual carriageway.

By car, the easiest route is to leave Harryville yard via Douglas Terrace, turn right onto the Larne Road and then right again at the mini roundabout into Wakehurst Road. The line crossed the road just past Wakehurst Park. At the end of Wakehurst Road turn left onto the Antrim Road and proceed to the Ballee Roundabout where you take the first exit (A26 Coleraine). About half a mile along Ballee Road East, at Irish grid D11640103, the trackbed can be seen on the north side if you pull onto the grass.

Ballymena–Kells

Continue along the A26 for another half mile, moving into the right-hand lane and turn right at the next junction into the Liminary Road for Kells. Less than a mile down this road turn right into the Ballylesson Road. This will take you past the remains of the old brickworks identified by a tall brick chimney in a field to the right. The railway passed under the road by a stone bridge, still extant and known as 'Brunty's bridge'. From the bridge the trackbed to the

Top left: *The railway bridge over the River Braid, viewed from the Fire station. The piers of the narrow gauge bridge are clearly visible.*

Top right: *A close up of one of the piers*

Left: *Paradise Avenue viewed from what was Harryville yard. In the distance is the broad gauge goods depot.*

Below: *No 28 Douglas Avenue. The space between the gable wall and the building on the right was occupied by the trackbed leaving Harryville for Larne.*

All N Johnston

north between fences can be clearly seen. There was a siding from the railway into the brickworks, an important source of traffic (see page 44).

Turn and retrace your steps to the Liminary Road and turn right towards Kells. The line is out of sight to the right but our road gradually converges with it. If desired, another overbridge can be viewed by turning right after three quarters of a mile into the Ballycowan Road. The bridge is adjacent to Country Garage. Near Kells, just after the 30mph sign, the point where the line crossed the road can be identified by a surviving abutment on the right. The line entered Kells station here. Unfortunately nothing of **Kells station** itself survives apart from the stationmaster's house. The site can

Top left: *'Brunty's bridge' which carries the Ballylesson Road over the trackbed west of Kells.*

Top right: *Trackbed of the railway, looking west from Brunty's bridge towards Ballymena.*

Left: *Surviving chimney and buildings at the brickworks, as seen from the bridge.*

All N Johnston

be viewed from the large garden centre across the river. Access is by turning left directly after the bridge. The café inside the garden centre is highly recommended! The station was across the river directly behind this building. To see the station master's house, return to the main road, cross the river again and take first right onto the B53 (the Kilgad Road). About 100 yards up this road are stone abutments where the line emerged from the station towards Moorfields. The large white house is the heavily rebuilt station master's house. Just here, another smaller garden centre is built on the site of the actual station.

Kells–Moorfields

Continue on up the B53, which runs roughly parallel to the Kells Water. The line also followed the river valley and crosses the river about a mile from Kells to follow its southern bank. If desired, another overbridge can be viewed by turning right onto the B59 at the next crossroads, the bridge being just after the road crosses the river.

After reaching Moorfields village, turn right onto the A36 and right again at McBirney's yard into Greerstown Road. **Moorfields station** is on the right just after the river bridge and is the best preserved on the line. It is occupied by a brother and sister who are the children of the last station master. Here the platform, station building, station house, signal cabin, water tank, and even a milepost, are all carefully preserved. The arch of the overbridge is filled in to make a wall.

Moorfields–Ballyboley Junction

On leaving Moorfields station, retrace your steps to the main A36 (Moorfields Road) and turn right for Larne. Two

Left: *Moorfields station viewed from the overbridge looking east. The platform is still discernible and the lawn occupies the trackbed. Note the water tower on the left and the signal cabin in the distance.*

Lower left: *Moorfields signal cabin. According to the plate it was built by Courtney, Stephen and Bailey, Dublin.*

Lower right: *The red brick down platform building at Ballynashee station. The main building, on the up platform, is still occupied.*

All N Johnston

miles on, at the Battery Inn crossroads, the Collin Road (B94) to the right (sign posted *Ballyclare*) will take you to the remains of a level crossing where the railway crossed just before the junction with the Whappstown Road, and this was the site of **Collin station**. The trackbed of the line can be seen across the fields to the left.

Return to Battery Inn crossroads and turn right onto the A36. Three and a half miles further on turn right at the next crossroads onto the Ballynashee Road. The railway crossed over this road after about one and a half miles, where Carnlea Road North diverges, and the abutments and embankments are well preserved.

Less than a mile beyond this is **Ballynashee station**, just on the corner of the Braepark Road. It can be viewed

by turning left here and parking on the overbridge. The attractive station building is still occupied and the red brick down platform building also survives, as does a section of the platform. Viewed from the bridge a line of hedge marks the eastern side of the trackbed.

The next station on the line was **Ballyeaston halt**. No trace of this now remains but the site of it is near McCleanstown. To get there, return to the Ballynashee Road (crossing the Sawmill Road) and travel a mile and a half south to Ballyeaston village. At the village turn left onto the Ballyboley Road and about 500 yards down this take the Ballyalbanagh Road to the left. The halt was just under a mile up this road, the trackbed running parallel to and just south of a lane which joins the road from the left.

The stone overbridge has been filled in on one side but the trackbed is visible on the right side of the road.

From Ballyeaston we head for **Ballyboley Junction**. Return down the Ballyalbanagh Road towards Ballyeaston and at the Ballyboley Road turn left towards Larne. Follow this road for about three miles and look out for the line from Ballyeaston, crossing the road diagonally from the left after about two miles. A mile after that look out for a small road to the right called Junction Road. This leads to a group of about six houses which occupy the site of Ballyboley Junction. Straight in front is a wide modern bungalow which occupies the site of the former station building and signal cabin, the Doagh branch diverging to the left of it and the main line climbing to the right. The tall two storey house on the left is the stationmaster's house, heavily rebuilt. The platforms are long gone.

Ballyboley Junction–Doagh

It is probably convenient at this stage in the journey to diverge from the main line to follow the Doagh branch. The first station on the branch was **Ballynure**. Turn left out of Junction Road and retrace your steps for just over a mile to turn left towards Ballynure. This road crosses the Sixmilewater and the branch after about 300 yards. At Ballynure village turn right onto the A57 and immediately right again into Church Road. The station is about three quarters of a mile down this road, on the left, at the bottom of a hill close to the river. The house and station building are occupied and in good order. The road crossed the line on a hump-back bridge here but this has been removed and the road lowered.

From Ballynure, continue the way you are heading, to the Ballyeaston Road, following it to Ballyeaston and on into **Ballyclare**. Proceed through the centre of Ballyclare until you come to the bridge over the Sixmilewater and the Asda store on the left. If you turn left into the carpark you are on the site of the former narrow gauge station. The distinctive point of reference is the Methodist church on the opposite side of the road, which appears in the photo on page 32. The Sixmilewater has an 'S' bend between the Asda store and the Leisure Centre. It was here that the railway crossed the river from the south bank to the north and this bridge appears in the foreground on page 32. If you walk through the grounds of the Leisure Centre you will see the trackbed of the line coming in from Ballynure.

On leaving Ballyclare for Doagh, the railway followed the river for the first mile, serving the **Ballyclare paper mill**, once a major source of traffic (paper pulp and coal in and finished paper out). This is long gone but was probably under the present Avondale Industrial Estate sited off Mill Road, just north of the Templepatrick Road (A57). Mill Road can be reached by turning left out of the Asda carpark and then right at each of the two mini-roundabouts. The entrance to Avondale is to the right, just before Mill Road joins the A57. However, no trace of the railway remains here.

Whether you visit the industrial estate or not, join the A57 towards Templepatrick and after two miles turn right for Doagh into Station Road (B59). As you enter Doagh, look out on the right for Exchange Avenue, sited between the Masonic Hall and the Texaco filling station. Exchange Avenue occupies the trackbed and if you drive or walk down it you can get your bearings from the photo on page 126, where the Masonic Hall is prominent. **Doagh station** occupied the ground to the left as you go down Exchange Avenue. Although no trace of the actual station now remains, the red brick station house on down the Avenue is still occupied (compare page 55) and is worth photographing. A small shop now adjoins it.

Ballyboley Junction–Larne

To resume following the main line, we now need to return to the vicinity of Ballyboley Junction. Return down Station Road to the A57 and head for Larne, bypassing Ballyclare and passing through Ballynure village after joining the A8 from Belfast. About a mile and a half after Ballynure, we pass the Junction, which is across fields to the left. The first thing to look out for on this section is **Headwood station**, which was where the line crossed the road diagonally from left to right, about half a mile after the Moss Road joins from the left at a staggered crossroads. The station house is on the left and is still occupied.

After Headwood, the line veers away from the road but then swings back alongside it. At this point there is a loop on the right called Stewardstown Drive (part of the old road) and here a crossing keeper's house survives on a side road. About half a mile beyond, the line swings east to join the valley of the Inver River and it is here that **Kilwaughter halt** was situated. To get there, turn right at Ballyedward onto the road for Glenoe (B100). A quarter of a mile down

Left: *Ballynure station viewed from Church Road. Both station building and station house are occupied. The cars are on the trackbed.*

Centre left: *The station house at Ballyboley Junction is the only surviving structure.*

Centre right: *The site of Ballyclare station. The Sixmilewater is on the left. Compare with page 32 where the Methodist Church also appears.*

Lower left: *The site of Doagh station looking towards the main street. The Masonic Hall on the left also appears on page 126.*

Lower right: *The station house at Doagh is further down Exchange Avenue.*

All N Johnston

Left: *Headwood station is alongside a former level crossing on the A57 to Larne close to Moss road.*

Centre left: *The much enlarged crossing keeper's house at Kilwaughter halt.*

Centre right: *Narrow Gauge Road, Larne, is about the only surviving reminder of the narrow gauge station.*

Both N Johnston

Left: *The flyover which carries the Harbour Highway through Larne is built over the former railway line up the Inver bank. This view looking towards St Cedna's Church is from the same vantage point as that on page 78.*

Opposite left: *The trackbed along the Inver bank is clearly identifiable today. This view is from the footbridge opposite St Cedna's Church.*

Opposite right: *The Inver bank looking back towards Larne, from a path leading up to the A8. This is roughly the curve featured on page 118, though blocks of flats have replaced the old terrace housing.*

All N Johnston

here the road divides and the left hand fork takes you past the crossing keeper's house, now much enlarged.

Return to the main A8 road and proceed towards Larne.

Larne–Larne Harbour

Unfortunately, major changes in Larne since 1970 have obliterated virtually all of the old narrow gauge infrastructure, and indeed much of the broad gauge as well. In 1974, to make way for the new Harbour Highway, the NIR railway to Belfast was given a new alignment on reclaimed land, to the east of the original. This led to the replacement of Larne town station, the site of the original being now the bus station and adjacent carpark. The Inver River was diverted to a new channel through the reclaimed land. The present Larne town station is a new one built in 1974 and is actually closer to the town centre than the original. A further change was the reclamation of most of the bay for an industrial estate.

The best way to explore the narrow gauge is on foot so, after passing Millbrook Roundabout, keep in the left lane and follow directions for the town centre and Larne town station. These will bring you to the Circular Road Roundabout where you should take the second exit and park near the Tourist Information Centre.

To make the most of this area you would benefit from studying and comparing the 2007 April Sky map of Larne and Alan Godfrey's historic map of Larne in 1903. Both are available in the Tourist Information Centre.

To understand what this area was like before 1974, you need to imagine the Circular Road running over the Tourist Information Centre and sweeping across the town side of the carpark and roundabout, with the broad gauge railway alongside. Circular Road crossed the narrow gauge line to Larne Harbour on a skew bridge, which features in several Larne photos in this book (see pages 53, 99 and 102 for example). The narrow gauge station was in the triangle of land between the river, the Circular Road and Narrow Gauge Road. The Tourist Information Centre is built over the passenger station and the engine shed and Works were under the Harbour Highway. Thankfully, Narrow Gauge Road is still there to help us get our bearings.

Leaving Larne for Ballyboley, the railway followed the north bank of the Inver and today you can follow the track for some distance as it is now a footpath. The first part of it, as far as Bridge Street, is under the concrete base of the elevated Harbour Highway. Bridge Street originally crossed the line and river on a much higher bridge than the present. The photos on pages 40 and 78 were taken from this.

Beyond Bridge Street the path emerges from under the Harbour Highway and it is much easier to visualise the railway. The low river bridge at St Cedna's church did not exist in railway days. Along this stretch the terrace houses seen in the background of Inver bank photos are long gone, replaced by tower blocks. The modern A8 partly encroaches the railway trackbed but at least the path follows the basic alignment.

Follow the path as far as you wish and then retrace your steps to the carpark at the Tourist Information Centre. As mentioned earlier, the narrow gauge line passed under

Left: *The NIR line to Larne Harbour as seen from Glynn View Avenue. The narrow gauge ran on the inland side of this track. This is from a similar vantage point as the picture on page 130 in 1937. Then, Larne Lough skirted the railway as seen in the bottom picture here.*

Below: *The view from the Curran Road bridge looking west today, showing the present NIR tracks. The headshunt on the right was the trackbed of the narrow gauge.*

Both N Johnston

Above: *Larne Harbour station, viewed from the Curran Road bridge. The chimneys are at Ballylumford. The narrow gauge yard was on the ground to the left and the British Aluminium Works was on the extreme left.* N Johnston

Right: *This view was taken in 1902 in exactly the same spot as the recent view centre right. 0-6-0T No 108 arrives at the harbour past the track to the narrow gauge turntable. Note how, in 1902, the railway was on a causeway across the lough.*

Ken Nunn collection, LCGB

the old Circular Road just east of the station and then ran alongside the broad gauge (on the inland side) to Larne Harbour. It can be followed by car if you return to the Circular Road Roundabout and take the second exit with the NIR station to your right. This leads to the truncated remains of Circular Road and hence the Main Street. Turn right into Curran Road and, after the police station, turn right into Glynn View Avenue. If you park here you can walk through the security barrier to the carpark. The railway is just through the fence. Here the line is back on its original alignment, the old line having passed through the present police station. Looking left you will see the sweep of the line round towards the harbour. It was near here that the view on page 130 was taken, though all the lough to the right is now reclaimed.

Our final viewpoint is the Curran Road bridge (or in some early maps the Olderfleet Road bridge). Turn right out of Glynn View Avenue and follow the Curran Road round the corner. There is a convenient parking spot on the right, opposite Bay Road. From the bridge you can see the present Larne Harbour station. The narrow gauge sidings were in the land to the left, now occupied by the harbour container park. The red brick building to the left of the bridge is a surviving part of the British Aluminium Works (compare page 133).

On the Larne side of the bridge you are looking down on the area where the narrow gauge turntable was sited (see page 65). In the early 20th century the railway from here to Glynn View Avenue was on a causeway (see opposite).

This ends our tour of the narrow gauge.

Industrial lines in Mid-Antrim

Dr Patterson's original 1968 edition of this book, titled *The Ballymena Lines*, was essentially a study of the narrow gauge lines which were owned by the NCC. However, it did include information on such industrial lines as the Glenariff Railway, the British Aluminium Company and those tramways to mines that were linked to the Cushendall line. The appendices included information on the Trostan Mineral Railway.

Maintaining this tradition, Chapter 13 of this edition includes photographic coverage of the Larne complex operated by the British Aluminium Company up to 1960 and of the completely unconnected Carnlough Lime Company Tramway which operated in four different gauges, thus hopefully documenting most significant narrow gauge lines to operate in the Mid-Antrim area, whether public or private. This chapter includes Dr Patterson's original appendix on the Trostan Mineral Railway.

British Aluminium Works, Larne

The British Aluminium Works at Larne had commenced operations in 1897, occupying land to the north side of the harbour, across the Harbour Road from the NCC yard. Bauxite came (initially) from the Glenravel mine at Cargan, on the Cushendall line. The processed alumina was shipped from Larne to the then new BAC smelter at Kinlochleven in Argyllshire. Within the works, an extensive three feet gauge railway system was constructed from 1900 on.

In addition to the main works on the north side of the Harbour Road, the BAC reclaimed approximately 28 acres of mud flats on the south side of the NCC railway, used as ponds for the removal of the residual red oxide from the bauxite by a process of settlement. These ponds were accessed from embankments along which another railway network was constructed. The ponds were reached from the Works by an arrangement with the NCC. A junction was formed at the old Ballymena and Larne turntable road west of the Curran Road bridge, from where the BAC carried its narrow gauge to a reversal point. From here a spur climbed to cross the NCC lines by a reinforced concrete bridge, before dropping to the level of the ponds. This bridge was just south of the road bridge and bore the date '1915'.

As local sources of bauxite declined, supplies began to be imported from France around 1910. However, the unavailability of French bauxite during the German occupation of 1940–44, led to extraction from Cargan being recommended, though by this time the Ballymena lines were lifted and the bauxite came to Larne by road.

The BAC ceased to produce alumini at Larne in 1947, but the firm diversified into recovering the red oxide from the ponds described above. This was dried out and bagged for sale to the Red Oxide Group at Bristol, where it was used for paint-making and in the plastics industry. Since the linen bags used for the powder were continually recycled, a works laundry was built to clean them.

In the 1950s the main functions of the internal railway system were to move the red oxide into the Works from the ponds and to transport loaded wagons of oxide powder from the factory to the harbour sidings. This activity kept the narrow gauge alive at Larne until closure of the works in 1960.

The BAC lines were operated by three Peckett 0-4-0Ts, Nos 1–3, built respectively in 1904, 1906 and 1914. Of these, two are now preserved. No 1 was saved by Bill McCormack in 1960, who ran it on a private railway in his extensive garden, before selling it in 1969 to Lord O'Neill for his Shane's Castle Railway, where it was named *Tyrone*. Lord O'Neill's railway closed in 1995 and No 1 is now on the Giant's Causeway Railway, Co Antrim. No 2 was purchased by the contractor who lifted the Larne Harbour to Ballyclare narrow gauge section in 1954-55, but is now the Ulster Folk and Transport Museum, Cultra.

No 3 became a stationary boiler at the afore-mentioned laundry in the 1950s (see photo). A four-wheel Planet diesel locomotive, from sent over from Kinlochleven in 1953, replaced it. Its cab bore the number '12/2'.

The wagons used on the BAC railway were a mix of German-built side-tippers, wooden wagons for bagged oxide, flat trucks from the BAC's Scottish operation and second-hand wagons from the NCC and the Clogher Valley Railway. BAC rolling stock used link and pin couplers which were not compatible with the NCC buck-eye system, known as the 'Norwegian' type.

Above: By the early 1950s the only operational steam engine was Peckett 0-4-0T No 1. Now preserved as Tyrone *on the Giant's Causeway Railway, the engine is seen at the weighbridge inside the Works entrance on 20 August 1950.*
DG Coakham

Left: BAC wagons in the NCC sidings with the Aluminium works in the background on 10 March 1951.
DG Coakham

Opposite top: *No 1 crossing the road from the quayside line on 4 July 1951.*

Right: *The reinforced concrete bridge (dated 1915) which carried the BAC line to the iron oxide ponds over the NCC tracks, adjacent to the Curran Road bridge, was photographed on 25 March 1955. The aluminium works is in the background.*

Below: *The bridge viewed from the direction of the ponds, with the Curran Road in the background. The man in the coat is the late John McGuiggan.*

All DG Coakham

Opposite bottom: *The Planet diesel which handled traffic between the Works and the quay in the 1950s was photographed on 25 March 1955.*

Right: *The boiler of 0-4-0T No 3 as a permanent fixture at the laundry on 25 March 1955.*

Both DG Coakham

0-4-0T No 1 propelling empty wagons across the Harbour Road into the Works on 20 August 1951.   DG Coakham

0-4-0T No 1 waits its next move in the NCC sidings on 4 July 1951. In the background is Harbour Road and the perimeter wall of the Works.
DG Coakham

Carnlough Lime Company tramways

Anyone travelling up the Antrim Coast Road between Larne and Cushendall will pass under a stone bridge at Carnlough. This bridge once carried another independent railway, which we can illustrate thanks to the extensive photographic record of DG Coakham and Richard Whitford.

This railway was opened in 1854 by the Carnlough Lime Company Limited as a 4'8½" gauge cable-operated line, about a mile in length. Its inclusion in this book is justified on the grounds that, in Ireland, anything under 5'3" counts as narrow gauge. (Only joking!) More seriously, it is included because parts of the ststem were genuinely narrow gauge.

The original 4'8½" gauge line was laid on a continuous gradient of 1 in 25 and was initially horse and gravity worked. However, as this was hazardous for both horses and men, the line was later altered to become two cable-worked inclines, the upper and lower slopes being of 650 and 750 yards respectively. The system used about 80 end-tipping wagons. Power was supplied by a winding house built half way up, adjacent to the lime kilns (disused from the 1930s). It was equipped with a Chaplin winding engine, but in 1952 steam power was replaced by a 35hp three-phase electric motor, and the upper incline reverted to gravity working, loaded wagons raising empty ones as they descended. Wooden disc signals at the head of the incline were used to communicate with the winding house.

Gortin Quarry was at the head of the main incline and from there a branch went off at right angles, in a north-easterly direction, to Creggan quarry where there were about half a mile of hand-worked sidings. Beyond Creggan was a third incline, which had a 100 yard tunnel but the top quarry was worked out about 1929 and the line above Creggan abandoned.

At the Carnlough end of the line, between the river and the present Gortin park, a Whiting Mill was built. Here the limestone was unloaded and crushed into powdered lime for export. Within the mill there were several internal narrow gauge systems – a 1'8" gauge system on the first floor and a 2'4" gauge one at ground level, mainly hand operated. The lime was loaded into wagons after processing and brought to the harbour for loading into ships. The line to the harbour crossed the town on two bridges, still in use today as a footpath.

A 3'6" gauge branch, two miles long, from Tullyaughter quarry to Carnlough was added in 1890. This joined the main line a short distance west of the mill, so between there and the harbour mixed gauge track was installed.

The Tullyaughter branch was probably horse-worked initially, though it is possible a locomotive was in use from the beginning. Certainly, in 1898 a second hand Andrew Barclay 0-4-0T called *Otter* (Wks No 770, 1896) was obtained from Hurst Nelson and Co, who had supplied the 20 wagons. The branch closed in 1922 but, since the 3'6" gauge wagons were retained, the mixed gauge tracks between the Whiting Mill and the harbour remained in use and *Otter* continued to work between the harbour and mill until 1930. It remained on site after that and was not scrapped until 1951.

Later, a Davy Brown tractor with buffers was used to move wagons of both gauges between the mill and the harbour. The Carnlough limestone railway remained in use until about 1965.

Thankfully, today the course of the line is preserved as a public footpath and the impressive views from the top make it well worth a visit.

Of the photographs which follow, those by DG Coakham were taken on 29 September 1950 (unless otherwise stated) and those by R Whitford on 6 October 1962, on the occasion of a visit by the Irish Railway Record Society.

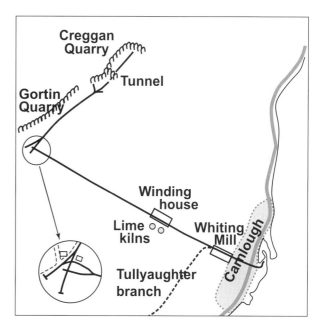

The north side of the harbour at Carnlough on 29 September 1950 showing a row of four wagon turntables leading to the staithes on the left and right. These turntables were four-rail in order to balance the narrow gauge wagons.

DG Coakham

Below: *A later view, on 6 October 1962, showing the facilities at the harbour, including mixed gauge track.*

R Whitford

Three 4'8½" gauge mineral wagons with differing wheel sizes. Note the conveyor belt for loading limestone on the ships.

R Whitford

Left: *An early 20th century view of the well known bridge at Carnlough, showing the 3'6" gauge locomotive* Otter *with a train from the harbour.*

National Library of Ireland

Below: *After leaving the harbour and crossing the main street, the line passed through the Whiting Mill, where most of the limestone was ground down into a powder before the final trip to the harbour. This view on 7 September 1955 shows the main line on the right climbing up to the hills beyond.*

DG Coakham

Above: *The bridge over the main street, viewed from the harbour side, showing mixed gauge track, with the second bridge and the Whiting Mill visible in the distance.*

Right: *Another view on the same visit, showing the Whiting Mill with mixed 3'6" and 4'8½" gauge track on the left running to the harbour, behind the photographer. On the right are 2'4" gauge tracks of the internal mill system. The footbridge in the foreground was the vantage point for the centre right photograph.*

Both R Whitford

Left: *The Whiting Mill viewed from further up the line.*
R Whitford

Above: *The line used rope haulage. Six wagons arrive at the top of the first incline.* DG Coakham

Below: *A magnificent view of Carnlough looking downhill from above the first incline. Whiting Mill chimney in the distance. The second incline climbs to the left.* R Whitford

Above: *The winding house was part way up the first incline towards Gortin quarry (visible in the background). This view shows its position above the track. Note the rollers for the haulage ropes, visible between the rails. The buildings on the left are the lime kilns.*

Left: *Creggan quarry, which was the destination of the second incline, is seen here in a view from the winding house, looking to the right (north).*

Both R Whitford

Below: *see overleaf . . .*

Above: *The reversing point at the top of the first incline. The white disk signal was rotated 90° to tell the winding house when a train was ready to descend. The second incline climbs up past the cottage. The track in the foreground and that occupied by the empty wagons are headshunts or sidings. By 1962 the weigh house had a flat roof.*

Left: *A close up of the complicated track work at the reversing point. The wagons on the right are waiting to descend the first incline. Note the haulage cable trailing across the tracks.*

Both R Whitford

Previous page left: *At the top of the first incline was a reversing point. Here it is viewed from the track leading to the second incline. The first incline is to the left.*

Previous page right: *Another view of the reversing point, but this time looking down the first incline with Carnlough in the distance. The stone building is a weigh house.*

Right: *Manual shunting of wagons at Creggan quarry in 1950. It was all very reminiscent of conditions on an 18th century plateway.*

All DG Coakham

Above: This 1950 view shows loaded and empty wagons at the top of the second incline at Creggan quarry. A third incline rose in the background and passed through a tunnel. Its route is just discernible above the empty wagons, rising diagonally to the tunnel mouth.

Below: An impressive photograph from above the tunnel mouth looking back towards the position of the top photograph. The overbridges carried tracks running to spoil dumps. The embankment carrying the first incline can be seen top left.
Both DG Coakham

Left: In the late 1940s a crushing plant was built at the head of the second incline for initial processing of the limestone and is seen here in 1962. Crushed stone was dropped into the wagons by the chutes seen here. The plant can also be seen in the general 1950 view above, just to the left of the wagons.

R Whitford

The Trostan Mineral Railway

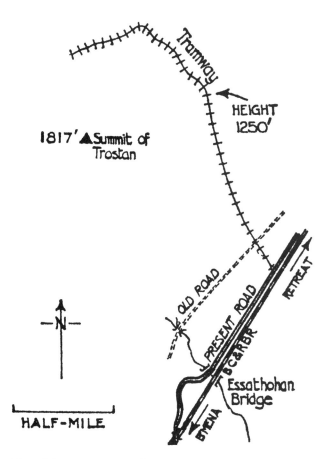

Plan of the Trostan Mineral Railway, based on aerial photographs and ground survey

Half a mile NE of Essathohan siding, between Parkmore and Retreat, the six-inch Ordnance Survey map shows a line of 'Mineral Railway (disused)' along the line of the ore outcrop, ENE and N of Trostan. At this place, both the county road and the BC&RBR are close together and the

Trostan mineral line began roughly at right angles to the two. The Cushendall railway lies at a lower level than the Trostan line and physical connection between the two would hardly have been possible.

The Trostan line started on an embankment, a few yards NW of the road, beside a flat area paved with random stones. Government mineral statistics record that mining was in progress here during 1872 and 1873, but was discontinued in 1874. It is therefore probable that the Trostan line predated the BC&RBR, and was a hutch line bringing ore down to a roadside loading area where carts would be filled. Examination of aerial photographs confirms this, and fails to disclose traces of any spur lines towards the Cushendall railway. Rising from the roadside, the Trostan mineral line entered a cutting, and, about a mile from the road, reached an altitude of 1250 feet above sea level. Over this distance a climb of about 220 feet would have taken place, corresponding to an average gradient of 1 in 22. Towards the end of its course of just under two miles, the line probably attained a height of 1,400 feet and was certainly the highest of all the Antrim mineral railways. Its gauge is not known, though it may well have been the same as the various mine tramways, namely two feet. Much of the Trostan line was in Barard townland, the last 350 yards were in Eshery townland.

In connection with the height of the Antrim railways, it should be mentioned that an error was perpetuated for many years in the pages of *The Railway Year Book*. This stated that the maximum height reached by the NCC was 1,250 feet above sea level, at Cloughglass. Cloughglass was an alternative name of Retreat townland, and at no point there was the Parkmore-Retreat section of the NCC much above 1,000 feet. The summit was at Essathohan, 1,045 feet above sea level.

Appendices

1: List of Stations and Halts

	Miles	Opened Goods	Opened Passenger	Closed Goods	Closed Passenger	Classification	Crane Power (tons)
Larne–Ballymena							
Larne Harbour	0	1878	1878	1950	1933	GPLH	–
Larne	1	1878	1878	1950	1933	GPLH	3
Kilwaughter	4	1878	1885	1933	1933	GP*	–
Ballygowan, *later* Headwood	6¼	1878	1878	1940	1933	P*	–
Ballyclare Jct, *later* Ballyboley Jct	7¾	1878	1878	1940	1933	GP	–
Ballyeaston	10	–	1880	–	1881		
		–	*1911*	–	*1933*	*P**	–
Ballynashee	12	1879	1879	1940	1933	GP	–
Collin	15½	–	1887	–	1933	P*	–
Moorfields	17½	1878	1878	1940	1933	GPL	2
Kells	20½	1878	1878	1940	1933	GPLH	2
Harryville	24¾	1878	1878	1940	1881	GLH	6
Ballymena	25¼	1875	1880	1940	1933	GPLH	5
Ballyboley Jct–Doagh							
Ballynure	9½	1878	1878	1933	1930	GPL	–
Ballyclare	11½	1878	1878	1933	1930	GPLH	3
Doagh	*13½*	*1884*	*1884*	*1933*	*1930*	*GPL*	–
Ballymena–Retreat							
Ballygarvey	2¾	–	1889	–	1930	P*	–
Ballycloughan	4	1886	1886	1940	1930	GP*	–
Rathkenny	6	1886	1886	1940	1930	P*	–
Clough Road	6¾	1886	1886	1940	1930	P*	–
Knockanally, *later* Martinstown	8¼	1886	1886	1937	1930	GP	–
Carrowcowan *later* Cross Roads	9¾	1875	1888	1937	1930	GP	–
Cargan	11¼	1888	1888	1937	1930	GP	–
Parkmore	13½	1875	1888	1937	1930	GP	–
Retreat	16¼	1876	–	1937	–	G	–

NOTE: Classification and crane power (except for Ballyeaston) is abstracted from *Official Handbook of Railway Stations*, published in 1912 by the Railway Clearing House. Abbreviations used are: G = Goods, P = Passengers and parcels, P* = Passengers but not parcel or miscellaneous traffic, L = Live stock, C = Carriages by passenger train. Distances are from the Working Timetables.

2: List of Chairmen and officers

Ballymena, Cushendall and Red Bay Railway Company

Chairmen: William Valentine 1872–73; John Shelly 1873–76; Thomas Valentine 1876–84

Secretary: Silas Evans 1872–84 (also Secretary Ballycastle Rly Co 1878–85)

Manager: Edward J Cotton 1875–84 (also Manager under BNCR)

Engineer: Robert Collins 1874–80 (also PW Inspector on Londonderry and Lough Swilly Railway 1866–74 and Engineer on Letterkenny Railway from 1880.

Consulting Engineer: William Lewis

Locomotive Superintendent: James Donaghey ?1872–84

Ballymena and Larne Railway Company

Chairmen: James Chaine, MP 1873–85; OB Graham 1885–90

Secretaries: WR Anketell 1873–74; CH Brett 1874–76; George Brett 1876–78; FW Rew 1878–86; JD Nott 1886–90

Managers: FW Rew 1877–86; JD Nott 1886–90

Locomotive Superintendents: William Pinkerton 1877–86; – Horner 1886–89

Engineers: William Lewis 1876–?; – Horner 1886–89

3: List of relevant Acts of Parliament

For ease of reference, the chapter numbers of the Acts listed below have been given in Arabic numerals though, strictly speaking, they should be listed in Roman numerals.

Ballymena, Cushendall and Red Bay Railway

35-6	Vc	85	(1872)
41-2	Vc	117	(1878)
43-4	Vc	105	(1880)
46-7	Vc	127	(1883)
46-7	Vc	128	(1883)
47-8	Vc	128	(1884)

Ballymena and Larne Railway

37-6	Vc	200	(1874)
41-2	Vc	227	(1878)
42-3	Vc	174	(1879)
48-9	Vc	75	(1885)
52-3	Vc	97	(1889)

Ballymena and Ahoghill Tramway

48-9	Vc	192	(1885)
49-50	Vc	46	(1886)

Ballymena and Portglenone Railway

42-3	Vc	210	(1879)
45-6	Vc	225	(1882)
49-50	Vc	46	(1886)

Ballyclare, Ligoniel and Belfast Railway

44-5	Vc	215	(1881)
47-8	Vc	126	(1884)
48-9	Vc	161	(1885)

Larne and Ballyclare Railway

36-7	Vc	240	(1873)
37-8	Vc	200	(1874)

Glenariff Railway and Pier

43-4	Vc	198	(1880)
48-9	Vc	166	(1885)

4: *Classification of engines according to their power (brake vans included) which can be worked by each engine up the inclines.*
(abstracted from the MR(NCC) Working Timetable July-September 1908)

NARROW GAUGE

				Class A 101, 102, 103, 104, 105	Class B 106, 107, 108	Class C 109, 110, 111
Larne	to Kilwaughter	...	...	6 Wagons and Van.	10 Wagons and Van.	11 Wagons and Vans
Kilwaughter	„ Ballyboley	...	...	10 „ „ „	15 „ „ „	17 „ „ „
Ballyboley	„ Ballynashee	...	...	11 „ „ „	16 „ „ „	18 „ „ „
Ballynashee	„ Ballymena	...	...	20 „ „ „	20 „ „ „	20 „ „ „
Ballymena	„ Larne	...	...	9 „ „ „	14 „ „ „	16 „ „ „
Parkmore	„ Knockanally	...	...	16 „ „ „	16 „ „ „	16 „ „ „
Knockanally	„ Ballymena	...	...	24 „ „ „	24 „ „ „	24 „ „ „
Iron Ore Sidings from Mines		...	...	16 „ „ „	16 „ „ „	16 „ „ „
Ballymena	to Knockanally	...		24 „ „ „	24 „ „ „	24 „ „ „
Knockanally	„ Parkmore	...	...	16 „ „ „ } Empty	16 „ , „ } Empty	16 „ „ „ } Empty
Iron Ore Sidings to Mines		...	...	16 „ „ „	16 „ „ „	16 „ „ „

The loads given above are for the guidance of Enginemen and Traffic Officials, and refer in all cases—where the load is fixed by the number of vehicles—to fully loaded standard vehicles, and they are such as will permit the Engine to stop and start from any Station or Siding without danger of stalling under ordinary circumstances. Under exceptional circumstances, or when an Engine from any reason is unable to work its proper load, the Driver must decide how many vehicles it can work, and his decision is to be final.

When the vehicles forming a train are not fully loaded, or when a train is timed not to stop at Stations situated at or near inclines, the driver must use his discretion as to what additional vehicles he may take, care being taken not to overload the Engine as to run the danger of stalling.

In calculating the number of vehicles in a train, the following rules must be observed:—

Each Long Broad-Gauge Passenger Vehicle will count as 2 Loaded Wagons in the case of mixed trains.
„   Short Broad-Gauge Passenger   „   „   „   „   1 Loaded Wagon   „   „   „
„   Long Narrow-Gauge Carriage   „   „   „   „   2   „   Wagons.
„   Short   „   „   „   „   „   „   „   1   „   Wagon.
*   Loaded 16 ton Ore Wagon   „   „   „   „   2   „   Wagons
Two   „   8 ton N.G. Hopper Wagons „   „   „   „   3   „   „
Three Broad-Gauge Empty Wagons   „   „   „   „   2   „   „
Two Narrow-Gauge   „   „   „   „   „   „   1   „   Wagon.
Two Long Bogie Broad-Gauge Carriages „   „   „   „   3 ordinary Passenger Vehicles.

5: Traffic Returns
(abstracted from Board of Trade Railway Returns)

Ballymena and Larne Railway

Year	Passengers			Goods Traffic (tons)		Train Miles		Dividend on
	1st	3rd	Season	Minerals	Gen Mer	Pass	Goods	Ord Stock
1877	–	–	–	5155	2596	7546		Nil
1878	2432	32,149	–	19,529	12,510	12,611	27,598	1%
1879	6121	101,415	26	34,168	24,812	46,536	41,133	Nil
1880	6797	126,049	70	52,794	29,218	53,704	47,669	2%
1881	5734	123,495	94	62,211	25,938	64,759	48,111	1%
1882	6944	138,297	57	75,844	33,740	63,915	47,427	2¼%
1883	6592	146,455	51	74,266	34,813	62,627	49,012	2%
1884	5707	166,495	61	74,445	34,655	67,167	54,292	Nil
1885	5838	163,460	57	65,833	36,686	68,079	50,403	Nil
1886	4321	158,643	88	62,043	32,884	112,477		Nil
1887	3290	150,044	11	66,664	32,294	110,337		Nil
1888	2959	142,894	71	69,583	42,579	119,376		¾%

Ballymena, Cushendall and Red Bay Railway

Year	Goods Traffic (tons)		Train Miles	Dividend on Ord Stock		
	Minerals	Gen Mer		A	B	C
1875	37,688	908	14,111	4%	–	–
1876	59,800	2154	23,128	4¾%	–	–
1877	88,315	2596	31,037	5%	–	–
1878	77,228	1539	29,616	43/8%	43/8%	43/8%
1879	79,663	2280	26,613	Nil	25/8%	Nil
1880	118,721	3273	43,522	3½%	4½%	2½%
1881	92,925	1958	33,939	3½%	4½%	2½%
1882	84,515	2980	30,648	2%	4%	Nil
1883	72,534	2637	28,300	17/8%	3¾%	Nil

B = Preferred Stock
C = Preferred Stock

Dr Patterson's Acknowledgements for the original edition

As in the case of the companion volume, *The Ballycastle Railway*, the gathering together of the factual material in *The Ballymena Lines* has only been possible through the encouragement and help of many people.

To present and former Northern Counties Railway staff I am especially grateful, for without their personal recollections and guidance the construction of this book would hardly have been possible. Inevitably, the target for many of my enquiries has been Harold Houston, who generously gave much effort and time to helping me. There must also be mentioned the assistance given by W Hanley, H Herron, W Hutchinson, WS Marshall, W McNinch and WJ Waterman. Their piquant reminiscences have, I hope, helped to make the book more than the mere bones of history.

Consultation of documents relating to the original companies was facilitated by JGT Anderson and Newton Compton, formerly of the Secretary's Department of the UTA. My thanks in this connection are also due to the staffs of the Public Record Offices in Belfast and in London, of the British Railways Historical Archives Offices in Edinburgh and, in London, and of the House of Lords Records Office.

My gratitude of due to Colonel Sit Basil McFarland, Bart, for permission to quote from letters written to his father by Basil McCrea on the Glenariff Railway auction. The Earl of Antrim also helped in amplifying the story of the Glenariff railway in allowing me to examine documents at the Antrim Estate office in Glenarm.

The illustrations owe much to the efforts of John Jamieson of Kells, N McCarter of Belfast, Miss Mary Millar of Ballymena and RE Russell of Ballyclare, all of whom supplied photographs of historic interest.

Brian E Crompton of Manchester gave me valuable unpublished information from his researches into Messrs Beyer, Peacock's records, and his notes were freely used in the chapter on the locomotives. Drawings and photographs were supplied by the former chief draughtsman of Messrs Beyer, Peacock. My father helped me on many occasions in abstracting information from newspaper and journal files in the Linenhall Library, Belfast.

While the sketches on station plans are my own, they are entirely based on detailed surveys and drawings made by DG Coakham of Bangor. He has also helped me in various ways in writing the elusive history of the carriage and wagon stock.

Space permits me only to list the names of others who have assisted me in one way or another, and my thanks are due to: HA Boyd (Ballycastle), HT Brown (Larne), J Butt (Glasgow), EN Carrothers (Belfast), RN Clements (Celbridge), DJ Dickson (Fahan), Lt-Cdr GMH Dinsmore (Kells), the late H Fayle (Bournemouth), PJ Flanagan (Dublin), L Hyland (Dublin), RH Inness (Darlington), W Lambden (Douglas IOM), GR Mahon (Dublin), DB McNeill (Southampton), DL Smith (Ayr) and J Wormwell (Larne).

Publisher's Acknowledgements

Colourpoint Books would like to thank the following, who have played a valuable part in the production of the second edition:

Desmond Coakham, Leslie Cooper, David Francey, Charles Friel, Brian Gallagher, Alec McKillop, Sean Magee, David Orr, Jack Patience, Nelson Poots, Ian Stewart, Richard Whitford. We are particularly grateful to those who made their photographic collections available for the compiling of the new edition, especially my ever-helpful friend, Charles Friel, without whose collection this book would have been impossible. For the section on the Carnlough Limestone Railway, I am indebted to Andrew Waldron for permission to use information from his forthcoming book on Irish industrial railways.

Dr Patterson's Original Bibliography

NOTE: Where a line precedes the date, the name of the author is not known

Dubordieu, J (1812) *Statistical Survey of the County of Antrim.*
_ _ (1873) 'Iron Mining in Co Antrim' *Engineer*, Oct 24 p281.
Lewis, W (1881) 'Narrow gauge Railways, Ireland' *Trans Inst Civil Eng Ireland*, **13**, 122.
Green, CF (1882) 'On light railways, or remunerative railways, for thinly populated districts.' *Trans Inst Civil Eng Ireland*, **13**, 31.
Symes, RG and A McHenry (1886) Explanatory memoir to accompany Sheet 14 of the Maps of the Geological Survey of Ireland.
Price, A (1894) 'The Location, construction and equipment of light or secondary railways in Ireland.' *Trans Inst Civil Eng Ireland* **25**, 93.
Timins, DJ (1897) 'The Belfast and Northern Counties Railway.' *Railway Magazine*, **1**, 560.
Livesey, RM (1912) 'Rolling stock on the principal Irish narrow gauge railways.' *Proc Inst Mech Eng* p599.
Cole, GAJ et al (1912) 'The Interbasaltic Rocks (Iron Ores and Bauxites) of North-East Ireland.' *Mem Geol Surv Ireland*.
Gairns, JF (1924) 'Northern Counties Section (Ireland) LM and SR,' *Railway Magazine*, **54**,121.
_ _ (1930) 'Narrow gauge corridor train, LM&SR – NCC.' *Locomotive*, **36**, 402.
Casserley, HC (1931) 'The Castlederg and Victoria Bridge Tramway.' *Locomotive*, **37**, 137.
McDowell, JH (1931) [Letter on Castlederg and VBT], *Locomotive*, **37**, 214.
_ _ (1931) 'The locomotives of the NCC, LM&SR.' *Railway Magazine*, **68**, 468.
_ _ (1932) 'Rebuilt narrow gauge compound tank locomotive, LM&SR NCC. *Locomotive*, p382.
Nock, OS (1936) 'The NCC Section of the LMSR, part III.' *Railway Magazine*, **78**, 413.
Nock, OS (1937) 'The Locomotives of the LMSR, NCC section.' *Railway Magazine*, **81**,119.
Kidner, RW (1937) *The Three-foot gauge Railways of Northern Ireland.*
Bruce, RHW (1944) ' The LM&SR in Northern Ireland.' *Railway Magazine*, **90**, 145 and 203.
Fayle, H (1945) *Narrow Gauge Railways of Ireland.*
Marshall, WS (1946) LMS-NCC *The Operating Department in War Time, 1939-1945.*
_ _ (1948) *NCC 1848-1948.*
_ _ (1949) 'The two-cylinder compounds of the Northern Counties Railway' *Railway Magazine*, **95**, 159.
Houston, JH (1949) 'The B&NCR and its locomotives part III,' *Journ Irish Rly Record Society*, **I**, 88.
Brown, HT and DB McNeill (1950) 'The Railways at Red Bay.' *SLS Journal*, **26**, 108.
McNeill, DB (1953) 'The Little Railway Mania in County Antrim.' *Ulster Journal of Archaeology* **16**, 85.
McNeill, DB (1956) *Ulster Tramways and Light Railways.* Transport Handbook No 1, Ulster Museum and Art Gallery.
Coakham, DG (1964) 'LMS(NCC) narrow gauge coaches, Part I, *Model Railway News*, **40**, 608.
Patterson, EM (1966, 2006) *The Ballycastle Railway.*

Directors' Minute Books of the various companies.
Shareholders' Minute Book of the BC&RBR, 1874-1884.
Half-Yearly Reports of the B&LR, BNCR and MR(NCC).
Board of Trade Railway Returns.
Board of Trade Railway Dept Inspecting Officers' Reports on New Lines and c.
Various Working and Public Timetables of the B&LR, BNCR, MR(NCC), LMS(NCC) and UTA.
Various Editions of *Bradshaw's Railway Shareholders Guide and Directory.*
Reports of the Vice-Regal Commission on Irish Railways, 1906-11
Minutes of Evidence and Report of the Commissioners, Railway Commission in Northern Ireland, 1922.
Relevant Acts of Parliament, and documents relating to Parliamentary Bills.

Index

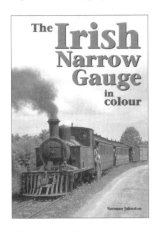 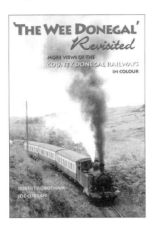  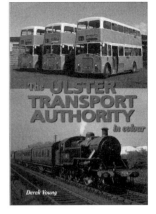
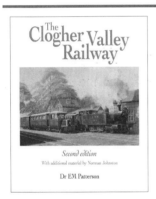
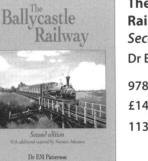
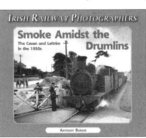 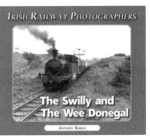